T0339791

A DAM IN THE RIVER

A Dam in the River

Releasing the Flow of University Ideas

Jeff Camhi

Algora Publishing
New York

Library of Congress Cataloging-in-Publication Data —
Camhi, Jeffrey M., 1941- author.
  A dam in the river: releasing the flow of university ideas / Jeff Camhi.
     pages cm
  Includes bibliographical references and index.
     ISBN 978-0-87586-987-2 (soft cover : alk. paper) — ISBN 978-0-87586-988-9 (hard
cover: alk. paper) — ISBN 978-0-87586-989-6 (ebook)
     1. Universities and colleges—United States—Public services. 2. Universities and
colleges—United States—Influence. 3. Community and college—United States. 4.
Communication in education—United States. I. Title.
     LB2331.44.C36 2013
     378.1'03—dc23
                                   2013004878

Front cover: Judith Margolis / Bright Idea Books

Printed in the United States

For Jane

TABLE OF CONTENTS

INTRODUCTION

A dam blocks a river's flow, creating a reservoir. The reservoir holds great potential benefit for the people downstream; just open the sluice gates and you irrigate farmlands, create hydro-electric power, control seasonal flooding, provide recreation areas, and enable river navigation. In many dams, it's really simple to open the gates, just by pushing a button. All that benefit, so easy.

A Dam in the River is about the flow, not of water, but of ideas. It tells of the huge and ever expanding reservoir of ideas in America's outstanding universities and colleges—arguably the world's deepest source of knowledge about the widest range of subjects. This reservoir holds great potential benefit for the people downstream—off campus.

This book focuses on universities and America's off-campus public. It explains how and why the public can benefit greatly from academic ideas. But as it also explains, the sluice gates for ideas at most American campuses have long been nearly shut. The coming chapters will show how this reduces the flow to a weak stream, able to water only an upper crust of the nation. And yet, like a real dam, increasing the academic flow can be easy—and inexpensive. Much can be done with no cost at all, just by thinking creatively about how to reallocate already existing resources.

You may be surprised to read that ideas flow from the campus to the American public only in a weak stream. You may have in mind, for instance, the great increase in online courses now available to the public via the "continuing education" divisions of many universities and colleges. But as I will show, most of these courses for adults are designed to develop specific career-oriented or technical skills (admittedly an important goal), not to stimulate the mind with ideas (the subject of this book). You will see that fewer than two percent of adult Americans take online, continuing education courses of this idea type—courses that are offered mainly in the humanities or arts and sciences division of a college or university. One should applaud the few existing courses of this type, in the spirit of viewing the cup as half full rather than half empty.

But two percent full? Unfortunately, most other efforts by universities to share their ideas with the public reach a similarly low percent of the population.

One clear indication that academics are not much out there mixing it up with the general public comes from a study by University of Chicago law professor (and currently US Court of Appeals judge) Richard Posner. He compiled a list of 546 intellectuals who received, according to his count, the most frequent media mentions (on TV and radio, in newspapers and magazines) and Web visits—"public intellectuals," as he and others call such people. Posner showed that just 100 of those on his list received over two thirds of these mentions and Web visits. Thus, a mere 100 people are the ones substantially in the public eye. Moreover, of the top 50 on this list, hardly any are academics. Most are journalists, freelance authors, politicians, and others.[1] This, in spite of the huge number— over 720,000—of full-time faculty, and a further 710,000 part-time faculty, in the degree-granting colleges and universities of the United States.[2] While these numbers indicate a potentially enormous academic media presence, the reality is a profound media absence. Posner's data were published in 2001. Since then, there has been some blog-objection to this analysis. But I have yet to see any actual data contradicting it.

The damming up of campus ideas amounts to a tragic waste of a vital national resource. Why? Because an idea can change a mind, change a life, change the world.

Ideas can broaden our horizons by connecting us to new areas of knowledge and leading us to new insights and interests. Seeing where ideas come from can enhance our understanding of, and perhaps our facility with, analytical thinking and complex reasoning. Ideas can stimulate us to test our points of view and beliefs. They can expand our sense of wonder at the universe and the human species, enrich our spirit, and bring us pleasure.

Ideas can benefit not only individuals, but also the nation as a whole. They can lead to a more enlightened citizenry, an elevated and more nuanced public discourse on complex issues, and improved decision-making on matters of national and global importance.

If you agree with me, or think you might, that ideas like these are important, then *A Dam in the River* is for you. This book includes a detailed set of recommendations for enhancing the current weak flow of ideas from campus in ways that are important for the public and the nation. If you are a university administrator, professor, or student, you are ideally positioned to help implement these recommendations; likewise if you are a university or college trustee, foundation or granting agency professional, educational policy maker, academic donor, or alumnus of a college or university. And if you are a school teacher, or simply are interested in education, you also have an important role to play.

I am *not* proposing that university ideas be used to try and change people's political, religious, or other orientations. I have no such agenda. Rather, I will show that whatever one's personal orientation, enrichment waits at the watering hole. And you can help dole out the water.

Making This Book

I have come to write *A Dam in the River* via a roundabout route. I am a professor of biology, born and raised in the New York area. After completing my doctorate, I taught at Cornell for fifteen years. Then, after a sabbatical year at the Hebrew University of Jerusalem, Israel, I accepted a professorship there in 1982. My family and I have been in Jerusalem ever since, though always in close professional and personal contact with the USA.

As I explain in Chapter 6, I founded and now direct an "open-campus museum" at the Hebrew University that uses both indoors and outdoors as venues for sharing academic ideas with the visiting public. As I began to note the positive effects of this museum, I asked myself the question that was to become the starting point of this book. Namely, how much do American universities—among the world's leaders in higher education—share their ideas with the public? This brought me full circle, back to the USA for an intensive period of research that included extended visits to 26 campuses and 13 additional academic organizations in the United States, and interviews with 155 academic leaders (listed in the Appendix), primarily university and college presidents, provosts, deans, and heads of campus outreach programs.

Ultimately, I switched my entire academic focus—my research, teaching, professional reading, the subjects of international conferences I attend and of visiting lectures I present, and my driving passion—to the subject of university ideas and the public. It was inspiring to enter a whole new field, and my entry became a contributing factor to my decision to write this book. It meant putting on a different thinking cap, since relating to the public is far more central to the culture of a museum than that of a university. In sum, my switch has allowed me to analyze and understand the sharing of academic ideas with the public far better than I ever could, had I not experienced the unique combination of an academic and a museum profession.

I was well aware when I began working on this book that the public intellectual was a rare breed at U.S. universities, and that campus intellectual life and the general public have long been far apart. This separation was already well-documented by Richard Hofstadter in his 1962 classic, *Anti-Intellectualism in American Life.*[3] However, I soon began to realize that in more recent decades, right up to today, this separation has actually been increasing.

This results in part from academic leadership's turning increasingly inward. As professor of literary theory Stanley Fish noted in the mid-1990s, "academics, at least a visible number of them, once did have...a pulpit, the college presidency or major deanship, offices that for a long time carried with them not only the possibility but the obligation of addressing issues of public concern." But for a variety of reasons, Fish claims, "People at the top have repudiated the very behavior that public intellectuals are supposed to engage in."[4] And in the late 1990s, former Stanford University President Donald Kennedy wrote that universities no longer "have much influence in the shaping of public awareness"; moreover, "the role of universities has been diminished in part by their own failure to exercise intellectual leadership...." They now need to "reconnect to the society that nurtures them."[5]

A recent well-argued analysis of the place of science in American society concludes that academic scientists increasingly talk among themselves, leaving the rest of society out of the discussion: "...[T]he rift between science and mainstream American culture is growing ever wider. Nearly a decade into the twenty-first century, we have strong reason to worry that the serious appreciation of science could become confined to a small group of already dedicated elites [such as science professors and their research students], when it should be a value we all share."[6]

Hurdles

Although small cadres of people on various campuses are working hard at increasing the flow of academic ideas, their efforts are blocked by several major hurdles, in the form of current trends both on and off campus. These hurdles include:

- Public disaffection with universities, stemming from diverse outlooks— including the political and religious right and the postmodernist left, and from the continuing crisis in the economy coupled with the ongoing rise in college tuition.[7]

- The increasingly narrow specialization of academic disciplines, leaving broad interpretations, more suitable for much of the public, in ever shorter supply. As a biologist colleague of mine puts it, "My kids, my wife, and my neighbors all know I'm a nerd, specializing in what seems a very narrow slice of the universe. When I want to find like-minded people—you know, other nerds—I just go to the campus."

- The continued growth of commercial influences on campus, directing much scientific research away from fundamental issues and their underlying ideas, and instead, toward specific industrial applications. Feeding this trend are public and political disappointments about the (so far) limited translation of the Human Genome Project, stem cell research, and some other high profile academic programs into medical cures, and the economic growth that such cures promise. As industry has both the cash needed for these expensive projects and a no-nonsense expectation of quick returns on investments, it is increasingly seen as essential to university research.[8] A further issue is that industrially supported university researchers are often forbidden by contract to speak about their findings with university colleagues or the public.

- An "arms race" among different universities and colleges, competing for the spoils of the best faculty and students. The "battle plan" is the building of ever greater research facilities for faculty and amenities for students. With many traditional funding sources shriveling up, lower priority programs such as those related to the general public are often left gasping for breath.

- A shift in educational goals on many campuses to career-oriented and technical courses at the expense of the humanities and other idea-rich subjects. As a result, faculty hiring in the humanities is at an all-time low, and several campuses have been closing their degree programs in foreign languages, classics, and other humanities subjects.[9]

These changes have several underlying causes, including the decreased funding for academia, especially at state-supported institutions; increased career concerns by the public, given both the recent economic downturn and the enhanced global job competition; and an increased tendency among many college administrators to follow short-term market trends rather than adhering to enduring academic principles and values as a basis for setting policy and practice. Professional and technical training, even at the expense of courses in the humanities and arts, is now regarded on many campuses as a benchmark of academic success. Every time President Obama mentions education, he stresses technology and career preparation, competition for global markets, and America's economic future. Important as these aspects are, more people need to stand up for ideas and the future of the American mind.

Given these ongoing and increasing trends, now is a critical moment in the history of academia's relationship with the public; today's weak idea stream is at risk of becoming the faintest of trickles. We need to be asking, "Will today's low flow of university ideas become tomorrow's no flow?"

I'm hardly the first author to comment on the flow from campus to the public, though my approach differs from most who have come before. Ever since the founding of America's colonial universities, the public purpose of the nation's higher education has sparked debate. Those sparks grew into flames during the social upheavals of the 1960s and 1970s. Since then, two opposing views have emerged regarding the appropriate form—and direction!—of idea flow. I state here somewhat extreme, yet frequently articulated, versions of these two opposite views.

According to the first view, universities should substantially overhaul much of their often esoteric and irrelevant research and teaching, and instead dedicate themselves to helping solve urgent practical problems facing society. In the framework of "civic engagement," faculty and students should work together, on an egalitarian basis, with civic groups to define the problems and seek solutions.[10] One can regard this as a call to dismantle the metaphorical dam and transform the flow into a sloshing of ideas back and forth, into and out of campus.

According to the second, opposing view, the university is not in the social welfare business. It's in the idea business. But its ideas, this view commonly maintains, are primarily for internal consumption, relevant mainly to academics and their students; sharing with a wider public is not part of the university's core mission.[11] This is a call to maintain or expand the reservoir and keep the sluice gates in their present state, or even more fully closed.

Many in academia have lined up somewhere along the axis formed by these two polar views. The argument I build in this book lies somewhat closer to the latter, idea-oriented view, beginning with a firm commitment to ideas as the core business of the university. But I will develop the case that sharing these ideas broadly with the public should likewise be a high priority. I regard helping to solve civic problems as a positive activity for academic involvement, but in moderation; and I offer an alternative approach by which universities could help, perhaps more effectively, to solve civic problems.

What Ideas, and Who Needs Them?

What, you might be wondering, do I mean by an "idea," and what sorts of ideas from academia is this book about? Many authors have written extensively on the definition of an idea, perhaps none more than philosophers. But the history of philosophy offers so many different definitions that I take the liberty of using the word "idea" in ways that will specifically apply to this book's discussion. I will discuss the following three important types, one in each of the first three chapters:

1) *The Idea of a University*. This is the title of a seminal 19th century book about what a university is and does, by British scholar John Henry Newman.[12] As I will show, what the modern American university is and does, though somewhat different on different campuses, can be formulated as an idea, and one that is both widely misunderstood and often criticized by the public. In a sense, this idea is the gateway to all the others on campus, really the gateway to the university as a whole; one who does not know what a university does will hardly recognize its wealth of knowledge and how this can impact on the individual and the nation. Therefore, clarifying to a broad public the idea of a university—something universities themselves rarely do—is an appropriate starting point for increasing the flow of academic ideas to society.

2) *Ideas from the Disciplines*—that is, from the various areas of academic study. By this I mean concise summations of things that academic experts have come to know or believe concerning subjects in their own and related disciplines, firmly supported by evidence, and interpreted in a manner that reveals their broader significance. Here is a partial list of areas rich in discipline ideas:

- New scientific knowledge about everything from quarks, to you and me, to the whole universe;

- New insights from the arts, humanities, social sciences and other fields about how to understand ourselves and the world in the 21st century;

- Analyses of particular political, cultural, technological, economic, historical, educational, literary, or other developments.

At the core of these ideas is forefront research in a very broad range of subject areas, from anthropology to astrophysics, Bach to biology, classics to chemistry. Many important ideas—in some ways the *most* important ones for academia to share with the public—concern the nature of the inquiry process itself in the different subject areas, and the nature of valid evidence. Only if one understands on what basis researchers come to accept a given idea can that idea be grasped fully and with conviction.

3) *Value-Based Ideas*—a set of core ideas expressing what the university fundamentally stands for, and holds most dear—ideas that underlie and support just about everything that happens intellectually and culturally on campus. If *the idea of a university* is the gateway to the university, *academic values* are its infrastructure. The public needs to understand these values in order to appreciate the context for the full range of academic ideas.

Who on campus should be sharing these ideas with the public? The people most responsible for the ideas—the faculty and the highest level administrators. But maybe you're thinking, there are people both on and off campus, aside from professor and president, whose job it is to share academic ideas with the public. You'd be thinking perhaps of the university's public relations department, or newspaper and broadcast journalists and other professional communicators.

Yes, these people make a valuable contribution. But there is something very special—irreplaceable, really—about getting ideas directly from their source, and not in a brief TV "moment". From the university president, provost or dean who, in the best of cases at least, helps define and maintain university goals and values; and from the professor of physics, political science, philosophy, or any other academic field, who has been at it not just for as long as it takes to write an article, blog, or book, but for a lifetime; who has taught the university course, maybe written the university textbook, tested the ideas time and again against departmental and disciplinary colleagues; who wakes in the night with an insight that's been percolating and could change forever the way people think; who filters academic content through a life-long story filled with memories and emotions, false starts and thrilling discoveries, personal failures and stunning successes. No one else can draw so deeply from the academic well. No one else truly knows this story.

But knowing a story doesn't mean that one can tell it engagingly. Unfortunately, although a small number of academics have natural talents and predilections for communicating with the public (a form of communication quite different from conversing with academic colleagues), a great many do not. Hardly any academics receive professional training in public speaking to a live, radio, or TV audience, or writing for the public. This is surprising, as almost any university community includes people able to provide at least some of this training. Sadly, then, most academics are inadequately prepared for sharing with the general public the deep well of their academic ideas. Much of *A Dam in the River* focuses on how to turn this sad fact around.

The public in particular need of academic ideas is the adult population—those over, say, 25 years of age. Adults not only encompass roughly two-thirds of all Americans, including the vast majority of voters; they are also helping to build the nation every day—making significant contributions to the workplace, the community, civic organizations, and family life. In this regard, the over-50 segment of society is particularly relevant. Typically, their children are grown or nearly so, their working lives have peaked or they have retired, many are seeking new ideas and activities, and some occupy positions of influence. (According to an old joke, human life begins not at the moment of conception, nor at birth; rather when the kids leave home and the dog dies.)

People are now living longer, healthier, more active lives. Remarkably, over half of the people born, in advanced nations, after the year 2000 are expected to live to celebrate their hundredth birthday! Moreover, it is not mainly life's final period of decline and disability that is lengthening, rather the preceding period of continuing health and vigor. Today there are more people than ever in their 70s and even 80s looking not for the country club and retirement community, but for a new challenge and a world problem to help solve. These older people could integrate new academic ideas with important life skills acquired through years of accumulated knowledge, experience, perspective, wisdom, and connectedness to other people.[13]

The contemporary rubric for sharing ideas with adults is "lifelong learning," or "continuing education." Yet as mentioned above, the percentage of the adult population engaged in these activities, as offered by academia, is minuscule. The potential of universities to engage the minds of the adult population is enormously greater than is currently the case.

Hearing People Out

During my research, as I began to realize the degree of damming up of academic ideas, I shared this realization with the people I was interviewing. Many agreed, though some raised specific objections to my claim. Let me share the five main objections I received. Although I did not reply during the interviews—I was there to gather information, not to object to it—I present here the replies I would have made, had these been open-ended discussions.

Objection 1: Universities and colleges effectively disperse their ideas throughout society by educating their students.

Reply 1: Currently, only about 6 percent of Americans are enrolled college or university students. The remaining 94 percent are not. Most Americans have not gone to college. Although 27 percent of those 25 years of age or older hold a bachelor's degree,[14] haven't we all heard of college students who don't fully engage in rigorous learning experiences? "No one in my family," you may be thinking. But on average, college students spend just 9 percent of their time in class, 7 percent studying outside of class (that's less than two hours per day!), and 51 percent in socializing and recreation! Most of the remainder is sleep time.[15]

Moreover, a recent study of cognitive advancement during the first two years of college showed that, except for students at outstanding research universities and liberal arts colleges (the ones focused on here), there was almost no improvement in the students' analytical thinking, complex reasoning, or writing skills—that is, in working with ideas, accepted by many in academia as the most important set of goals of a college education.

Furthermore, a large and increasing number of students are so focused on career preparation that they expose themselves to few of academia's great ideas. The most popular undergraduate major, attracting 19 percent of all students, is business, a distinctly practical and career-oriented subject. Furthermore, 19 percent of college seniors state that business is the lifetime career they most likely will pursue.[16] Business majors showed the least growth in analytical thinking, complex reasoning and writing skills of majors in eight different subjects studied. Education and social work, two other practical majors, showed the next least growth.[17]

After college, few graduates maintain any significant relationship with their alma mater or any other college or university. For most alumni, their contact with college was but a brief, often quite care-free and learning-limited, moment in a long life.

Given all this, the claim that, by educating their students, universities and colleges effectively disperse their ideas throughout society seems plainly wrong.

Objection 2: American campuses have several categories of service programs which increase their contact with the public. One category is "civic engagement," mentioned above.[18] A second is "cooperative extension" at land grant universities,[19] which provides outreach services to communities throughout the home state. A third category is continuing education courses, both online and in the classroom.[20] And a fourth is a set of public-oriented academic initiatives in defined subject areas, two prominent examples being "public history"[21] and "science, technology and society."[22] Surely these programs share ideas effectively with the public.

Reply 2: Civic engagement programs usually connect students with small public committees, working groups, or even just with one individual, whom they may tutor—situations neither intended for, nor conducive to, a broad sharing of ideas. Cooperative extension of land grant universities shares primarily technical and practical information, not the great academic ideas, mostly with farmers and their families. As mentioned above, continuing education courses that stress ideas, though very positive, engage only a tiny fraction of adult Americans.

Public history and science, technology and society are two other positive ways of sharing ideas with the public. There are questions, though, about the extent of these activities and the breadth of their effect on society. I explore all these subjects in depth in Chapter 4.

Objection 3: Given universities' limited financial and other resources, they should focus their efforts not on sharing ideas with the general public but rather on their core missions of teaching and research.

Reply 3: I show in several chapters that many potentially useful means of sharing, not widely employed, would not stress university finances at all. Most of the necessary resources already exist on campus. What's lacking is original thinking about how to implement the sharing. Yet doing so could enrich people's lives and the nation at large, while elevating the university to a position of greater prominence and leadership. Why would a university turn its back on such a possibility?

Objection 4: Although universities should try to influence society, the best way is to influence politicians and other leaders, and this is already being done. Educating Mr. and Mrs. Smith of Main Street is much less effective.

Reply 4: Yes, influencing politicians is extremely significant. Much of the political influence universities exert is designed to maintain or increase their funding from state and federal budgets—important and indirectly useful to society, though not to be confused with promoting the flow of ideas. Those activities that attempt to educate politicians are to be praised. One notable example is the Saguaro Seminars: Civic Engagement in America, initiated by Prof. Robert Putnam of the John F. Kennedy School of Government at Harvard. One of the seminar's activities, the "Executive Sessions Program," invited future public leaders and scholars to a series of weekend meetings held between 1995 and 2000. One attendee was an up-and-coming Chicago politician named Barack Obama.[23] Such advanced training in democracy, offered to a future president (of any political orientation), seems like a really good deal for the nation. Other forms of university influence on political leadership, such as professors being consulted or employed by government, also have a positive impact on politics. But it is, after all, Mr. and Mrs. Smith—and America's increasingly diverse population—who put the politicians in office. If they do not vote on the basis of well-informed positions—irrespective of their political leanings—in local, state, and national elections, as well as in civic organizations, what level of democracy, and what sort of government can Americans expect? Moreover, the public deserves attention simply because it comprises, by definition, the majority of the people.

Objection 5: Universities will never succeed in sharing their ideas broadly with the public, because much of the public couldn't care less about university ideas. Most people are not as cerebral as academics. Besides, a growing number of people, including political conservatives and religious fundamentalists, actively resist academia.

Reply 5: Yes, this is part of the picture. But I suggest academia can do much to bridge such gaps, including learning to relate better to people of different orientations, and extending an open hand[24]—something museums generally do better than universities. We won't know how effective such efforts by academia can be until we give them a serious try. But we already know that ignoring those who "couldn't care less," or those of political or religious outlooks outside the campus norm, has not worked very well.

A Dam in the River, then, points to a problem in America's universities and colleges, and offers a broad range of solutions. Part 1 presents the problem. It unravels and attempts to simplify the complex subject of academic ideas, and tries to correct some common misconceptions about them (Chapters 1–3). It also backs up with detailed evidence my claim that ideas do not flow with any intensity from campus into society (Chapter 4). These chapters also begin the process of offering some specific solutions to the problem of idea flow.

Part 2 deals primarily with the solution. It offers a wide range of ways to open the sluice gates for academic ideas, including how to upgrade the experience of visitors to university and college campuses (Chapters 5 and 6), improve academic writing for the public (Chapter 7), expand the use of radio and TV broadcasting to share academic ideas (Chapter 8), and enhance the use of the Internet (Chapter 9). And finally, Chapter 10 organizes all 35 solutions suggested throughout the book into a coherent and readily usable format. This chapter is aimed at helping universities and colleges develop their own plan of action to increase the flow of their ideas to a broad public.

Notes

1. Richard A. Posner, *Public Intellectuals: A Study of Decline* (Cambridge, MA: Harvard University Press, 2001), Table 5.3.

2. National Center for Education Statistics, US Department of Education, 2009 tables. http://nces.ed.gov/programs/digest/d11/tables/dt11_263.asp.

3. Richard Hofstadter, *Anti-intellectualism in American Life* (New York: Vintage, 1962).

4. Stanley Fish, *Professional Correctness: Literary Studies and Political Change* (Oxford: Clarendon Press, 1995), 120.

5. Donald Kennedy, *Academic Duty* (Cambridge, MA: Harvard University Press, 1997), 278.

6. Chris Mooney and Sheril Kirshenbaum, *Unscientific America: How Scientific Illiteracy Threatens Our Future* (New York: Basic Books, 2009), 6.

7. Remarkably, today 94 percent of those earning a bachelors degree borrow money to pay for it, up from 45 percent in 1993. Average student debt at graduation is $23,300. From 2001 to 2011, tuition and fees at private, non-profit universities increased 29 percent, and 72 percent in state universities. http://www/nytimes.

com/2012/05/13business/student-loans-weighing-down-a-generation-with-heavy-debt.html.

8. http://www.theglobeandmail.com/news/opinions/opinion/why-science-has-to-promise-profits/article2409571/.

9. Lisa W. Foderaro, "Budget-cutting Colleges Bid Some Languages Adieu," *New York Times*, December 3, 2010. http:www.humanitiesindicators.org; Lee McIntyre, "Making Philosophy Matter—or Else," *The Chronicle of Higher Education: The Chronicle Review*, December 11, 2011.

10. Adrianna J. Kezar, Tony C. Chambers, and John C. Burkhardt, *Higher Education for the Public Good: Emerging Voices From a National Movement* (San Francisco: Jossey-Bass, 2005).

11. Stanley Fish, *Save the World on Your Own Time* (New York: Oxford University Press, 2008).

12. John Henry Newman, *The Idea of a University* (Dublin: James Duffy, 1853). Repr. Notre Dame, IN: University of Notre Dame Press, 1960.

13. Sara Lawrence-Lightfoot, *The Third Chapter: Passion, Risk, and Adventure in the 25 Years After 50* (New York: Farrar, Strauss, Giroux, 2009); Marc Freedman, "Preparing Boomers to Transition Into New Roles," (lecture, Annual Conference, University Continuing Education Assoc., San Francisco, April 7-10, 2010); James W. Vaupel, "Biodemography of Human Aging," *Nature* 464 (2010): 536-542.

14. U.S. Census Bureau, http://www.census.gov (Data from 2008).

15. Richard Arum and Josipa Roksa, *Academically Adrift* (Chicago: University of Chicago Press, 2011), 97.

16. Victor B. Saenz and Douglas S. Barrera, *Findings From the 2005 College Student Survey (CSS): National Aggregates* (Los Angeles: Higher Education Research Institute, UCLA, 2007); Ray Franke and others, *Findings from the 2009 Administration of the College Senior Survey (CSS): National Aggregates* (Los Angeles: Higher Education Research Institute, UCLA, 2010).

17. Arum and Roksa, *Academically Adrift*, 105.

18. Kezar, Chambers, and Burkhardt, *Higher Education for Public Good*; Scott J. Peters and others, eds., *Engaging Campus and Community: The Practice of Public Scholarship in the State and Land-Grant University System* (Dayton, OH: The Charles F. Kettering Foundation, 2005); Joseph Huber and Ira Harkavy, eds., *Higher Education and Democratic Culture: Citizenship, Human Rights and Civic Responsibility* (Strasbourg: Council of Europe Publishing, 2007).

19. Peters and others, *Engaging Campus and Community*.

20. Mary Lindenstein Walshok, *Knowledge Without Boundaries: What America's Research Universities Can Do for the Economy, the Workplace, and the Community* (San Francisco: Jossey-Bass, 1995); Michael Shinagel, *"The Gates Unbarred:" A History of University*

Extension at Harvard, 1910-2009 (Cambridge, MA: Harvard University Extension School, 2009).

21. Michael Frisch, *A Shared Authority: Essays on the Craft and Meaning of Oral and Public History* (Albany, NY: State University of NY Press, 1990).

22. Thomas Easton, *Taking Sides: Clashing Views on Controversial Issues in Science, Technology and Society* (New York: McGraw-Hill, 2008).

23. Interview by the author of Thomas Sander, Executive Director, Saguaro Seminar, at Harvard University, September 4, 2007; Robert D. Putnam, *Bowling Alone: The Collapse and Revival of American Community* (New York: Simon and Schuster, 2000).

24. For an interesting example of how academics might improve their communication with the public see Randy Olson, *Don't Be Such A Scientist: Talking Substance in an Age of Style* (Washington, DC: Island Press, 2009).

Part 1. University Ideas and Their Low Flow

At this point, I have a question for you. But first, please think about one subject that greatly interests you. Any subject. Something in the news perhaps, or how to stay healthy, or about history, science, art, sports, a movie recently seen, a piece of music recently heard, something recently read. If you work or study at a university or college, please select a subject *not* related to your work or studies.

Now the question: From where have you most recently learned something that interested you about this subject? From TV? Radio? Internet? Newspapers? Books? Magazines? Conversations with friends or family? Academia?

Academia? Probably not. Not for most people, at least. Yet as the chapters of Part 1 illustrate, America's universities and colleges create arguably more knowledge, and a greater range of ideas, about more subjects—probably including the one you just thought about—than any place else on earth. In the four chapters that follow, we'll explore these ideas, and we'll see why they don't reach most Americans, and why they should.

Chapter 1. The Idea of a University

Many Americans just don't "get" the idea of a university. They're not quite sure what universities do, aside from offering courses and playing football; and what role they play, or could play, in American society. While many people follow what's happening in Washington, in their local communities, workplaces, and perhaps their places of worship, and while some follow current events, sports, music, movies, art, technology, business, globalization, the stock market, or other subjects, how many people actually "follow" academia?

How many, for instance, encounter new ideas in the natural or social sciences or humanities coming out of Columbia, Harvard, Stanford, or other great institutions? Or important campus issues being discussed at the Universities of Chicago, Pennsylvania or Michigan? How many are aware how university administration (as opposed to governmental or business administration) works; for instance, where is the power on campus—with the board of governors, president, provost (and what *is* a provost, actually?), deans (and just what do *they* do?), faculty, students, parents, alumni, major donors, city or state governments? How many could define a university's mission in one brief sentence? Answer: Very few people, whether or not they happen to be associated with academia.

It has been claimed that "cultural literacy" is a self-fulfilling prophecy. That is, if you know about a certain subject today, you tend to continue learning about it, so that you'll know more about it tomorrow; your mind has an open channel for this subject. But for subjects that you don't know about today, without an open channel in your mind, you are unlikely to know more about them tomorrow.[1] By this reasoning, unless people were to get a jump-start at "literacy" about academia, the campus will remain, for many, foreign terrain.

This chapter attempts to help people "get" academia. Hopefully, if you have not been intimately associated with quality universities or colleges you will find a useful discussion about what these institutions are and do. Even if you are closely connected to such a campus, you may find this material useful; as Jonathan Cole, former Provost of Columbia University, recently wrote, "The faculty and students of great universities typically know very little about their histories, about their structures, or more broadly, about the values that form the foundation of these institutions. They are *at* the institution, but not *of* the institution."[2]

It's not surprising that so few people are literate about academia. Only a modest fraction of Americans have had direct experience with colleges or universities. And even a smaller fraction have attended the more distinguished universities—the ones most fully involved in the creation of ideas. Also, whereas current affairs, sports, music, and the rest are all around us—on TV, on the Web, in the newspapers—academia is far less so. As Cornell's Dean of Arts and Sciences G. Peter LePage told me: "Universities need to explain to the nation what a university is and what it does. Many people are attacking universities now, through profound lack of awareness of what this institution actually is."[3] Former Cornell President Frank Rhodes concurred, "We need to do a better job at informing people what universities are all about. We in academia haven't done a good job with education beyond the campus."[4]

But if universities are potentially as important to the general public as I am suggesting, then academia should become a matter of substantial public interest. People outside America seem to know this better than those inside its borders. US universities are recognized around the globe as the gold standard of idea creation, and newly developing foreign universities mimic American academic models. At a recent conference of the World Universities Forum in Davos, Switzerland, academics from Africa, Asia, and Latin America described their visions for their own universities' future; their models were not Oxford, Cambridge, or the Sorbonne, but Harvard, Princeton, Berkeley and other great American institutions.

This admiration of American academia is also expressed by the large number of foreign students in American universities and colleges—over 720,000 in 2010, with each year showing an increase. Approximately half of the graduate students in engineering in American universities are from overseas, as are more than a third of those in the physical sciences, and more than a quarter of those in biology. China sends the most students, and India sends the next largest contingent.[5] In an internationally recognized ranking of the world's universities in 2011, seventeen of the world's twenty highest ranked institutions were American.[6]

Given all this, an awareness of idea-producing academia should be regarded as a feature of good US citizenship, along with an awareness of national, state and local government. High schoolers should be learning, and adults should be asking themselves, not only how will their lives be affected by the political orientation of the White House or City Hall, but also how will academic ideas affect their lives? (If only these ideas would reach the high schoolers and adults!)

Of the more than 4,000 institutions of higher learning in America, in this book I discuss but a tiny fraction—the most distinguished ones, about 100 major universities deeply engaged in research (and thus generating most of the university ideas), usually called "research universities," of which about 40 are private and the rest state-sponsored. I also discuss the 50 or so leading liberal arts colleges, mostly private. Together, these amount to roughly 3 percent of all American universities and colleges. As such, I am leaving out the great majority, including two-year community and vocational colleges, comprehensive universities offering a wide range of undergraduate and masters, but not doctoral, programs, universities that offer mostly online courses, and others.[7]

Is College For Getting a Good Job?

Recent national surveys revealed some striking results regarding the public's idea of a university. One survey asked adult Americans to identify the most important roles that universities and colleges perform. The answer selected by a whopping 92 percent was "preparing undergraduates for a career."[8] A similar survey of over 250,000 college freshmen showed that 73 percent regard "being very well off financially" as "essential or very important" in their lives. The only other category that scored higher in the freshman survey was "raising a family," at 76 percent. By contrast, "developing a meaningful philosophy of life" scored just 46 percent.[9] It seems, then, that for most people, academia is a job training center for creating young, rich families lacking a particularly meaningful philosophy of life. Or, as Matthew Goldstein, Chancellor of City University of New York, commented, "We need to be concerned that so many of our best students only want to get an MBA, work for an investment bank, and make a lot of money. Where are their values?"[10]

University faculty don't tend to see things as the freshmen do. In a national survey of faculty that paralleled students' survey, only 43 percent of professors (compared to 73 percent of freshmen) stated that "being very well off financially" is "essential or very important" in their own lives. The three goals regarded by the professors as most important were being a good teacher (which scored an amazing 98 percent), being a good colleague (92 percent) and serving as a role model for students (88 percent). Raising a family weighed in at 70 percent (similar to the 76 percent of the freshmen). And 70 percent of the faculty selected "developing a meaningful philosophy of life" (much higher than the 46 percent of freshmen). Moreover, only 30 percent of faculty agreed with the statement, "The chief benefit of a college education is that it increases one's earning power."[11]

In short, the freshmen and the faculty in whose classes they sit have flip-flopped notions about why they are both there. So who "gets it" about universities: The professors? The freshmen (and more advanced students)? Their parents? Or, as in the standard exam format, none of the above? In other words, what is a university, and what is it supposed to do?

Lots of different definitions of the university's role waft through the halls of academe and appear in scholarly writings. Here's one I think is right on target: *The university creates, stores, and disseminates knowledge.* This idea of a university, as I suggested in the Introduction, is the gateway to all academic ideas, and to the university itself.

So it's all about knowledge, which I divide into two sub-categories—practical expertise, which is not central to my subject, and ideas, which are the core of this book and, in my view, the core of the university. Thus, we can now restate what the university mostly does—it creates, stores, and disseminates *ideas*. Notice that this definition says nothing specifically about careers, wealth, raising a family, teaching, colleagues, or philosophy of life. It does, however, recall the image of the reservoir of stored ideas, and begs the question of whether they are disseminated, in any substantial degree, to people off campus.

Let's elaborate on these three roles of a university. The *creation* of ideas is largely through research and the interpretations of its findings—thus, the prominence I give to research universities. The *storage* of ideas takes place in libraries, archives, university museum collections, computers, file cabinets, and more abstract forms of stored ideas such as schools of thought and intellectual traditions in various disciplines. Idea storage also takes place in the brains of professors and other scholars. The *dissemination* of ideas occurs mainly through publishing and teaching. Some courses do help students on their way to careers, though it can be argued that other educational missions are more important, at least in an undergraduate program, such as improving analytical thinking, complex reasoning and both written and spoken communication, broadening horizons, enhancing old and developing new areas of interest, and developing in the personal, social, and civic, as well as intellectual, realms.[12]

If the issue at hand had been defining a college—specifically a liberal arts college—I would have begun my definition with disseminating ideas through teaching, since education is a college's main function. In the next section, I discuss the idea of a college, and how college faculty might communicate especially well with the public. Following that, I explore the unique idea of a university. Both colleges and universities are frequently, often passionately, criticized, often out of a lack of understanding of academia. Such criticism is damaging to academia's public image, and to the prospect of drawing on- and off-campus populations closer together. Therefore, unsubstantiated criticisms must be corrected, a task taken up in the last section of this chapter.

The Liberal Arts College and the Public

A liberal arts college, loosely defined, is a small institution, with a student enrollment of about 500 to 3,000, who generally reside on or near the campus. Given the small population, often in a rural setting, the campus becomes the focus of most academic and social activities. Thus, the liberal arts experience is often highly communal, cohesive, and intense—for both students and faculty.

Another cohesive factor is that, unlike universities, most liberal arts colleges are not subdivided into separately administered colleges, institutes, or centers—just different academic departments representing the various subjects taught. To quote one study, "When student population rises above three thousand, it seems common for a 'college' to proclaim itself a 'university' and for different schools or colleges to develop (e.g. a college of business), and it becomes less common for, say, a faculty member in geology to have as her closest colleagues and friends on campus professors of French literature, economics and special education." This study adds, "In a small academic setting, faculty members [have] a constant intellectual cross-fertilization with other academics whose ideas are stimulating and exciting precisely because they are not those of fellow specialists."[13]

At liberal arts colleges, professors "specialize" in being unspecialized—that is, in expanding the breadth of their intellectual scope. Often, they teach courses far outside their core fields of expertise, for which, of course, they need to prepare extensively. Quoting former President of Amherst College, Anthony Marx, "It remains the faculty's responsibility to inform teaching with scholarship that is deep but also broad—in a way it can be only at a great liberal arts college."[14] In our discussions, President Marx repeatedly stressed this point about the scholarly breadth of his faculty members.[15] His predecessor, President Tom Gerety, speaking about liberal arts colleges in general, referred to "our flexibility in moving across and among fields [and] a curiosity that does not stop at the boundaries of one's discipline but pushes on to ask about the disciplines of our colleagues."[16]

This breadth of scope that characterizes many college professors is precisely what Richard Posner, cited earlier, claimed is missing in many university professors, and limits them in generating broad ideas. Thus, many professors at liberal arts colleges may be especially well-suited to address the public about broad concepts. (This is not to denigrate university professors, some of whom are very broad in their scope. But in general the tendency of faculty members in universities is more toward depth of specialization, and in colleges more toward breadth of interpretation.)

A second relevant feature of colleges vis-à-vis universities concerns how faculty relate to their role as teachers. College professors are usually more strongly committed to the classroom than are university professors. In a national survey, faculty were asked to compare their interest in teaching versus research; 85 percent of college faculty put classroom over research, whereas university faculty were split 50/50 in their interests.[17] Moreover, college professors often employ innovative and interactive pedagogical styles. (Chapter 5 has some remarkable examples I witnessed at Amherst.) This is possible in part due to the relatively small and intimate nature of college classes. A standard class at a major university is a 50 minute didactic lecture that can be given to any number of listeners, even thousands in a huge auditorium. The introductory biology majors course at Cornell, where I taught for many years, had 1,200 students. At one point, to make the experience more "intimate" it was decided to divide the class into two sections and give the lecture twice—to 600 students each! College classes, by contrast, often have a handful of students, who engage deeply in dialog with the professor. Also, I was pleasantly surprised to learn that, just prior to my visit to Swarthmore College, several of its faculty members had been away, taking part in a workshop on innovative educational methods. In 45 years of my work on university—not college—campuses, I have never taken part in such a workshop, even though I have always regarded teaching as both a pleasure and a serious commitment.

These general tendencies of college faculty toward a broader scope, greater commitment, and more interactive and innovative communication styles may render some college professors particularly well-suited to engaging the public in academic ideas. Quoting Gerety again, "...we believe in teaching as conversation because the best teaching is conversation; except by dialogue we cannot do our work. The college, unlike the university, takes the dialogue of professor and student as a master principle."[18] President David Oxtoby of Pomona College told me something I would be much less likely to hear from a university president: "We don't hire brilliant scholars if they can't communicate really well." One can speculate that professors who have chosen employment at institutions that stress conversation (colleges) over those that stress more private, isolated research (universities) might be naturally inclined to interact well with the public.

The Unique Idea of a University

Universities implement more extensively than colleges the three core roles of academia mentioned earlier—more creating of knowledge through research, more storing of knowledge, for instance, by maintaining larger libraries, and more disseminating of knowledge by publishing more articles and books and offering a wider array of undergraduate and graduate course subjects. Let's examine the resources of major research universities in these three core areas that could support a fuller sharing of ideas with the public.

Research

At the leading universities, most faculty members spend roughly half-time engaged in research, although there are seldom any written rules or contractual statements about this. As university professors tend to work long hours, that's a lot of research. To permit and encourage this activity, universities provide state-of-the-art research labs, research hospitals, libraries, supercomputers, and often a university press. American universities carry out an estimated 57% of the nation's basic research, and 34% of its applied research, with a total budget of around $42 billion per year.[19]

As research is the source of a university's greatest number and widest range of ideas, it is an almost unlimited resource for potentially increasing idea flow to the public. However, I defer a detailed discussion of this subject to the next chapter.

Storing knowledge

One of the main means of storing knowledge at major universities is through their libraries. Harvard's library system, distributed among 90 different spaces in many campus buildings, and containing more than 16 million volumes, is America's largest academic library. Twenty-eight libraries of American universities have over 5 million volumes each, whereas only eight non-university libraries in the USA have this many.[20]

It is now widely known that several university libraries, including Harvard, Stanford, University of California, University of Michigan and Oxford, together with the Library of Congress and the New York Public Library, have entered into an agreement with Google to make their books available for reading directly on the Internet. This project involves scanning many millions of books page by page. The scanning began in 2006, and six years later, millions of volumes have already been fully scanned. The process continues, in spite of an ongoing legal battle with the Authors Guild and other groups over claims of copyright infringements.[21]

Books online are certain to change libraries and reading habits forever. Online professional journals have already done so. For instance, in the science library on my own campus, what was, until recently, the journals room is now filled with computer stations, not journals. And I read far more professional articles sitting right where I am now, in front of my office computer, than in the library.

The Google project is a great step forward for the democratization of knowledge. Opening public access to academic libraries constitutes a massive sharing of university resources. Yet this is not quite the same as opening the campus sluice gates and sharing university ideas. That would mean providing interpretation of the books by the academic faculty, not only the books themselves which were already widely available, though less accessible than they are becoming.

Many university libraries are housed in magnificent buildings rich in architectural and cultural history. The term "temple of learning" comes to mind. Walking the open stacks of a major library with its miles of book shelves, and settling into a seat in a beautiful reading room among a diversity of scholars engaged in a variety of intellectual pursuits can be inspirational both for those on campus and for visitors who are permitted to use some—but not all—university libraries.

As universities contemplate the future of their libraries, and their digitally dictated re-design, I hope they recognize what a loss for everyone it would be to abandon the sacredness of learning's temple.

Disseminating knowledge

Here I restrict the discussion to educating graduate students in the arts and sciences, as well as the professions. This is an area in which research universities very substantially dominate colleges. Although the public tends to be aware primarily of undergraduate activities at universities (perhaps owing to intercollegiate sports, general familiarity with undergraduate admissions, or news items about undergraduate education), the proportion of a university's students who are undergraduates can vary very widely, from 0% (in the unusual case of the Rockefeller University in New York) to about 35% at Harvard, about 65% at University of Michigan, and about 75% at Dartmouth, which approaches the 100% of the strictly undergraduate college.[22] Some graduate students focus on scholarly subjects, often administered by a graduate school of arts and sciences, and earn an MA or PhD in literature, history, anthropology, religion, mathematics, biology, physics, or many other subjects. Others study professional subjects, such as medicine (leading to an MD degree), veterinary medicine (DVM degree), law (JD), business (often an MBA), or many other fields, including dentistry, nursing, architecture, education, and library science. Just about anything there is to learn is represented by world experts on the faculty of a major research university.

In the case of arts and sciences graduate students, the PhD is a necessary, though usually insufficient, station along the route to an academic faculty job. Rather, as has been true for decades, especially in the sciences, a postdoctoral training period is required. This period typically lasts from two to four years in the sciences, often less in other fields. It is informally organized and concludes with no awarded degree.

A "postdoc" (the term most commonly used for a postdoctoral fellow, especially in the sciences), informally apprenticed to a given professor, is usually a key worker in a science professor's lab. Postdocs usually work very long hours, and as they are not required to take or teach courses, they generally devote themselves almost exclusively to research. As such, they hone their research skills in preparation for a life-long academic career. It is primarily from this post-doc pool across the nation that colleges and universities hire new faculty members. Thus, this pool, at any given time, represents the future of American higher education.

The nation's postdoc pool offers a significant potential resource for relating to the public. Many are both idealistic and youthfully energetic, yet well enough along in their training to be conversant with the many ideas being generated in their fields. True, some percentage of postdocs would not be appropriate for this task, including foreigners struggling with English, and others who just aren't interested, or whose talents lie elsewhere. This still leaves a sizable population. And although they are very busy, postdocs do not usually teach or sit on academic committees or carry out the many other duties that can make it difficult to convince a professor to take on added tasks.

Although the postdoc's youth has its advantages, it also has its limitations. Often the maturity born of years in the field is necessary to be able to conceive and convincingly express broad intellectual ideas. However, postdocs could, perhaps together with advanced graduate students, correct misinformation and provide missing information in the public realm. There's a lot of both mis- and missing-info that can lead people to accept ideas that either have no evidential support or are opposed by evidence. Responding to errors or lapses in newspaper and magazine articles (via letters to the editor), radio talk shows (via phone-ins), and blogs (via blog comments) are among the ways postdocs could provide a valuable public service. Organizing this as a campus-wide program, sharing experiences across departments, learning from one another, and perhaps offering annual prizes for the best work, with official recognition by the university administration and faculty would provide this program with the recognition necessary to attract participants and to survive. This activity would also encourage postdocs, once they become faculty, to continue their relationship with the public.

Critics of Academia

Universities and colleges receive frequent and often strident criticism. I am not referring to complaints about particular institutions for some action or inaction, but rather about academia collectively. Some of this criticism is a direct challenge to the main theme of this chapter, and even this book; for where I state that academia does a, b, and c, and these would be good things to share with the public, a critic might say, "no they don't do a, b, and c," or "yes, they do, but poorly, making them not worth sharing with anybody."

An unfortunate result of such criticism is that it can snowball among popular opinion, and create widespread distrust of academia, making people less open to receiving its benefits. It is difficult to judge the extent of this effect, but there is reason to believe that the public image of academia is not good. True, in one national survey, 93% of adult respondents agreed with the statement, "Colleges and universities are among the most valuable resources to the U.S."[23] But this was the survey quoted earlier, that found nearly the same level of agreement (92%) with the statement, "Preparing its undergraduate students for a career is the most important role a college performs." Thus, it could well be that when most people think of academia as a valuable resource, they're thinking about how college helps their kids get good jobs.

A more recent survey gives more equivocal results. For instance, although 42 percent of randomly sampled adult Americans stated that they have "a lot of confidence" in American colleges and universities, an even greater number, 49 percent, said they had "only some confidence." The remaining 9 percent reported "hardly any confidence at all." In the same survey, a college or university professorship was regarded as a "very prestigious" profession by about half the respondents (53 percent), about equal to elementary school teachers (50 percent), and considerably less than doctors (72 percent).[24]

I now present four common criticisms of academia, and my replies to them.

Enormous damage?

The first criticism is the claim that academic campuses, especially the more elite ones, are hotbeds of radical leftist political orientation, and that professors attempt to manipulate students' thinking to match their own. If this criticism is valid, what's to prevent professors from trying to manipulate the public, rather than, as I suggest should happen, openly sharing academic ideas with them?

In a recent survey of US adults, 38 percent of respondents stated that the politicization of campus is a "very serious problem," and 8 percent even said it is the "biggest problem facing higher education."[25] It is true that American academic faculties lean toward the political left. In national surveys of thousands of full-time faculty in hundreds of four year colleges and universities, only 17 percent declared themselves "conservative" (and less than 1 percent "far right"), while about three times as many, 47 percent, identified themselves as "liberal" (and 9 percent as "far left"). A further 27 percent identified themselves as "middle of the road."[26] Moreover, in surveys of Berkeley and Stanford faculties, approximately ten times as many professors were found to be registered Democrats as Republicans.[27]

Some high profile critics have gone so far as to claim that academia is not only manipulating its students, but in the process is destroying our youth. David Horowitz makes this claim in his book, *The Professors: The 101 Most Dangerous Academics in America*. I take Mr. Horowitz's central point seriously—some fraction of professors do use their academic position as a platform for promoting personal political or other beliefs, delivering in-class monologues that may stifle student objections, or leave little room for students or others to engage in (to quote again Amherst's Gerety) "dialogue of professor and student." This goes against core academic values discussed in Chapter 3. But listen to Horowitz's strident language: "My most difficult task in writing this book was living daily with the knowledge it provides of the *enormous damage* several generations of tenured radicals have inflicted on our educational system...."[28] (Italics added.)

I have made some calculations, based on data Horowitz provides, about the frequency with which students at distinguished liberal arts colleges or universities are likely to encounter a radical professor who stifles student expression. On average, a student taking a wide range of course subjects during four college years *might* enroll in one course in which the professor stifles expression. That's one course out of a student's 30 to 40 courses taken in college. This is one course too many for such inappropriate faculty behavior. But "enormous damage" to "our educational system"?

Horowitz does not mention the many professors who abide by the instructional principles described by Penn State literature professor Michael Bérubé:

> I would be selling students short if my classes did not reflect some of my beliefs about literary theory or feminism or postmodernism or multiculturalism, since I have spent my entire adult life studying such things and am familiar with a wide range of opinions about them, quite apart from my own; just as I am duty-bound to make this argument or that under my own name when it is relevant to the mate-

rial, so too I am duty-bound to inform students of some of the most cogent critiques of the positions I favor....it is not my job to change students' minds about this policy or that, this person or that....[29]

Bérubé's teaching doesn't make headlines. Horowitz' claims do. Yet there are probably many more Bérubés than Horowitz would acknowledge.

Regarding "enormous damage," historian Zachary Karabell states, "Given how few of Berkeley's graduates go on to careers as leftist activists and how many of them become lawyers, bankers, doctors and engineers, one could conclude that radical professors have had remarkably little success in converting students...."[30] Perhaps Horowitz and others of like mind are doing just what they claim of their opponents—projecting their own political, religious, or other biases.

Lazy professors?

The second criticism, leveled perhaps more frequently against colleges than universities, goes something like this: Unlike those of us who work hard for a living and come home tired at the end of a long day's work, professors are lazy— they work just a few hours a day and take long vacations—and this pattern is guaranteed for life by tenure. How, such critics must wonder, could people who do so little be true scholars, rather than mere dilettantes? Why should I want them sharing their academic ideas with me?

"Are the profs here lazy?" I asked sociology professor Jan Dizard at Amherst, over tofu salads in the faculty cafeteria. He laughed, "Oh, we get that a lot. Folks in town frequently ask me, 'Just what is it you do all day, besides the few hours you teach? And you get summers off, right? And they pay you a full salary for that, right?'"[31] He proceeded to fill me in on his busy schedule of preparing and updating course lectures, checking and commenting on student papers, meeting individually with students about their papers, term projects, and future plans, attending departmental and committee meetings, advising extra-curricular student organizations, meeting with visiting alumni, reading extensively within and outside his field, carrying out research, and more. Summers, he pointed out, are for more intensive focus on his research, and for the books and articles in and around his field that he hasn't gotten to during the year. I received similar replies to similar questions from faculty at Bennington, Pomona, Smith, and Swarthmore colleges. There are lax people everywhere, to be sure, but the typical college professor is highly motivated and engaged.

Ridiculous research?

The third criticism is of university research. Of the three main things universities do more than colleges—graduate education, research, and the storage of knowledge—research, the activity responsible for the greatest number of new university ideas, which could most fully inform the public, is the one most ridiculed.

The most common criticism goes something like this: "So much university research is esoteric, featherheaded, and a ridiculous waste of national resources because it doesn't contribute to creating a new 'widget' you can sell, or to curing diseases, or anything else useful." One can expect such a comment from about half of all Americans, as 52 percent of those recently surveyed agreed with the statement: "Too much of the research conducted by professors is irrelevant to the needs of society."[32]

This criticism has a long history. Between 1975 and 1988, it even spilled forth from the US Senate, when the late Senator William Proxmire selected specific federally funded research projects that he regarded as "ridiculous," or "irrelevant to the needs of society," to receive his monthly, derogatory "Golden Fleece Awards." I always wanted to win one of these accolades, and I had some pretty abstract-sounding grant titles that should have put me in the running. I guess it's who you know.

What the senator may not have realized, nor others who continue on his path, is that conceptually, most research in science—and in many other fields— has the shape of an hourglass—broad on top and bottom, narrow in the middle. When one positions the wide, sand-filled portion upward, the sand flows slowly down through the narrow waist and into the broad bottom.

How does the hourglass shape explain the senator's error? The specific subject of research, at least in science, is nearly always quite narrow, like the narrow waist of the hourglass. That's because the two key conceptual tools of science— experiments and observations—usually work only on specific and narrow questions. There's no experiment, for instance, that will answer the broad though interesting question, "How does the brain work?" Rather, a researcher, whose interest may well have begun with this broad, top-of-the-hourglass question, must narrow the question. This may involve selecting one part of the brain, probably of a particular animal species—since invasive brain experiments generally can't be done on people—and defining both a specific function of that brain region to study, and a specific experimental procedure to carry out—that is, narrowing down to the hourglass' waist.

Many scientists and other researchers arrive at their narrowly defined questions in this way, following the path of the sand from an initially broad question of both scientific and general interest, through perhaps a series of narrowing steps to the specific experimental question, and then broadening out again at the bottom to the scientific and general insights and implications obtained. This hourglass shape describes not only research, but also seminars and lectures about the research, scientific articles, and grant applications. If they're good, they follow the flow of sand.

Something similar occurs as far away from science as the opposite end of the academic campus, in the writing of fiction. Novelist and Middlebury College English professor Robert Cohen pointed this out in a public interview at the annual Jerusalem Book Fair. At a given moment in a story, Cohen may wish to convey a universal idea or widely held belief or feeling. To do so, he focuses on the "narrow-waisted" particularity of the moment. Perhaps a specific character carries out a specific action within a specific environment—perhaps just a glance, or the utterance of a single word. To the reader, the particular reveals the general. So again we have a flow of sand from broad (the author's intended broad meaning) to narrow (a character's specific action) to broad (the reader's receiving the author's intended broad meaning). And doesn't this same pattern underlie most art forms, like theater, film, dance, or painting? Doesn't the merest brush stroke sometimes tell a whole story?

Here, though, is a problem faced by some, especially beginning, scientists, and some of the public, with the hourglass concept. They tend to get stuck in the narrow waist and forget how the sand got there, and where it is going. People who think the main question being asked is the narrow one at the waist should realize that this is just a tool for addressing the broader question at the top of the hourglass. If academics don't make this clear to the public, the public will have good reason to believe that much academic research is indeed "ridiculous."

> *Normal, down-to-earth guys.*

The fourth and final criticism I'll discuss, perhaps the most significant of all, is a wider criticism, as its target is the entire rational approach to knowledge, and very large numbers of Americans are taking target practice. Several recent authors have bemoaned this development.[33] To quote one, "During the past four decades, America's endemic anti-intellectual tendencies have been grievously exacerbated by a new species of semiconscious anti-rationalism, feeding on and fed by an ignorant popular culture...at odds [with] modern scientific knowledge...."[34] Surely anti-rationalism is running rampant. Recent Harris polls report that nearly half of adult Americans believe in ghosts, about three quarters believe in angels and miracles, and about a third believe in UFOs, astrology, and witches.[35] To this list we could add belief in astrology, reincarnation, communication with the dead, the emotions of plants, and abductions by aliens. These are not viewpoints one typically acquires with an Ivy League degree. Not one of these beliefs is backed up by responsible, rational evidence, yet all are believed by huge numbers of Americans.[36]

But are irrational beliefs really growing in America? Although difficult to quantify, and thus to prove, several developments on both the socio-political right and left suggest so. From the right comes the extraordinary growth of religious fundamentalism. And from the left comes the postmodern notion (which I discuss in later chapters) that everyone is an expert, empowering just about anybody to share their "ideas" with the world.

Some people, rather than feeling they themselves are experts, seem to believe that not being an expert is actually more legitimizing than being one. To quote the host of a Minneapolis-based paranormal radio show that promotes the existence of ghosts, "That's why people like our show....We never claim to be experts." And TV "star" Jason Hawes of the show *Ghost Hunters* concurs, "I think the main appeal of our show is we're normal, down-to-earth guys. We're not scientists out there talking over everybody's heads." Both these avowed non-experts claim that more people than ever now believe in ghosts. The radio man again: "It just seems like everybody came out of the paranormal closet....Especially after 9/11, people were seeking more of an interest in the spiritual side of life. Back in 2000, if you talked about ghosts at the water cooler at work, people rolled their eyes at you. Now you talk about ghosts and everybody seems to have a story they want to share."[37]

While ghosts and witches, with the help of "normal, down-to-earth guys" who "never claim to be experts," seem to be gaining traction across the land, the CEO of the prestigious American Association for the Advancement of Science recently announced some bad news. Namely, "15-year-olds in the United States ranked 17th on science tests and 24th on math tests, compared with teens from 29 other wealthy nations. The United States is failing to address the problems of science education for tomorrow's work force."[38] And the US ranks only 21st among these nations in the percentage of its youth who finish high school.[39]

So while universities, as I have claimed above, are not strongly connected with the general public, much of the public seems to be in an anti-rational downward spin. Nor are school students showing much promise that the next generation will reverse the spin. Although this does not say that the limited academic connection with the public has *caused* society's regression, academia has done little to reverse it. Academia may find it difficult to connect with the ghost-believing segment of the population. However, positioned as it is at the head of the nation's rationally-based educational hierarchy, it can hardly escape the need to try. But how?

It is important to recognize that irrational and unsubstantiated beliefs are, at least in part, intellectual matters, and thus approachable in part on intellectual grounds. I don't mean that ghost belief is necessarily a matter of intelligence. There are lots of intelligent and capable people out there who, however, simply have little idea of how evidence works to support or refute an idea, why evidence matters, and how to make one's way along a path of even modestly complex reasoning. Unable, thereby, to come to evidence-supported conclusions, they will believe just about anything. Half of America ready to believe just about anything is a very serious and dangerous problem, in need of urgent attention.

Defining ghost belief as partly a problem of intellect, analysis, and evidence differs from the way some people define it, as a sign of a "culture war." One leading scholar describes the "soldiers" of a culture war as having "basic commitments and beliefs that provide a source of identity, purpose, and togetherness for the people who live by them."[40] According to this view, ghost believers derive personal benefits from their beliefs. Perhaps so, just as most academics I know appear to derive personal benefits from their academic culture, and most would want nothing to do with ghost believers.

But is this war? Must it be war? War is a strong word—and, I believe, the wrong word. When you're at war you have an enemy. You attack. You kill. And while doing so, it's a tad difficult to sit down to tea with your enemy and explore ideas together. By regarding certain people as "other," as belonging to a different culture, academics can conveniently convince themselves that there's no possibility of meaningful interaction, and thus no point in trying. So most don't.

This raises an important problem, pointed out by Harvard Law Professor Cass Sunstein in his book, *Going to Extremes*. When groups of like-minded people come together to discuss their views (such as ghost believers or others discussing shared irrational beliefs), their views almost invariably become even more extreme as a result of the group interactions.[41] That is, leave like-minded groups to their own devices and they will, in Sunstein's terminology, "go to extremes" of belief. But if people with a different outlook interact with these groups, their extreme views can be moderated. We all tend toward those of like mind. But what Sunstein underlines is that doing so not only creates divisiveness, but provides a breeding ground for extremism.

I don't regard ghost believers as my cultural enemy. I regard them as people I should listen to and try to understand better. How do they come to their beliefs, and how do these fit into their life patterns? I would like to share my ideas, as a scientist, that led me to be a ghost non-believer. Specifically, I would like to share how inquiry works in science, including what kinds of answers it can provide, what kinds it can't, what kinds of evidence scientists regard as legitimate, and why.

I doubt that many ghost believers, on hearing my ideas, would jump right up and whoosh ghosts from their minds, just as I, hearing their ideas, would not whoosh them into mine. Rather, this conversation may produce four other types of goals. First, it can lead the "warring" parties to sit at the same table, something that hardly ever happens. Second, it can possibly moderate extreme beliefs, as Sunstein's book suggests. Third, it can create greater mutual understanding—if not convincing—of positions that initially seem foreign, or even abhorrent. And fourth, it can open the door to other conversations, on less controversial or non-controversial ideas based on shared interests. There are a great many such interests, as even those who belong to separate cultures also belong to the same overarching culture—namely, the shared American experience in "one nation, indivisible."

It's a bit like a family in which some members hold political, religious, or other ideas radically different from everyone else. The family may have discovered there's little point in trying to convince one another, or perhaps even to talk about these topics. But there are still lots of other things to talk about, and other ways to be a family. And in the course of time, as world views and experiences are shared and appreciated, as confidence builds across boundaries, there may be some softening of outlooks and shifting of ideas.

This book calls upon universities to alter how knowledge is delivered to the nation, thereby generating a major change in the nation's character. Skeptics may say such a character change is not possible. But people of my age (I'm now 71) could never have imagined in our youth the extent of change America would undergo in the course of a lifetime—consider just the subject of segregation, a word that sounds strangely old-fashioned today. Yes, creating a major change can take a long time, and may seem daunting. But it will take even longer if we don't start now.

Whereas this chapter has dealt primarily with just one idea—the idea of a university (and a college), as well as its critics, most academic ideas that have the greatest capacity to change our lives result primarily from research in the various academic disciplines. Research-based ideas are the subject of the next chapter.

Notes

1. E. D. Hirsch, Jr., *Cultural Literacy: What Every American Needs to Know* (New York: Houghton Mifflin, 1987; rev. ed. Vintage, 1988).

2. Jonathan R. Cole, *The Great American University: Its Rise to Preeminence, Its Indispensable National Role, Why it Must be Protected* (New York: Public Affairs, 2009), 500.

3. Interviewed by the author at Cornell University, September 12, 2007.

4. Interviewed by the author at Cornell University, September 13, 2007.

5. American Institute of Physics, *Bulletin of Science Policy News* 135 (September 19, 2005). http://www.aip.org/fy/2005/135.html; Karin Fischer, "Number of Foreign Students in U.S. Hit a New High Last Year," *Chronicle of Higher Education* (Nov. 16, 2009); University Continuing Education Association, *The New Face of Higher Education: Lifelong Learning Trends*, 10th ed. (Washington, DC: University Continuing Education Assoc., 2009); Beth McMurtrie, "International Enrollments at U.S. Colleges Grow but Still Rely on China," *The Chronicle of Higher Education* (November 14, 2011); Karin Fischer, "Chinese Students Account for About Half of All international Applicants to U.S. Graduate Programs," *The Chronicle of Higher Education* (April 3, 2012).

6. htpp://www.shanghairanking.com/ARWU2011.html.

7. The Carnegie Foundation for the Advancement of Teaching has categorized the many different types of institutions of higher education. htpp://www. Carnegiefoundation.org/classifications/.

8. Jeffrey Selingo, "U.S. Public's Confidence in Colleges Remains High," *Chronicle of Higher Education* 50, no. 35 (May 7, 2004), A1.

9. John H. Pryor and others, *The American Freshman: Forty Year Trends* (Los Angeles: Higher Education Research Institute, UCLA, 2007).

10. Interviewed by the author at CUNY, July 24, 2007.

11. There were only slight differences in these percentages for faculty at different types of universities and colleges, including public versus private research universities and colleges. Jennifer A. Lindholm and others, *The American College Teacher: National Norms for the 2004-2005 HERI Faculty Survey* (Los Angeles: Higher Education Research Institute, UCLA, 2005), 40.

12. For a trenchant discussion of undergraduate learning goals, see Richard P. Keeling and Richard H. Hersh, *We're Losing our Minds: Rethinking American Higher Education* (New York: Palgrave Macmillan, 2011).

13. Samuel Schuman, *Old Main: Small Colleges in Twenty-first Century America* (Baltimore: Johns Hopkins University Press: 2005), 46, 124.

14. Inaugural presidential address, Amherst College, October 26, 2003. http:/www.amherst.edu/-president?/.

15. Interviewed by the author at Amherst College, March 13, 2007.

16. Tom Gerety, "Except by Dialog: 1994 Inaugural Address," Amherst College Archives. http://www.amherst.edu/aboutamherst/news/archives/gerety/inaug94.

17. Lindholm and others, *American College Teacher*, 29.

18. Gerety, Except by Dialog.

19. National Science Foundation, http://www.nsf.nsb.

20. American Library Association, http:///www.ala.org/tools/libfactsheets/alalibraryfactsheet22

21. Jennifer Howard, "Google begins to scale back its scanning of books from university libraries," *The Chronicle of Higher Education* (March 11, 2012).

22. Dartmouth, in fact, refers to itself as Dartmouth College. But in spite of its small student population—5,700, close to the range of liberal arts colleges—its several separate graduate and professional schools place it squarely in the category of a university, albeit a small one.

23. Selingo, "U.S. Public's Confidence"; Another survey that generally concurs with these points is John Immerwhar, *Public Attitudes Toward Higher Education: A Trend Analysis, 1993-2003* (San Jose: National Center for Public Policy and Higher Education, 2004).

24. Neil Gross and Solon Simmons, "Americans' Views of Political Bias in the Academy and Academic Freedom" (lecture, American Association of University Professors, Washington, D.C., June, 2006), http://www.aaup.org/surveys/2006/Gross.

25. Ibid.

26. Lindholm and others, *American College Teacher*, 44.

27. Daniel Klein and Charlotta Stern, "Surveys on Political Diversity in American Higher Education from the National Association of Scholars: How Politically Diverse are the Social Sciences and Humanities?" http://www.studentsforacademicfreedom.org/news/1909/Surveys.html.

28. David Horowitz, *The Professors: The 101 Most Dangerous Academics in America* (Washington, DC: Regency, 2006), xlviii.

29. Michael Bérubé, *What's Liberal About the Liberal Arts? Classroom Politics and "Bias" in Higher Education* (New York: Norton, 2006), 12.

30. Zachary Karabell, *What's College For* (New York: Basic Books, 1998), 101.

31. Interviewed by the author, March 12, 2007.

32. Gross and Simmons, "Americans' Views."

33. Chris Moody, *The Republican War on Science* (New York: Basic Books, 2005); Morris Berman, *Dark Ages America: The Final Phase of Empire* (New York: Norton, 2006); Al Gore, *The Assault on Reason* (New York: Penguin Press, 2007); Susan Jacoby, *The Age of American Unreason* (New York: Vintage, 2008).

34. Jacoby, *Age of American Unreason*, xi.

35. The Harris Poll, *The Religious and Other Beliefs of Americans*, 2003-2008. http://harrisinteractive.com.

36. Michael Shermer, *Why People Believe Weird Things: Pseudoscience, Superstition, and Other Confusions of Our Time* (New York: Henry Holt, rev. ed., 2002).

37. Aaron Sagers, "Haunt Hunters," *Providence Journal* (October 26, 2008). http://www.projo.com/tv/content/artsun-ghost-hunters_10-26-08.

38. Alan I. Leshner, "A Wake-up Call for Science Education," *Boston Globe* (January 12, 2009), A 11.

39. UCEA, *New Face of Higher Education*, 17.

40. James Davison Hunter, *Culture Wars: The Struggle to Define America* (New York: Basic Books, 1991), 42; James Davison Hunter and Alan Wolfe, *Is There a Culture War: A Dialogue on Values and American Public Life* (Washington, DC: Brookings Institute Press, 2006).

41. Cass R. Sunstein, *Going to Extremes: How Like Minds Unite and Divide* (New York: Oxford University Press, 2009).

Chapter 2. Ideas from the Disciplines

What kinds of ideas, from the vast array of research disciplines studied at universities, are important to the general public? Given that these ideas are at least as diverse as the disciplines themselves, universities are relevant to almost anyone's favorite subject. It would be nearly impossible in this chapter to cover such a broad range of subjects, and I do not attempt it.[1] Rather, I begin with one prominent idea from my own discipline, neurobiology, as a kind of case study. This idea is the outcome of research about how our brains create and store memories. We'll briefly trace where this idea came from, beginning with speculation and moving on to experimental evidence, then how this idea influenced later thinking in this discipline, and finally how this idea can be a powerful force in people's lives.

Next we will explore three factors that threaten the notion of sharing ideas from the academic disciplines with the public. The first is a misunderstanding—or worse, a rejection—by large segments of the public, of academic expertise and the evidence underlying research in the academic disciplines. The second is the steady decline on campus of idea-rich basic research, which is continuously displaced by industrially driven applied research with more specific goals. The third is a common claim that non-academic institutions are replacing academia as the wellspring of research-based ideas. The chapter concludes with an analysis showing that, in spite of these factors, much of the public appears ready to receive research-based ideas from universities, if only they would be appropriately presented.

Before diving in, I offer a comment about the word "research," which is sometimes reserved for the natural and social sciences, and replaced by the term "scholarship" for the humanities. I believe this constitutes a subtle denigration of the humanities. Academics in all fields seek out new truths. That different methods are used, and that different forms of expression result, in different fields, are of secondary significance. Therefore, I apply the term, "research," to the seeking of new truths in all fields of academic study. But with two provisos—first, that the truths be new not only to the seeker, but to the world of knowledge, and second, that the truths be well-supported by research, rather than being mere opinion. I use the word "scholarship" for the wider range of intellectual activities that all academics engage in while creating, storing, and disseminating ideas and knowledge.

You Sculpt Your Own Brain—A Case Study Idea

Where do our memories come from? What happens in our brain when we consciously learn something, or simply experience something that we can later recall? This question has been a source of wonder and speculation for centuries. And the wonder increases when we realize just how effective our memory storage can be—how many thousands of remembrances a brain can hold, and how long it can hold them. Many people recall in intimate detail experiences they had even 50 or more years ago. (My earliest, quite detailed, memory is of the US Air Force fly-over on V-J Day, celebrating the end of World War II—67 years ago!)

What physical or chemical changes take place in the brain to encode and hold a memory for later recall? Years of speculation produced three main ideas. First, perhaps some specific chemical substance is created at the time of the initial experience that somehow encodes and stores the memory. Second, as the brain's information travels in the form of electrical impulses, perhaps some form of long-lasting electrical signal holds the memory. And third, perhaps some long-lasting structural change in the actual substance of the brain constitutes the memory's code.

Speculations can stimulate thinking. But the first concrete evidence about these questions came through the laboratory research of Eric Kandel of Columbia University and his associates. Kandel won the Nobel Prize in Physiology and Medicine in the year 2000 for these and other extensive studies of memory.

Recall from Chapter 1 the concept of the hourglass shape of research, with its broad upper and lower portions and its narrow waist. The narrowness of the waist expresses the highly specific (and seemingly narrow) nature of the research activities carried out, though these are intended to help answer the very broad question represented by the wider top of the hourglass. In the research of Kandel's lab, the waist became *really* narrow; Kandel selected for study neither the human brain, nor that of a species closely related to us, but rather a squishy, slimy, sedentary sea-slug called *Aplysia*. He did so because early studies, mostly in his own lab, had shown that this simple animal learns, and that the learning involves just a handful of nerve cells, which would greatly simplify the analysis. Moreover, each of these cells is large enough to identify under the microscope as the same unique cell in every *Aplysia*, just as you can identify a given finger— say the left thumb—on your hand and anyone else's. Thus, it was possible to carry out repeated experiments on copies, in different *Aplysia* slugs, of the same cell—like studying the left thumb of lots of people. And that's what Kandel and colleagues did—the narrow waist of their studies on the huge subject of memory was one particular nerve cell in a sampling of sea-slugs—a much more manageable research subject than the horrendously complex human nervous system.

But the resemblance to our own learning is real. For instance, Kandel's research group showed that *Aplysia* engages, as we humans do, in learning that is stored in "short-term memory" (quickly and easily learned, quickly forgotten), and if the learning is a bit more intense this can transform into "long-term memory" (remembered for a duration long by sea-slug standards—three weeks or more). This resemblance indicates that *Aplysia's* memory is a good model for studying human memory. This common strategy of studying a simpler system to understand more complex systems is often called the "model systems approach" to research.

What happens in the particular nerve cell studied in *Aplysia* when this cell takes part in creating a long-term memory? The Kandel research group looked for structural changes in the nerve cell. Since the contact points among nerve cells—the synapses—are known critical points for controlling the flow of information through nervous systems, the researchers looked for changes specifically in the number of synaptic structures from the single nerve cell studied onto other nerve cells in *Aplysia's* nervous system.

In general, one nerve cell contacts another not just at one, but at a great many synapses. So this became a grueling study, counting under the microscope hundreds to thousands of tiny synaptic structures by which the nerve cell studied connects up with other nerve cells. But the work paid off. The researchers found that during the creation of a long-term memory, the nerve cell developed about twice as many synaptic structures as the same cell in other *Aplysia* that had not experienced long-term memory (about 2,700 versus 1,300 synaptic structures). Moreover, the establishment and maintenance of these new synaptic structures followed the same time course as the establishment and maintenance of the sea-slug's long-term memory itself, as determined from the animal's behavior. This and subsequent studies by the same researchers strongly suggest that when *Aplysia* creates a long-term memory, it does so by creating more synaptic structures between particular nerve cells, thereby strengthening the functional connections among these cells.[2]

As mentioned earlier, the question of how this process occurs had been the source of speculation for centuries. But speculation doesn't answer questions. Only actual evidence does, such as the evidence described here.

It's a long way from *Aplysia* to you and me. But the sea-slug findings, first reported in the 1980s, stimulated researchers to look for similar increases in synapse formation during long-term memory creation in mammals. And they found them. It was not possible to perform these tests on the human brain, because the brain tissue would need to be removed and examined microscopically to search for the new synapses. Nevertheless, the fact that what works in *Aplysia* also works in mammals—the animal group to which we belong—strongly suggests that it works in our brains as well.

Apparently, we each rebuild a portion of our own brain, sculpting it anew, every time we create another long-term memory. This rebuilding is on the microscopic level—the new synaptic structures are tiny. But given the huge number of memories we carry around, what is microscopic for one learned event becomes macroscopic for all learned events. It's not that we develop bumps on our skulls when we learn, as was once claimed in phrenology, a long-discredited approach to brain study. Rather, the rebuilding on the microscopic level can add up to a macroscopic amount of our brain tissue.

What can the knowledge of this idea—that apparently we sculpt our brain as we learn—do for us? Quite a lot, I believe.

First, it could impress upon each of us that, being our own neural sculptors, we hold our brain's structure and function, and thus in a sense, our life, largely in our own hands, to do with as we like. This could encourage school and college students to take their studies, their life, and themselves a bit more seriously; it could lead educators to dedicate themselves more fully to their task (they're not just throwing knowledge at students, they're helping them build their brains); and it could remind us never to give up on our potential to learn, grow, and find improved ways of living.

Second, knowledge of our brain sculpting could encourage us to provide positive, reinforcing experiences, rather than negative, painful ones, for our children, other loved ones, friends, co-workers, and perhaps even strangers. Each time we act nasty to someone, that person might end up with nasty built into a little corner of the brain. Realizing this, we might think twice about acting in this way. The alternative claim that, "He'll/she'll get over it" now seems harder to maintain. Perhaps this realization could even help lead to a more compassionate society.

Third, as each of us experiences and learns different things, each brain becomes a unique sculpture, in a sense, a one-of-a-kind work of art. Nobody else's brain is quite like yours. This realization can enhance our awareness of our unique individuality, which might well help some people develop more self-confidence and personal pride, which surely can change one's life.

If just one idea from one academic discipline can potentially have such positive effects, think what the wide array of discipline ideas can do to enhance our lives. For sure, academia's discipline ideas comprise a huge resource for personal fulfillment, and for the benefit of families, communities, the nation, and the world. And recall, our case study's research was carried out on nothing more grandiose than a squishy little sea-slug!

Experts and Evidence

In the Introduction, I defined ideas from the disciplines as "concise summations of things that academic experts have come to know or believe about subjects in their own and related fields, firmly supported by evidence, and interpreted in a manner that reveals their broader significance." This statement includes two critical words—"experts" and "evidence"—hot-button terms, the first rejected, and the second misunderstood, by many people.

What have people got against experts these days? Three things. First, in this postmodernist, Wikipedia, social networking era, some people claim that *everyone* is an expert, a claim I examine in some detail in Chapter 9. Second, some people who know they are *not* experts seem nevertheless to regard their thoughts as more legitimate than those of experts—recall from Chapter 1 the radio and TV ghost hunters who claim that their success results from their being "normal, down to earth guys" who "don't claim to be experts." And third, some people seem to regard an expert the way I did while growing up, as someone with an encyclopedia in his head—who simply knows a great deal of stuff. In this section, I will counter these three concepts about experts. I will argue that only some people, not all, are experts; that in addition to normal, down-to-earth guys, we also need real experts; and that although many academic experts do know a lot, this isn't the main thing that makes them experts or makes them good at their jobs.

One person I came to admire as an expert during my doctoral training was the late Steve Kuffler, who assembled, and then headed, Harvard Medical School's Department of Neurobiology, perhaps the finest such department in the country at the time. I had the honor of being one of six graduate students attending a summer lab course run by Steve and two other professors from his department. We students got to know the profs pretty well.

You didn't get the feeling that Steve knew a great deal of stuff—he didn't spout species names, reel off long lists of books he'd read, or engage in philosophical debate. Encyclopedic wouldn't describe his mind. Incisive would. He recognized clearly the most important unsolved problems regarding how nerve cells and brains work, and had a knack for designing remarkably effective experiments to solve these problems. He also had a knack for recognizing this knack in others, whom he hired as members of his department. That is, for Steve, knowing it was not the essence; figuring it out was. Being an expert, for him, was about the process of coming to know something through research evidence. Through Steve, I came to realize that figuring it out is the heart of science, and the essence of academia.

Does the word "expert" express the idea of "figuring it out?" I'm not sure, but I'm also not sure there's a more fitting word—none of the following seem to work: Analyst (calls up the image of a couch); scholar (brings up the encyclopedia image again, or dusty manuscripts in the library basement, which are only one part of university research); intellectual (a bit pompous); authority (even more pompous); researcher (perhaps not pompous enough); academic (used here as a noun, too vague). So in this discussion, I will stick with the word "expert," for lack of a better alternative.

The nature of the evidence that experts seek is often misunderstood. In my judgment, this is the single most important subject that academia could get across to the public. Although not everyone will learn about evidence by actually doing research, understanding how researchers think about, organize, strategize, and implement their work, and how they interpret their results, could empower people to understand, and to some extent judge, a given research claim. It could help people improve their own analytical thinking and problem solving. Unfortunately, though, there is a dearth of explanation of the nature of research evidence explained appropriately for the non-expert.

As research evidence is a very broad subject, with variations among the different disciplines, I restrict this discussion to scientific evidence, itself a subject of considerable breadth. There is a whole field of academic study—much of it carried out in philosophy of science and science education departments—concerned with exploring the "nature of science."[3] While scientists often abbreviate jawbreaker technical terms to ease discussion, like DNA for deoxyribonucleic acid, I find it amusing that those studying the easy-on-the-jaw "nature of science," likewise abbreviate, perhaps aping the scientists. So their subject becomes NOS. In my view, a core concern in this subject is the nature of scientific evidence—which I suppose we could call NOSE.

Rather than attempting to review the entire subject of scientific evidence, I will simply offer some FATNOSE ("facts about the nature of scientific evidence") that I've picked up by sniffing around my own and others' research labs and classrooms.[4] These are simple points, though they are probably foreign to most of the general public. I believe they could help the public, as they help me, think about how scientific research comes up with its results. Perhaps they will even help my academic colleagues think about how to present scientific evidence to the public.

Most scientific evidence is acquired by the use of just two types of procedures, or conceptual tools, irrespective of the field of science. One is called an observation—you look at something, some object or process. The object may be a molecule, cell, animal, forest, or even a distant galaxy. The process could be some movement of any of these objects, or some transformation occurring within them. Makes no difference—in all these examples, you're just looking. You may go to great lengths to place the object or process under conditions suitable for both the object and your viewing of it, perhaps maintaining it under particular conditions of temperature, light, humidity, etc. (This doesn't work for a galaxy, of course.) You may do your "looking" not with the naked eye, but rather indirectly with the aid of a microscope or telescope, X-ray crystallography (which, incidentally, is how the structure of DNA was first discovered), or by reading out numbers from some type of meter. But basically, all you're doing is looking, and by looking carefully, you can sometimes discover important new things about the object or process of interest.

The other type of procedure, slightly more complicated and potentially much more powerful, is an experiment. In any experiment, you give some kind of push to an object or process, and look at what it does in response. Again, the object or process could be of any type, though in this case it needs to be something you can "push," which again excludes galaxies. (Actually, though, as I write this, a missile is on its way to the moon to bombard its surface, giving it a pretty hard "push," to see if underground water is released—less ambitious than pushing a whole galaxy, but still impressive.) Again, you may go to great lengths to place your object or process under suitable conditions. You may "push" it with your hand, or more likely in a precisely controlled, physically or chemically defined way, say with electric current, or by injecting a certain amount of a specific drug, or by any of a thousand other types of defined "push." In an experiment, the object or process is often referred to as a "system" or a "black box" or, if you are experimenting on a person, the slightly more humanizing term "subject". Your push in the experiment is usually called a stimulus or an input, and the action evoked in the experimental system is called a response or an output. By examining in detail the response of the system to the stimulus, you can sometimes discover new things about the system—what's inside the black box and how it works. But recall, all this is just an experiment, which is just pushing and looking.

Perhaps you see that observations and experiments are, in principle, so simple that we probably all do them every day. We probably did a lot of both, even as babies. Crawling on the floor, we might have looked at that nice, brightly colored ball our parents placed before us. By looking, we discovered roundness (an observation). By pushing, we discovered the rolling of round objects (an experiment). Scientists are big babies, still just pushing and looking.

The clever reader will jump in here and say, "But you've forgotten about theoretical research—like computer models." Not really. When you create a computer model, or any other kind of model of the real world, even one made of paper and chewing gum, the model becomes your "system" and you have the same two ways of researching it. You can look at it, or first push it (for instance, by putting numbers into your computer model and clicking on "go") and then look at it, to see what it does—that is, you either observe, or experiment on, your model.

Several seemingly unrelated varieties of research can also be understood within the observation/experiment format. Two examples of observation are the use of questionnaires to survey public opinion, and the study of historical documents. An example of an experiment is a "natural experiment," in which nature has produced some type of stimulus to a definable system—for instance, the arrival on an isolated island of a species of vertebrate predator, where none had previously existed. One could examine the response of the "system" under study (such as the populations of the island's plants and non-vertebrate animals) following the arrival of this "input"—the vertebrate predator. Another example is the "thought experiment," in which you don't actually look at or push anything, rather you imagine doing so, and try to figure out what would happen. Einstein was really good at this and changed the world of physics through his thought experiments.

If looking, or pushing and looking, were all there were to science, it would just be rote work. It's not, of course. Although observation and experiment are the underpinnings of science, the actual process can be tremendously complex, and offers great opportunities for originality and creativity. It also offers many potential intellectual pitfalls that could easily entrap the unwary.

To mention one common pitfall, in an experiment, when one presents a stimulus to the system under study, many unintended and unwanted components are often included in the stimulus. It is important to recognize these components and, if possible, eliminate them and thereby present a "pure" stimulus containing only the intended component. A complementary approach is to rule out the influence of the unintended components by means of control experiments, in which only the unintended components are presented as a stimulus, to see if they, in the absence of the intended component, can evoke a response. Without paying careful attention to these matters, one can never know whether the unintended components of the stimulus were responsible, or partly so, for the response. Many of the pitfalls encountered by novice scientists, or novice interpreters of science, fall into this category of not recognizing unintended components of a stimulus, and not checking whether their possible effect has been eliminated.[5]

Scientists spend their lives learning their way around these and many other pitfalls, coming to recognize solid evidence derived from well executed observations or experiments, and distinguishing it from weak or no evidence. This is part of what makes them experts. Moreover, as observations and experiments in all fields of science are very similar in principle, and somewhat similar to research methods used in the social sciences, there exists "general research expertise," shared by many in academia. It's not, as some people seem to believe, that scientists and other academics claim expertise out of a desire for authority or power or any of the other contemporary mantras. (Some do, of course, but they are rare.) It's just a matter of practice—expertise you develop by doing your work day after day. An auto mechanic gets better by repairing more cars, a pianist by playing more sonatas. It's like that, too, in academia.

Most academics have done little to get explanations about their evidence flowing out through the academic sluice gates. There seems to be a channel blockage regarding the "nature of scientific evidence"—a kind of "stuffed NOSE." There have been efforts over the decades to improve such understanding among school students, and a limited number of academics have discussed, in language appropriate for the general public, how they gather evidence. Unfortunately, though, academics have made little *concerted* effort in this important area.

The public should also realize that academic experts continually help each other refine their understanding of evidence, and thus become even better at it. One way they do this is through peer review. Even before any evidence is acquired in a research project, a grant application to support the proposed re-search is peer reviewed. The agency or foundation that receives the grant pro-posal selects a group of academic experts in the subject area and requests that they carefully judge the research plan and the applicant's ability to carry it out. Many applicants see this as a hurdle, which is, of course, one way to view it. Craig Venter, leader in the Human Genome Project, even calls it "a pointless, annoying, and frustrating distraction from science."[6] But it can also be a richly rewarding source of feedback, as the applicant receives the anonymous report of these experts' deliberations. Moreover, after the research is finished, written up, and sent off for publication in a professional journal, or perhaps as a monograph to a university press, the editors send it out for peer review to academic experts in the field. Again there's the hurdle and the reward. Academics, then, receive twice feedback from some of the best minds in their field, helping them to re-think and refine their ideas and means of obtaining evidence. And it's all free! I have never understood why some academics complain about this remarkably helpful process.

Academics cooperate in many more ways that refine their understanding of evidence. There are departmental seminars followed by discussion periods, "journal club" meetings in which one or more research groups discuss profes-sional research articles, informal hallway chats and national and international conferences.

What's going to make the "normal, down-to-earth guys" in America realize that the ghost hunters and others who "don't claim to be experts" are correct in not claiming so, and that experts and their evidence offer a more reliable basis for understanding? I believe the ghost hunters have given us at least part of the answer—stop "talking over everybody's heads." We should not dumb down in talking to the public, however. Finding the balance between talking over peo-ple's heads and dumbing down is not easy. (I suggest several ways to find this balance in Part 2.)

What effects can we expect a broader public acceptance of academic exper-tise and evidence to produce in American society? Suppose that more people understood and acknowledged how expert evidence for ideas is acquired. And suppose that more people tried to build their world view around evidence-based ideas, striving to understand themselves, their environment, our world, exist-ing threats, and our best responses to those threats, on the basis of responsibly acquired evidence. (Living by this approach does not mean relinquishing one's imaginative, creative, artistic, right-brain nature, which exists in parallel to left-brain rationality). What might be the overall effect of this? For an answer, I borrow an insight from history professor Robert Cherny of San Francisco State University:

> History is a social cement; it's what holds together a society, that
> you know your common past and by virtue of that are better able to

function as a member of the society and take part in forming some kind of a common future. It gives people a sense of who they are by knowing where they are coming from.[7]

Social cement—a nice phrase. And it applies not only to history, but more broadly to expert evidence in all areas of inquiry. Wider public acknowledgment and understanding of expert evidence could give rise to "social cement," holding together a better informed, more analytically aware and thoughtful people, engaging with one another on an elevated level of public discourse. People would not get bogged down debating the existence of ghosts. Surely this is a worthwhile goal, and surely, opening the academic sluice gates has the potential to help bring it about.

The Slide to Applied

A common criticism of universities addressed in Chapter 1 claims that much academic research is esoteric and wasteful of national resources because no practical outcome is produced. The question of how to justify academic research calls for a broader discussion of basic versus applied studies. To clarify, applied research is oriented toward creating practical outcomes such as medically, socially, industrially, or militarily useful, or commercially salable, products or processes. Basic research consists of explorations to discover the fundamental nature of things, and is not motivated by, or oriented toward, practical outcomes. Phrased differently, applied research looks at a part of the world and asks, "How can I make this work for a given purpose?" whereas basic research looks at perhaps the same part of the world and asks, "How is this built?" or "How does this work?"

The results of basic research, especially in the natural sciences, are widely regarded as essential for providing a kind of intellectual infrastructure necessary for applied research to proceed. This idea was famously codified in a report written by Vannevar Bush (no family connection to the two US presidents) that had been commissioned by President Franklin Roosevelt near the end of World War II. Bush was former Vice President of MIT, and deeply experienced in academic, industrial and governmental affairs. After FDR's death, Bush submitted the report to President Truman in 1945. It stated: "Basic research leads to new knowledge. It provides scientific capital. It creates the fund from which the practical applications of knowledge must be drawn. New products and new processes do not appear full-grown. They are founded on new principles and new conceptions, which in turn are painstakingly developed by research in the purest realms of science."[8]

Bush's idea was later buttressed by a 1976 analysis of the types of research that had led to the then most advanced medical treatments of cardiovascular and pulmonary diseases. Two university medical experts on these subjects found that 41 percent of the research projects that led most directly to the advanced medical treatments were basic, not applied, research. (Their criterion for basic research was that the journal articles describing a project did not mention "an interest in diagnosis, treatment, or prevention of a clinical disorder, or in explaining the basic mechanisms of a sign or symptom of the disease itself."[9]) These 41 percent were studies that Vannevar Bush would have considered "in the purest realms of science," and that for the purpose of this discussion, are examples of basic research. Given the importance of these studies to the ultimate development of cardiac and pulmonary medical treatments, the financial cost of this basic research probably paid for itself many times over in lives saved, and in the continuing productivity of those whose lives were saved.

More than half a century after Bush's report, Princeton University political science professor Donald Stokes introduced a very different view in his book, *Pasteur's Quadrant*.[10] Stokes claimed, contra Bush, that it is not basic research, but rather "use-inspired basic" that provides the most useful infrastructure for applied research. Here the researcher studies fundamental principles, as in basic research, but has practical outcomes clearly in mind—perhaps a particular societal need or some commercially viable, or medically, or militarily useful product. Unlike those engaging in basic research, the use-inspired basic researcher continually dialogs with industrial, military, medical, or other potential implementers, reads their applied research articles, and orients his or her own research to provide the knowledge necessary for developing these applications. Yet this is not strictly applied research, Stokes clarifies, because its immediate outcome is not implementation itself, rather providing basic knowledge needed for the implementation. In short, use-inspired basic research sits squarely between basic research, which is fundamental and often abstract or theoretical, and applied, which is production-oriented.

Stokes correctly reminds us that use-inspired basic research is often an important intermediate category between basic and applied, a point that Bush had not included in his report. However, I have two objections to Stokes' analysis. First, I take issue with his seemingly low esteem for basic research's contribution to applications. Although neither Bush nor Stokes is alive today, I can envision them in a heavenly debate, Bush reminding Stokes of any number of examples, but most notably the atomic bomb, whose development during World War II was derived fundamentally from basic research in physics. Like the bomb or not, it was certainly a major invention.

My second issue with Stokes's analysis is that, by implication if not by direct statement, he measures the importance of a given research project primarily in terms of its ability to promote, directly or indirectly, practical applications. This is a common practice, in both professional and lay circles. For Stokes, as purely basic research is not terribly effective in leading to applications, its significance, if any, must lie elsewhere. He does state, "Nothing in this analysis is meant to diminish the case for pure research in terms of the intrinsic, civilizing value of knowledge." And he does add: "A civilized people will seek knowledge for its own sake...."[11] But these two sentences are about all he offers in support of basic research in his entire book.[12]

I must add that the reference to basic research as producing "knowledge for its own sake," which is often expressed as "knowledge for knowledge's sake," has always boggled me. Is an idea that changes the way people understand themselves and their place in the universe just an idea "for its own sake," whatever that may mean? Or is it for the sake of all humanity? Let's agree right now to expunge from the English language the absurd expressions, "knowledge for its own sake" and "knowledge for knowledge's sake." Voooooom. Gone.

A related statement frequently heard about basic research is that it is "curiosity-based," implying that the only reason for doing it is that the researcher is curious, as compared to an applied researcher whom we are perhaps to conclude may or may not be curious, but is clearly more useful. The value judgment is easy to detect. Are we to surmise, for instance, that Copernicus, a very curious chap, did nothing useful because no product or process was implemented as he (together with later help from Kepler, Galileo and Newton) "only" showed that the earth rotates around the sun, not the reverse? This, together with many other discoveries that have radically changed human history resulted from basic research carried out with no thought for practical use of the results. To quote former Harvard President Derek Bok, it is "social critics, philosophers, and the purest of scientists who have left the most enduring mark on our civilization."[13]

Jonathan Cole's recent book, *The Great American University* muddies the water on the basic/applied issue, in my view, by claiming that there is a "false dichotomy between basic and applied research" (one hears this a lot these days), and specifically that "the class of problems belonging to the biological sciences is far and away the most difficult to fit into either a basic or applied framework." For Cole this difficulty is far more widespread, given his claim that, "blurred boundaries between curiosity-driven and use-based research extended to almost all of the physical, biological, and social and behavioral sciences."[14] He seems to be saying that purely basic research is a thing of the past. Yet elsewhere in Cole's book he states the importance of basic research in the sciences, social sciences and humanities for the university's (not society's) health.[15] Is the present and future role of basic research to keep the university campus a thoughtful place, while society-at-large becomes ever less thoughtful and more technological?

It seems clear that there are three reasonably distinct categories of scientific research—basic, use-inspired basic, and applied. It is usually fairly easy to assign a given research project to one of these categories. Recently I asked a gathering of colleagues in my university's Life Sciences Institute into which category their own work falls, and hardly any had a problem answering—most responded, "use-inspired basic."

It is true that a strong, decades-long trend is leading to less basic research in universities. In biology, my subject, there are still a few holdout basic fields, such as paleontology, evolution, animal behavior, and taxonomy. But many other fields within biology and other disciplines have moved substantially away from basic work. Nowadays, this type of research occurs as if on an archipelago of "Basic Islands," dotting a "Use-inspired Basic Sea," that opens into an "Applied Ocean." And the tide is rising. In short, exceedingly important research—basic research—is drowning and in need of resuscitation—for the good of humanity.

What happened during the past several decades to bring about this change? Initially, events during the 1960s and 1970s associated with student activism helped set the stage for the slide toward applied. Paradoxically, while many student activists were demanding an end to applied, military-oriented research on campus, there arose a desire for more applied research of other types—to help cure what were increasingly perceived as society's multiple ills. In response, interdisciplinary centers and research institutes sprang up like mushrooms on campuses, many dealing with urban, racial, ethnic, feminist, educational and other social issues. These were generally committed to applied research and often to implementing the results of this research in society. The centers and institutes differed in several administrative ways, not relevant to this discussion, from regular academic departments. Many faculty who had previously focused on strictly basic research within their departments began drifting over to the new centers and institutes and shifting at least part of their research to more applied concerns. In time, with the "center culture" in place, it became relatively easy to create still more centers to deal with newly emerging issues. Applied research snowballed.

For the slide toward applied, 1980 was a watershed year. Two major developments that year were the Bayh Dole Act[16] and the creation of the hi-tech firm Genetech.

The passage of the legislation sponsored by Democratic Senator Birch Bayh of Indiana and Republican Senator Robert Dole of Kansas was probably the single most supportive event for applied research on campus. Previously, when a university research project, funded by a federal research grant, had resulted in an invention, the property rights to that invention usually reverted to the granting agency, which seldom did anything to implement or promote it commercially. This amounted to a big loss, economically and production-wise, for all concerned, including the nation as a whole. No general governmental policy existed on this matter. The Bayh-Dole act made it possible for the university to obtain the property rights, apply for a patent, and commercialize the invention. Royalties from sales could be shared by the university and the campus researcher/inventor, the latter often receiving both a salary supplement and further funds supporting the ongoing research. Most research-oriented universities ultimately developed an "office of technology transfer" to encourage patentable inventions by their researchers, help secure patents, obtain venture capital, and develop means of market implementation. This quickly became an academic win-win. Many inventions implemented in this manner are now in general use. Universities and faculty members have earned handsomely from commercialized inventions, and research activity has been enhanced by the portion of the profits fed back into campus laboratories to support the research.

Also in 1980, the first of many new academic biotech companies was established—Genetech, created by Professor Herbert Boyer of the University of California at San Francisco together with a venture capitalist. Boyer successfully used genetic engineering methods to synthesize the hormone insulin. From then on, an increasing stream of molecular biologists and others were drawn to commercial enterprises. This has strongly influenced the work of many molecular biologists; some of the very best have left academia to take full time positions in the biotech industry. Many others, remaining primarily on campus, are working, in essence, as much for industry as for their home universities, their research and part of their personal income supported by hefty industrial contracts. Viewing the overall involvement of industry in academic research, it is fair to refer to this arrangement as an "academic-industrial complex."

This raises several risks relevant to the sharing of academic ideas with the public. One is the trend of academics giving over to industry their choice of research aims and activities, often narrowing their focus from broad concerns with basic ideas to specific concerns about creating particular products. This amounts to giving up part of one's academic freedom, a foundational value of the university, which includes freedom to determine one's own research, rather than this being determined by industrial goals and markets. A second risk is giving up the right to speak openly about one's ongoing research, a centerpiece of academic freedom, but often prohibited by industrial contracts. A third risk is an altered public perception of the academic research enterprise, from one where profs seek truth to one where profs seek to prof-it.

A more benign aspect of the slide to applied concerns funding of research by federal granting agencies. It had long been the case that a grant application to NIH (the National Institutes of Health) or NSF (the National Science Foundation) required a statement of the potential public benefits of the proposed research. But these were general requirements with little impact on the evaluation of grant applications, which were judged more on their strictly scientific value. Now these agencies focus more intensively on a statement of the grant's "pre-defined societal benefits," specific contributions the research will make to society. These statements are taken much more seriously than ever before.

Of course, benefit to society is a proper expectation for federal research support. One type of benefit that sometimes satisfies NSF grant administrators is educating the public about the research supported by the grant, and about the general field of science. This type of benefit is consistent with the central theme of this book.

But this is not the whole story. Benefit to society also implies that a grant application for applied, or at least use-inspired basic research, has a much higher chance of being funded than an application for basic research. This again reflects the attitude that basic research is not especially beneficial. Whereas in the past I had grant support from NIH for nearly 20 years for purely basic research, I've recently been told that this same research, today, would have "a snowball's chance in hell" of being funded. Likewise at NSF, where I also had several years' funding, I am told that the same type of research would now have a very hard time finding funds.[17] As a result of these granting realities, many researchers have re-oriented the motivations, goals and methods of their research. Many of my colleagues now carry out studies less attuned to their own interests and driving curiosity, in order to bring in the necessary grant support.

As I have asked my students rhetorically each year in the final moments of the final lecture of my Introductory Biology course, "If university researchers don't study how the bird flies, so that our hearts and minds can soar along with it, how the forest grows, so that we can stand in awe of its majesty, how a single fertilized cell becomes you or me, with hearts and minds that can soar and feel awe, then who will study these things?" The rhetorical answer, "no one" is understood—no one will study them, and no one will share them with the public.

Off Campus Discipline Ideas

Some contemporary scholars have observed that today the creation of knowledge through research, rather than being university-centered as in former times, has moved at least partly off campus. Knowledge, they say, is now widely distributed among many types of institutions and organizations, including industrial, governmental, and independent research centers, think tanks, foundations and other non-profits. To quote one report, "Universities are coming to recognize that they are now only one type of player, albeit still a major one, in a vastly expanding knowledge production process."[18] According to this analysis, the role of the university as a creator of ideas has been diminished. What does this say about my claim for the importance of universities sharing their ideas with the public?

The statement that knowledge creation is moving partly off campus is a responsible one, not the irresponsible "everyone's an expert" variety mentioned earlier, and discussed in a later chapter. Here are five factors that have contributed to the growth of off-campus knowledge sources:

- The switch of much of the world's economy from manufacturing-based to knowledge-based has led industry to enter more fully into the knowledge market.

- An over-production of PhDs, beyond those who can be absorbed into academic jobs, provides a highly trained off-campus work force.

- University-based academics, increasingly engaged as consultants in various off-campus research activities, carry their knowledge off campus.

- "Trans-disciplinary research"[19] creates partnerships among faculty members and ad hoc groups of experts working in industry, government, think tanks, law firms, the media and elsewhere. Trans-disciplinary partnerships strive to solve problems that may or may not have applied outcomes. The relationships are often fluid, changing as the research progresses and new skills are required. (Trans-disciplinary is distinguished from inter-disciplinary research, which more often involves on-campus work by members of different academic departments who join forces, often through a university "inter-disciplinary center," to explore subjects not fully encompassed by any one academic department or discipline.)

- Various other types of new off-campus venues draw together academics and off-campus intellectual leaders. These include virtual venues where leading edge ideas are discussed and interpreted, such as the TED lectures and the Edge website.[20] Real venues include the growing number of major research institutes not formally connected to universities, some very generously funded by private capital. An example is the new Allen Institute for Brain Science in Seattle, driven by Microsoft co-founder Paul Allen's half billion-dollar contribution. This level of private funding allows the Allen Institute to draw outstanding researchers away from academia, especially given the ongoing decrease in funding for academic research.[21]

Allen is hardly alone among mega-donors. America's top 50 philanthropists donated a total of $10.4 billion in 2011, often via their family mega-foundations. Like Allen, many are now focusing their funds on a just few major recipients, and are expecting quick results. This is a shift from the approach of earlier giving by standby foundations such as Ford, Rockefeller, Mellon, and Carnegie—seeding many projects with smaller donations and continuing for many years to fund the successful ones. To quote a recent analysis, this shift in strategy "has substantially reduced direct foundation investment in university research, previously the largest single category of investment. Disillusioned with the slow pace of most university research, grant makers are redirecting their research investments to nonacademic centers, think tanks, and the like, which...are more likely than universities to produce what is wanted, and on time."[22]

But off-campus research does not significantly reduce the prominence of the university as the nation's greatest source of ideas. When a professor partners or consults with, or works for an off-campus organization, or engages with others via TED or Edge, that professor returns to the home university enriched by newly acquired insights. These enter the academic arena via collegial conversations, writing, teaching, and research. Thus, the on-campus reservoir of ideas actually expands, making it an even richer resource for the public than before. Although focused research centers like the Allen Institute are poised to make major research advances, they are generally devoted to a specific area of research, unlike a university that covers nearly all areas of knowledge.

A personal incident recently brought home to me the continued wealth of academic ideas. While visiting Cornell, I met a new graduate student specializing in natural resources and forestry. Later, we met again by the frozen foods counter in a local P&C Supermarket, as we both reached for the last frozen pizza. He was newly arrived from New Zealand, and I asked him casually, "So how do you like it here?" His response, paraphrased, was, "It's totally amazing. Anything you could possibly want to find is right here." (He meant on campus, not in the deep freeze bin.) I fully agree. Look at the Cornell website and you'll find a listing, for its Ithaca campus (not including its medical school, in New York City) of 94 academic departments (including, just to hint at the range, The Departments of Crop and Soil Science, Mechanical and Aerospace Engineering, and Russian Literature), plus over 100 inter-disciplinary research centers and institutes (including The Center for a Sustainable Future, The Institute for Women at Work, and the Center for Vertebrate Genomics). "And the range of courses is dazzling," he continued. "I can take anything I want," a phrase that rang true as he picked up the last pizza and headed for the cashier.

Is America Ready for Academia's Ideas?

There are several reasons to wonder whether, if academia opened its sluice gates for ideas, these might float right past a disinterested populace. Here's a reminder of five reasons for this concern that I have already mentioned. First, for many people, what's important about universities and colleges are career-relevant matters, not necessarily ideas. Second is the notion that everyone is an expert, so academia has nothing special to offer. Third is the perception that university people are "talking over everyone's heads," making "normal, down-to-earth-guys" more valuable to society than academic experts. Fourth, many people oppose universities on political or religious grounds. And finally, some people just couldn't care less what some professor has to say about Hamlet.

I believe, however, that there are two powerful reasons why, despite all this, many people are truly ready for an influx of academic ideas. The first reason has to do with America's strong democratic tradition, and the second relates to how people learn.

America's democratic tradition, as explained in an insightful book by Harold Shapiro (former President of University of Michigan, and subsequently of Princeton), promotes "personal autonomy [as] an almost supreme value, the source of individual self-realization, and both a reflection of an authentic inner self and the source of our liberty." Freedom means, among other things, personal development of one's self, one's family, and one's affinity group. People become, in Shapiro's words, "the authors of their own destiny."[23] (This recalls the parallel concept that people sculpt their own brains.) Self-fulfillment occurs largely through experiencing new things, including new ideas. American democracy thus creates a mass market for ideas.

The second reason people are ready for ideas is based on academic research about learning. Until a few decades ago, learning was almost always a somewhat rigid and formal process. Kids sat at rows of desks in classrooms and were taught things adults thought they needed to know. If adults wanted to learn something, the first thought would be to make bigger desks. The underlying notion, spoken or unspoken, was: You want to learn? Take a course, and a teacher will teach you.

Although courses serve an important role for school or college students, and for some lifelong learners, it is increasingly recognized that learning and self-fulfillment, especially by adults, needn't involve courses or other formal procedures at all. Rather, "informal learning," or "free-choice learning" is becoming for many a preferred option, as people search out what interests them and access it in diverse ways, most notably via the Internet. To quote John Falk of Oregon State University, a leading expert on informal learning, "There is a revolution going on in America and it is all about learning. Yes, lifelong learning is alive and well. And the vehicle propelling this long sought-after societal goal is free-choice learning."[24] Given these developments, there is a strong and growing thirst for various types of knowledge, and for a wide diversity of ideas.

Two related concepts, both originating from universities, about how learning occurs, lend further support for free-choice learning, and thus for the importance of a diversity of available ideas. The first of these concepts is "multiple intelligences," often abbreviated MI, developed by Harvard psychology professor Howard Gardner.[25] MI defines a set of broad skills, referred to as different "intelligences." According to Gardner, we all possess all these intelligences, but each of us is strong in some and weak in others. Gardner has defined eight intelligences—linguistic, logical-mathematical, spatial, bodily-kinesthetic, musical, interpersonal, introspective, and naturalistic. (Which of these are your own areas of strength and weakness? It can be both instructive and fun to profile oneself. Do the same for your spouse or your kids, siblings, or others, and see how different even close family members can be.) Each person's own profile of these different "intelligences" helps define what that person will likely want to learn, and how successful the learning is likely to be. Given the range of inter-personal differences, a wide diversity of ideas is needed to satisfy all people.

The second, related, concept about how we learn, which has been central in the field of education for decades, is "constructivism."[26] It posits that each of us "constructs" our own inner mental world. (Although this is an abstract notion of construction, it again recalls the sculpting of our brains.) We carry out this construction through our own individual experiences, within the capabilities set by our own genetic endowments. There are many types of relevant experience, including our formal schooling and myriad encounters with the world and its people. It is widely held in educational circles that a person will want to learn something new, and will succeed in learning it, to the extent that there is a match between the thing to be learned and the inner mental world the individual has already constructed for him/herself. If there is an appropriate "hook" on the "mental skeleton" you've built for yourself, on which to hang a new idea, that idea will likely stay put in your cognitive world. Without a hook to catch a new idea, it will likely fly in one ear and out the other. So again, multiple ideas are called for, to hang on the many different mental hooks of people, all different from one another, based on individual differences of experience and innate abilities.

We can conclude that: a) Lots of people have a yen for ideas of different types, from different subject areas; and b) Lots of ideas are afloat in the campus reservoir. So here's a thought—let's connect a) with b).

In the next chapter, we make a switch from ideas based on the experimental evidence and the rational logic of academic research to ideas that engage our emotions—ideas that people have stood up for, fought for, and in the extreme even died for. I refer to values, in particular, the values that underlie and guide the university. What ideas could be more important, and more powerful, than these?

Notes

1. Jonathan Cole, former Provost of Columbia University, lists a large number of findings from university research, some phrased as ideas. http://university-discoveries.com.

2. Craig H. Bailey and Mary Chen, "Morphological Basis of Long-term Habituation and Sensitization in *Aplysia*," *Science* 220 (1983): 91-93; Craig H. Bailey and Mary Chen, "Long-term Memory in *Aplysia* Modulates the Total Number of Varicosities of Single Identified Sensory Neurons," *Proc. Natl. Acad. Sci. USA* 85 (1988): 2373-2377; Craig H. Bailey and Mary Chen, "Time Course of Structural Changes at Identified Sensory Neuron Synapses During Long-term Sensitization in *Aplysia*," *J. Neurosci.* 9/5 (1989): 1774-1780; Eric R. Kandel, *In Search of Memory: The Emergence of a New Science of Mind* (New York: W. W. Norton, 2006).

3. American Association for the Advancement of Science, *Science for All Americans* (New York: Oxford University Press, 1989); Moti Ben-Ari, *Just a Theory: Exploring the Nature of Science* (Amherst, NY: Prometheus Books, 2005).

4. One of my most interesting opportunities to discover the nature of scientific evidence came when I developed an introductory biology course for 60 especially advanced Cornell freshman. I had them carry out, in groups of 2 to 4, experiments in many different areas of biology. The research was low on technology and high on thought. Most projects were original research, in that the teaching assistants and I did not know in advance what results they would obtain, though often we made good guesses. To my great interest, students researching plant physiology, animal behavior, bacteriology, and many other biological subjects all faced the same conceptual stumbling blocks, and for this reason often made the same procedural errors. I developed a "NOSE" for this kind of student errors.

5. This was the single most common pitfall of the students in the research course mentioned in footnote 4 above.

6. J. Craig Venter, *A Life Decoded: My Genome, My Life* (New York: Viking, 2007), 127.

7.   Robert Cherny, personal communication.

8.   Vannevar Bush, *Science the Endless Frontier* (Washington, DC: United States Government Printing office, 1945). http://www.nsf.gov/about/history/vbush1945.htm.

9.   Julius H. Comroe, Jr. and Robert D. Dripps, "Scientific Basis for the Support of Biomedical Science," *Science* 192 (1976): 105-111. A later British study found that 21 percent of research papers had contributed importantly to clinical practice in a different field, neonatal intensive care—Jonathan Grant, Liz Green and Barbara Mason, "Basic Research and Health: A Reassessment of the Scientific Basis for the Support of Biomedical Science," *Research Evaluation* 12, no. 3 (2003): 217-224. The latter paper claims the methodology of Comroe and Dripps was faulty, but differences in the methods used in the two studies to define a given research project as basic would strongly affect the outcome, as would differences in the research histories of different medical fields. The question of the utility of basic research has generated controversy, fueled in part by competition over who should receive research funding, academic scientists or medical researchers.

10. Donald E. Stokes, *Pasteur's Quadrant: Basic Science and Technological Innovation* (Washington DC: Brookings Institute Press, 1997).

11. Ibid., 100.

12. One might wonder whether Bush undervalued the broad importance of basic research to society, regarding it primarily as a service to applied research. However, Roosevelt's letter to Bush (which is included in Bush's report *Science the Endless Frontier*) had requested specifically the means for "the improvement of the national health, the creation of new enterprises bringing new jobs, and the betterment of the national standard of living." And that's what Bush provided. Roosevelt's letter also included the statement: "...we can create a fuller and more fruitful employment and a fuller and more fruitful life." He did not clarify what he meant by these lasts three words. Fruitful economically? Culturally? Personally? Interestingly, in Bush's cover letter accompanying his report, he states: "Scientific progress is one essential key to our security as a nation, to our better health, to more jobs, to a higher standard of living, and to our cultural progress." These last three words by Bush may be his reply to the last three by the President, "more fruitful life."

13. Derek Bok, *Universities and the Future of America* (Durham, NC: Duke University Press, 1990), 9.

14. Cole, *Great American University*, 97-104.

15. Ibid., 173-74.

16. Council on Government Relations, http://www.cogr.edu/docs/Bayh_Dole.pdf.

17. This analysis of the current granting situation is based largely on personal communications from Susan Volman, a grants administrator at NIH and Chris

Comer, formerly a grants administrator, and currently an advisor, at NSF. The quotes are from Comer.

18. Michael Gibbons and others, *The New Production of Knowledge: The Dynamics of Science and Research in Contemporary Societies* (Los Angeles: Sage Publications, 1994), 11.

19. Ibid.

20. www.ted.com; www.edge.org.

21. Peter Monaghan, "Microsoft Co-founder's Brain Institute Attracts Top Academic Researchers," *The Chronicle of Higher Education* (April 1, 2012).

22. Stanley N. Katz, "Beware Big Donors," *The Chronicle of Higher Education* (March 25, 2012).

23. Harold T. Shapiro, *A Larger Sense of Purpose: Higher Education and Society* (Princeton, NJ: Princeton University Press, 2005), 142. Shapiro reminds us that liberal democracy can conflict with one's personal autonomy. For instance, we need to respect the pursuit of personal autonomy by others, even when their pursuit may conflict with our own.

24. John H. Falk and Lynn D. Dierking, *Lessons Without Limits: How Free-Choice Learning is Transforming Education* (Walnut Creek, CA: AltaMira Press, 2002), 6.

25. Howard Gardner, *Frames of Mind: The Theory of Multiple Intelligences* (New York: Basic Books, 1983); Howard Gardner, *Multiple Intelligences: The Theory in Practice* (New York: Basic Books, 1993).

26. Leslie P. Steffe and Jerry Gale, *Constructivism in Education* (Mahwah, NJ: Lawrence Erlbaum Associates, 1995).

CHAPTER 3. VALUE-BASED IDEAS

Academia is widely criticized today for its supposed lack of values. In this chapter, I show that universities and colleges are actually among the most value-based institutions in America. Several of their core values are among the very ones that inspired the Founding Fathers, themselves inspired by Enlightenment thinking, to develop the world's first democratic nation. These shared nation-building and university-supporting values include freedom of speech (called on campus "academic freedom"), tolerance of diversity (originally religious diversity, expanded today to include ethnic, racial, gender, and other forms of diversity), rationality, and progress. I will show how daily life at universities and colleges, including the activities that give rise to their wide range of ideas, is strongly influenced by these institutions' core values. To repeat a statement from the Introduction, if *the idea of a university* is the gateway to the university, *academic values* are its infrastructure. Thus, public awareness of a university's values, or "value-based ideas," is essential for a well-grounded understanding of the university.

Most university ideas, being the outcome of research in various disciplines, as described in the previous chapter, are evidence-based. We relate to these on a cognitive level. Our emotions, belief system, sense of good and evil, and what we consider important in life generally has no bearing on our accepting or rejecting such ideas. This is especially obvious regarding research in the natural sciences; if an experiment clearly demonstrates that medicine x cures disease y, it doesn't matter whether you like modern medical practice or not—x cures y.

But value-based ideas are much less cognitively germane, and do depend on such things as what we feel is important in life. These ideas often engender strong emotional reactions. For instance, I happen to feel strongly—no surprise here—that democracy is a better form of government than totalitarianism. I can't prove rationally that it's better. Rather, I hold dear democracy and the freedom it offers, as they are in line with how I believe people should live and government should treat them. The idea of democracy, then, is a value I endorse. You too, I'm guessing.

Given their importance for understanding universities, academic values are ideas that should be flowing full force from campus into society. Academia should be saying loud and clear, for these principles we stand. Yet most of these values and their importance for academic work are rarely shared with the public. In my experience, the subject of values is rarely even discussed by faculty. Most academics seem too busy to engage in seemingly abstract, philosophical discourse. They want to get on with their work, be it research, teaching, or administering. Former Columbia University provost Jonathan Cole agrees: "Universities do not often talk about the core values of the university—the values at the heart of university culture....Somehow, we assume that people have considered these issues, have come to understand them, and don't need to discuss...how to reinforce or challenge appropriately [the university's] core norms and values."[1]

In this chapter, we'll dig beneath the surface in search of the values infrastructure that supports, motivates, facilitates, and even makes possible, the everyday work on campus. This discussion is based in part on my years of involvement with universities (silent though these institutions usually are on the subject of values), and on the writings of colleagues on this subject.[2]

Here is my list of ten academic values, which also serves as an outline of this chapter. Some items will need an explanation to reveal how they are actually values: 1) Discovery, 2) Truth, 3) Progress, 4) Rationality, 5) Simplicity, 6) Academic Freedom, 7) Civil Discourse, 8) Diversity, 9) Excellence, and 10) Service.

1) Discovery

A friend, a professor of neurobiology, tells me he will never retire because he "will always want to look around the next corner" of his research field. Many academics have such intense curiosity about their subject that it's not clear how they could ever stop discovering, as long as they are physically and mentally able. The drive to discover can be very powerful, sometimes bordering on addiction.

Discovery can be an aesthetic, long-remembered experience. Here is how noted physicist Freeman Dyson recalled the beauty of lectures by mathematician Godfrey Hardy at Cambridge University, heard more than fifty years earlier! "He lectured like Wanda Landowska playing Bach on the harpsichord: precise and totally lucid, but displaying his passionate pleasure to all who could see beneath the surface. Each lecture was carefully prepared, like a work of art...." Dyson quotes Hardy himself: "A mathematician, like a painter or poet, is a maker of patterns. If his patterns are more permanent than theirs, it is because they are made with ideas...." Dyson again: "His mathematical papers are beautiful in style as well as in content."[3]

One often speaks of a beautiful experiment, scientific article, or seminar presentation. The seminar slides may be quite ordinary, the article printed in an everyday black font on plain white paper. The beauty is not in the graphics, but in the elegant process of discovery and the findings produced.

The intensity of the drive to discover and of its aesthetic expression signifies how deeply discovery is ingrained in the academic experience, marking it as a central academic value.

2) Truth

Truth is tricky. Sorting it out, in all its dimensions, would take a whole book, or a shelf of books. I touch on three aspects—whether truth exists, seeking truth, and truth-telling.

Does truth exist?

Some postmodernist commentators claim that it is no longer possible to define a standard of truth. They claim that in any subject there are multiple, equally valid, truths. For example, a given historical event can have multiple interpretations, some conflicting with others, yet all true.

Reasonable as multiple interpretations can be, some postmodernists have exaggerated their claims against truth to the point of absurdity. If everybody's truth were really equally valid, if graffiti, pregnant with cultural relevance, were really in the same category as Rembrandt, if rap or hip-hop, because they come from the heart, were right up there with Beethoven, if the opinions of scientifically untrained people about global warming, the causes of autism, or the dangers of genetically engineered tomatoes were regarded equally with the judgments of highly trained scientists, then "anything goes" would be our approach to truth.

Yes, truth is more complex than previously realized, and the postmodernists have made us see this. But as Oxford Professor of English Christopher Butler says, "Postmodernist relativism needn't mean that *anything goes*....What it does mean is that we should be more skeptically aware, more relativist about, more attentive to, [our] theoretical assumptions...."[4] That is, truth exists, and is distinguishable from falsehood, but it may come in more than one form, making it trickier to pin down than we previously realized.

Truth seeking

The first item on this list of ten values was "discovery" by academics. This second value is about *what* they are trying to discover—truth. Truth seeking requires putting aside preconceptions and desires as to what answers one will find. If one does have preconceptions, and the research results happen to differ from these, then one must put one's preconceptions not just aside, but in the trash, and replace them with the new understanding. Trashing our cherished ideas can be difficult—the more so, the more we cherish them. Thus, best not to cherish them too much.

An aspect of truth seeking that troubles some people is its often temporary nature. My experimental result of today might lead me to think that a particular scientific idea is true; but tomorrow a researcher with a more powerful technique or a new insight may prove my result wrong. I would then have no choice but to revise my understanding of what is true, and would hold this revised idea only as long as no other new experiment sweeps this one away. There is reason to believe that, as these revisions of our understanding continue, we are approaching a final, lasting truth, but there is no guarantee of its permanence. At any moment in history, then, our scientific truth is our current best understanding, or working model, or hypothesis, or theory. That's why many researchers, myself included, are cautious about using the word "fact," which has the sound of finality.

Consistent with this cautious attitude, some scientific theories that have held firm and not been disproved for a long time are still called theories. One example from biology is the "cell theory," which states that all plants and animals are made up of cells, and these all derive from pre-existing cells. Anyone who has taken an introductory biology course knows that this theory is so well established that we can be pretty sure nobody will disprove it. Yet the cellular basis of plant and animal life, first discovered about 170 years ago, is still called the cell theory, not the cell law, principle, or fact—this in respectful recognition that new truths can supersede older ones. Some people who oppose Darwinian evolution are quick to point out that evolution is *only* a theory, and thus not firmly established. But the word *only* is misplaced, as evolution is about as firmly evidence-based as any scientific finding. Evolution is called a theory for the same reason that the cell theory is called a theory—respect for the ongoing nature of the search for truth, not belief in a legitimate basis for doubting evolution's validity.

Yet some scientific findings are referred to as laws—Newton's laws in physics, for instance. Let's recall, though, that Newtonian physics, the scientific standard for two centuries, was partially superseded by quantum physics in the 20th century. Perhaps physicists should act, like biologists, a bit "unlawful."

In the humanities, rather than attempting to approach some lasting truth about the natural world, scholars often re-examine their understanding in the light of new ideas and insights, reaching for a modified, or broader, more all-inclusive truth. Like scientists, many humanists resist the temptation to believe they have found truth's final version.

For people who desire the consistency and permanence of ultimate truth, as provided, for instance, by religious faith, the shifting sands of academic truth can be troubling. But that's just how it is as we do our best with the tools available at any moment, to understand ourselves and the world around us.

Truth telling

I was introduced to the importance of truth telling in the university context during my first week as a Tufts undergraduate. All new freshmen were required to attend a lecture on plagiarism. Plagiarism, we were told, was the greatest of all sins. "What happened to rape and pillage?" I heard someone whisper, a few rows behind me. I imagined some in the student audience (those with SAT scores high in math but low in English) might have been unsure what plagiarism meant—you know, copying others' ideas and passing them off as your own—and some might have worried that this "sin" was something they were already doing.

What Tufts didn't make clear, at least to me, was why all the focus on plagiarism. They should have explained that the reason the campus and the university exist is for the opposite of plagiarism, the opposite of cheating on tests, or copying someone else's lab reports, or co-opting ideas from books into your essays without digesting and interpreting them, and without citing the sources—in short, the opposite of lying. The college or university, we should have been told, is a place where every word a student or professor utters or writes needs to come from deep within a personal center of truthfulness; it mustn't be something casually whipped up to complete an assignment, to fill an hour-long lecture, or to impress others. They should have told us we need consistently to give our very best effort for the truth, as we would tell it to our best friend in a moment of utter confidence and sincere intimacy. We must be the most excellently truthful we can be.

None of us were. At least not all the time. But the more years I have spent on university campuses, the more I have come to appreciate the deep significance and multi-faceted nature of truth, its seeking, and it telling.

Fitting that the word *Veritas*—Latin for truth, appears in the mottoes of many American universities. It has long been the entire motto of Harvard.

3) Progress

Discovery, truthfully sought, can bring progress. On the individual level, by obtaining a college education, each student opens up new personal opportunities to progress through life. The sum total of all post-graduate activities confers progress on society. In the opinion of several college presidents, creating progress in the world through alumni's enlightened activities is their institution's overall function. Former Amherst President Anthony Marx defines "...what the college was founded for—to enlighten, care for and advance society as a whole...."[5] On a stone wall viewed upon entering Pomona College is inscribed, "Let only the eager, thoughtful, and reverent enter here." And on the wall's opposite side, viewed upon leaving the college, is inscribed, "They only are loyal to this college who, departing, bear their added riches in trust for mankind." Former Cornell President Frank Rhodes adds: "[The university] contributes to the nation's well-being as it nurtures and trains each new generation of architects, artists, authors, business leaders, engineers, farmers, lawyers, physicians, poets, scientists, social workers and teachers...."[6] Given all this, the commitment of a professor to teaching can be seen as a commitment to the idea of progress. Of course, university research also generates progress of many types, in many directions.

Over the centuries, the concept of progress has been redefined many times. Currently, it is held by some in rather low regard; many conservatives stress instead enduring religious or political values, while many liberals claim that the materialism associated with what others call progress bespeaks a socially and environmentally retrograde process. While some enduring values are surely positive, and excessive materialism is surely negative, most of us are pleased by the university-based progress in fields that touch our lives directly—medical research, for instance, which helps keep us alive. With new knowledge and ideas in a wide array of subject areas deriving from our universities, we ought to be optimistic that academia will continue to serve as a springboard for progress.

4) Rationality

Although subjective qualities such as creativity, inspiration and intuition play a role in university life, rationality is the hallmark of the academic enterprise. I relate here to two aspects—the historical development of the rational American university, and the rational approach to understanding.

A brief history of the rational American university

The idea that people can use reason, or rationality, to discover new truths derives, as does the idea of progress just described, from the 17th-18th century Enlightenment era. Democratic America, including its Declaration of Independence, Constitution, and governmental institutions, were all born of Enlightenment rationality.

Surprisingly, though, at the time of America's birth as a nation, its universities were anything but sources of rationality. The same was true throughout most of Europe, with the exception of certain German institutions that could already be defined as research universities. Of the nine academic institutions founded in America prior to 1781 that survive—Harvard, William and Mary, Yale, New Jersey (later renamed Princeton), Kings College (renamed Columbia), Rhode Island (renamed Brown), Queens College (renamed Rutgers), Dartmouth (initially an Indian mission school), and Pennsylvania—all but the last were either founded and then maintained by, or at least closely associated with, some branch of the Christian church. In place of the church, Penn had rational promoter Benjamin Franklin.[7]

The main mission of most colonial universities and colleges was to educate an elite class who would run business, government, and the church, with Protestant religious values informing their professional and personal lives. Most students were white, Christian males from reasonably well-to-do families. About half of Harvard's graduates during this period became ministers. To quote a leading scholar of academic history, "all learning ultimately was to coalesce into the values and actions of a Christian gentleman."[8] Hardly any original, rational research in science or other fields, as one would recognize it today, was carried out in these early institutions.

Anglican minister and British philosopher George Berkeley, a forceful opponent of Enlightenment rationality, crossed the Atlantic and, desiring to evangelize America, gave assistance to both Harvard and Yale. His American protégé Samuel Johnson (not Dr. Johnson of Boswell fame), also an Anglican minister, became President of Kings College. Congregational minister Jonathan Edwards became President of Princeton (though he died in his first year of office)—the same Edwards who famously sermonized: "The God that holds you over the pit of hell, much as one holds a spider over a fire, abhors you and is dreadfully provoked. His wrath towards you burns like fire....You are ten thousand times more abominable in His eyes than the most hateful and venomous serpent is in ours."[9]

Were Jonathan Edwards alive today, he might not be our best choice for commencement speaker.

Not until approximately a century after American independence did the modern, rational, American university begin to take shape. Four factors were involved:

- The acquisition of enormous wealth by leading American industrialists, resulting in greatly enhanced philanthropy, much of it supporting new and expanding academic institutions.

- The Morrill Act, signed into law by Abraham Lincoln in 1862. It led each state to establish at least one university dedicated to providing practical education, generally in agriculture and/or engineering, among other subjects, and with a distinct de-emphasis on religious training. These were called land grant universities, because the federal government granted large plots of federally controlled land to the states, which many then sold to bankroll the universities' construction and maintenance. The land grant universities were to admit students not just from wealthy, educated families. Rather, children of farmers, shop keepers, and others of modest means and educational backgrounds were to flood these campuses. Moreover, these universities developed ways of extending their education about farming and family matters to the public. Today, many land grant universities are among the finest in the nation.

- The emergence of a number of university presidents of especially great talent, vision, and leadership. These included Daniel Coit Gilman of Johns Hopkins, Nicholas Murray Butler of Columbia, Andrew Dickson White of Cornell and Charles William Elliot of Harvard.

- The influence on several American university presidents and other academics of the rationally-oriented German research universities. All four American university presidents just mentioned—Gilman, Butler, White and Elliot—had spent time in German universities prior to their own presidential appointments. With the opening of Johns Hopkins by Gilman exactly one hundred years after the Declaration of Independence, America's first research university was born.[10]

But the American research university reached maturity as a center of rationality only after World War II. One factor in this maturation was the absorption into American academia of many outstanding German and other European scholars, in an unprecedented intellectual migration following that war. Another factor was the wide recognition that scientific and technological research by American universities had contributed significantly to winning the war. One important outcome was the development of new means of federal support for university research, which helped drive the development of today's outstanding academic centers of rational thought and research.

The rational approach to understanding

A key concept intimately connected to the modern rational approach is reductionism—the idea that an object or phenomenon can be understood by first recognizing its component parts, then analyzing how each of these parts works, and how they fit together and interact with one another. Our bodies provide a good example. We can think of all our organ systems—circulatory, respiratory, muscular and other systems—as our bodies' main parts. To understand how the body works, we can ask how each organ system works, and how they work cooperatively to form the whole you or me.

Hand-in-hand with reductionism is the concept of hierarchy, again well-illustrated by our bodies. That is, each organ system has its own parts—namely, our organs (for instance, for our respiratory system, there's the nose, trachea, bronchi, and lungs). And each organ is made up of parts—tissues, and tissues of cells, cells of sub-cellular structures, and so on down to molecules, atoms, and sub-atomic particles. If you wanted to discover how a structure at a certain level of this hierarchy works you'd most likely examine the one or two hierarchical levels just beneath it. For instance, to understand how the contraction of a muscle works, biologists first examined the muscle's cells and their sub-cellular particles, especially their myosin and actin filaments, whose sliding motions cause muscle contraction. This reductionist, hierarchical approach to the human body has been responsible for most of the great medical discoveries since the Enlightenment, including those that have helped, since that time, to more than double human longevity.

Reductionism isn't the only legitimate approach to research. A common criticism of academic research is that it is too reductionist, and in focusing downward on component parts, tends to miss the forest for the trees. Some critics urge a holistic approach—looking upward in the hierarchy, toward a larger picture.

Let's examine this notion briefly using the example of forests and trees. Imagine that on some pleasant Saturday, you take a walk through a forest and note its trees and other plants, animals, and non-living elements such as soil, rocks, water, and climate. You might ask yourself how these various elements function together to form the whole, integrated forest. This would be a legitimate holistic research question, as it begins with one level of the hierarchy (individual plants, animals, rocks) and moves upward in attempting to understand the whole forest.

Now imagine that on an equally pleasant Sunday, you take another walk, this time in a meadow, and you view a forest from a distance. You might wonder how the forest's component parts function together to form the whole forest. This would be a reductionist question, as it begins by considering one hierarchic level (the whole forest) and moves downward to consider a lower level on the hierarchy (the forest's parts).

But note that once your Sunday question has led you to define the forest's parts—its trees, other plants, animals, soil, rocks, water and climate—the Saturday and Sunday questions become the same question: "How do the parts explain the whole forest?" (Saturday's question) is the same as, "How is the whole forest explained by its parts?" (Sunday's question). The only difference is where you were located when you first viewed the forest—inside it on Saturday, outside it on Sunday. Thus, reductionism and holism are not opposing, but largely overlapping, approaches.

Some people with little or no training in science who find the reductionist approach unpalatable on aesthetic, spiritual, or other grounds regard holism as more open, appealing, and valid. Some may fail to recognize the hierarchic organization of nature, which is the basis for recognizing the similarity of the two approaches. Clearly, both approaches are legitimate, though each is only as useful as the degree of rationality and rigor with which it is applied.

Some systems are so complex, with so many component parts interacting in so many ways that it can be daunting to define a hierarchy. The actions of such a system may appear to "emerge" from all these multi-directional interactions. The system's activity is said to be of an "emergent" type. Sounds mysterious, maybe even irrational, but it's not. It's just that the many parts of the system are talking to each other so much that it's hard to tease them apart. Hard, not necessarily impossible.

I believe that universities have been lax in conveying an understanding of rationality, reductionism, hierarchy, holism and emergence in academic work. At most universities, hardly any science or engineering undergrads or graduate students are required to take courses in the history or philosophy of science. Rather, most absorb the scientific approach willy-nilly from their physics, biology, chemistry, and engineering professors, who probably never had such a course either. Thus, the future academics among these students, who may become academia's future messengers to the public, will probably have little idea of how rationality developed historically, how it differs from other philosophical approaches, what are its overall strengths and limitations, and how one can best explain these and related matters. If academic institutions are hardly explaining these important ideas to their students, numbering 6 percent of Americans, how much are they explaining these ideas to the other 94 percent?

5) Simplicity

Many of the research problems that academics tackle are complex—figuring out how the brain works, or how to solve world hunger or AIDS can be daunting. Consider the human brain, for instance, the most complex bit of matter on earth. Over 30,000 brain scientists, most from universities, attend the annual conference of the Society for Neuroscience in the USA. I would guess that many, like me, went into the field of neuroscience out of awe at the brain and its amazing complexity.

And yet, the attempt to understand such complex things as the brain is all about simplicity, in two ways—simplifying the *process* of research and simplifying the research *goals*.

One simplifies the *process* of research to reduce an overly complex problem to manageable proportions. The hourglass metaphor of Chapter 1 includes the simplifying step of moving from a broad, highly complex question to a more focused, narrow, and simplified question that can be answered by research. Often this simplifying step requires selecting a totally different system to study than the one that first attracted the researcher's attention. (Like Eric Kandel, I spent my research career studying the nervous systems of relatively simple, invertebrate animals. While Kandel chose squishy sea-slugs, I chose crunchy insects.)

The research *goals* are also about simplicity. One tries to find, within the complex and apparently disorderly subject, a simple explanation for the complexity. What simple rule might underlie all this messiness? This approach is not always successful; systems with complex, emergent behavior sometimes appear to defy simple explanation. Yet it is remarkable how often simplicity wins out, from the genetic code comprised of just four letters that spell out the form and function of every living thing on earth, to the hierarchic order of the human body discussed above, that explains how all our complex parts form an integrated whole, to thousands of other examples.

Posted on my office door is a humorous statement attributed to Albert Einstein: "We should make things as simple as possible, but not simpler." A contemporary revision of this statement is the abbreviation "KISS," for: "Keep it simple, stupid."

Physicists since before Einstein have been longing for a KISS—a single, presumably simple, unified theory that will explain all the major physical forces of the universe. Some biologists feel that we already have a unified biological theory, namely, evolution by natural selection—a simple idea that explains so much. It can explain how every species has come into existence, how all species are related to one another (which, through the modern study of taxonomy assisted by molecular biology, itself brings simplified order to the great diversity of evolution's living products), and how all living things are distributed geographically in the world's different environments. What evolution does not explain, however, is how the body of a plant or animal, or any part of a body down to the molecular level, actually functions, issues that comprise most of contemporary biology. Therefore, I believe evolution does not qualify as a unified biological theory, and perhaps no such theory is out there awaiting discovery.

6) Academic Freedom

What could be more central to the American democratic ethos than the idea of freedom? Academic freedom is a quintessentially democratic value, central to the functioning of American colleges and universities.[11] It includes the freedom of a professor to make verbal and written statements, determine research subjects and methods, decide on course content and reading assignments, and grade student work, all without fear of censure. (Of course, there are occasional excesses, which are open to investigation and appropriate response).

Faculty tenure is inseparable from academic freedom; if you can be fired for what you say, you're not really free to say it. Some people object to tenure on the grounds of its being a final evaluation following which a faculty member is said to have a free ride for life. But that's not quite the case. Subsequent advancements of academic rank and salary are generally based on an annual performance review, often incorporating evaluations by both the students in a professor's classes and the department chairperson.

Increasingly, universities and colleges are hiring full-time or part-time faculty on renewable, short term contracts, and not on a "tenure track." These "contingent" faculty account for 68 percent of all academic teaching posts,[12] though considerably less in research universities and liberal arts colleges than in other institutions. Contingent faculty's academic freedom is at risk, as firing or non-renewal of a contract can easily be arranged and rarely requires explanation.

The principle of academic freedom was first stated formally at the founding meeting of the American Association of University Professors (AAUP), held at Columbia University in 1915. The meeting dealt with the atmosphere on America's campuses at the time, in which a professor could be fired if someone high up in the university's power structure—or even someone closely associated with such a person—didn't like his opinions. That's what had happened to Edward Ross, a well known Stanford University economics professor when, in 1900, the widow of university founder Leland Stanford, herself President of university's Board of Trustees, differed with Ross on matters of politics.[13]

Academic freedom and faculty tenure were established to protect professors from such actions. This was codified in the particular form currently employed in legal cases, in the 1940 "Statement of Principles of Academic Freedom and Tenure" of the AAUP together with the Association of American Colleges and Universities. From that time through the mid-1960s, most challenges to academic freedom were initiated outside the campus—usually by conservative politicians or citizens' groups disapproving of something a professor had said or done. But ever since the student activism of the 1960s and 1970s, and the resulting increased racial, ethnic and gender diversity on campus, most academic freedom challenges have been initiated from within the campus. One person or group says or writes something inflammatory and another person or group objects; or a university administration increasingly motivated by the bottom line, and increasingly divorced from university values, violates some cherished aspect of the faculty's academic freedom. New cases arise almost daily on campuses around the country, and are a central concern of the AAUP, working through its national office and especially its campus chapters to protect academic freedom.

In no other type of institution in America does freedom of speech occupy center stage to the extent it does in colleges and universities. Not in government, for instance. As for the national legislature, former President Jimmy Carter has described the decline in free and open discourse in Congress: "Probing public debate on key legislative decisions is almost a thing of the past. Basic agreements are made...often within closed party caucuses where rigid discipline is paramount. Even personal courtesies, which had been especially cherished in the U.S. Senate, are no longer considered to be sacrosanct."[14] In the judiciary, courtroom discussion is guided by the principle of competition between lawyers out to win cases, witnesses are not free to say all that comes to mind, and jury members are silent. In the executive branch in Washington, somewhat depending who's in the White House, everyone gets behind the views expressed by the President.

Nor does one commonly find much freedom of speech in the worlds of business (where profit rules), religion (where liturgy rules), or public school education (where the curriculum rules, and teachers and students are often discouraged from expressing extreme opinions). Newspapers, once ruled by freedom of the press, are increasingly ruled by highly opinionated media owners who hire like-minded reporters. Even independent news outlets keep an eye on the economic bottom line, and accommodate public tastes and interests in their decisions about subjects to cover and how to cover them.

Academic freedom is perhaps the most widely discussed value on today's university campuses. There the battle for the fundamental American value of free speech is played out day by day. Those critics of academia who hold the Constitution, personal freedom, and the American way of life in particularly high esteem might take special notice of this point.

Given the central importance of academic freedom for colleges and universities, academics would seemingly be writing extensively and sharing this subject with the public. But in my search for books on the subject, during the decade from 1995 to 2005, I found only one book about academic freedom written by a university professor in a popular style and published by a non-university press.[15] Ten others were clearly written for an academic readership. During those years and since, professors and academic administrators wrote extensively on academic freedom in professional magazines and journals such as The *Chronicle of Higher Education* and *Academe*. Hardly anyone in the general public reads these. In effect, for years, academics have written for other academics on the important core value of academic freedom—a lost opportunity for sharing one of academia's most cherished ideas with the public.

7) Civil Discourse

Imagine if everyone regarded others, including those clearly different from themselves, according to these four sentences:

- "I notice that your outlook is different from mine."

- "I have no interest in trying to convert you to my way of thinking."

- "Rather, my awareness and understanding are broadened by my knowing you, learning of your experiences, and considering your ideas."

- "I invite you to know me, listen to and consider my ideas, which may likewise broaden your outlook."

Imagine further if everyone were courteous, gentle, and compassionate. Now pinch yourself awake. If all this were really so, human interactions would be based on civil discourse and behavior, characterized by mutual respect, equality, fairness, and dignity. What would the world be like if more people held such attitudes toward their colleagues, students, teachers, spouses, children, parents, employees, employers, and those from other ethnic groups, cultures and nations?

I believe universities and colleges have the potential to lead the way toward a greater degree of civil discourse. (A good case for this is made in Harvard professor Sara Lawrence-Lightfoot's book, *Respect: An Exploration.*[16]) I believe this because the campus is an environment where, in general, these values are expressed in some significant measure, and this measure can be further expanded. True, some people on campus don't exemplify this type of discourse. We can call them the three "p's"—the *prima donnas*, who seem to believe the campus was built for them; the *posturers* who are busy trying to show they're smarter or more powerful than everyone else; and the *propagandists* who harangue others and try to recruit them to their point of view. Although these people are highly visible, giving the impression of large numbers, they actually comprise a small minority of the faculties, at least at universities with which I have been associated.

It's no surprise, then, that a group of academics are leading the way toward an upgraded approach to public discourse.[17] Their approach is called "deliberative discourse." (I'll risk trading one jargon for another, but at least I'll save five syllables, by calling it DD.) These DD people recognize that public debate is often aimed at assuring the rights of individuals and groups—we want more parks in our city, not more highways, or we want low cost housing for young people, not expensive high rise buildings. What often develops is that the rights of different individuals or groups conflict. The points of disagreement are then debated among these groups.

These debates usually conclude with a decision that defines—and here is the main point—a winner and a loser. It is a zero sum game. Everyone is arguing for their own, or their group's own rights, usually with little concern for the rights of the opponents. Lawyers are out to win cases, not to be nice. This behavior is deeply ingrained in American society.

A more liberally minded debater might hold a tolerant attitude toward an adversary's position. However, for DD, tolerance is a form of deprecation, as it says something like, "We of Group X can accept that Group Y hold that opinion, even though we realize they're full of baloney." Realistically, the DD people recognize that expecting Group X to *respect*, not just tolerate, Group Y's opinion may be expecting too much. Rather, they avoid this whole issue and strive instead for a completely different process—the process of DD (recall, that's "deliberative discourse"), that has different goals.

Here's how it works. In DD, members of different interest groups begin their encounter not by debating, or even discussing, the issue that brought them together as adversaries. Rather, they begin by getting to know one another, establishing relationships, seeking out common experience, mutual friends, shared values and purposes. Each side can then begin to understand where those on the other side are coming from, and on the basis of which concerns, and perhaps what pain, they have defined their goals. As a result, the two sides may come to realize that they share some common goals and values that run even deeper than the issues over which they initially were in conflict. Maybe, for instance, it's not the height of the high rises that bothers one group, but rather the high cost of apartments in those high rises, and maybe the other group agrees with this. Then they could actually join forces to promote their common goal of low-cost high rises—a win-win result of their deliberation. The deliberation becomes a process of discovery, sharing, and coming together, not debate, conflict, and separation.

Judith Rodin, former President of the University of Pennsylvania, is a leader in DD who recognizes the central role of academia in this process: "If we can actualize the potential of universities to define civility and community for the twenty-first century...universities can be truly powerful forces for the opening of a robust discourse and the changing of public culture."[18]

The central question here for *A Dam in the River* is whether universities present the DD idea to the public. A book co-edited by Rodin, impressively titled *Public Discourse in America: Conversation and Community in the Twenty-First Century*, reports the results of several years of thought and research on DD by a distinguished group, mostly of academic scholars. However, this book, published by the University of Pennsylvania Press, is oriented toward academics, not the general public. Several other academic books have been written about DD and related subjects, intended primarily for academic readers. Few are addressed to a general audience.

Since DD is all about public discourse, someone might have thought to tell the public about it—a pointed example of the lack of outward flow of university ideas. Many academics' initial response to a good idea seems to be, "Let's get a group of intellectuals to debate it, and get a university press to publish it." Just one problem—who's going to read it?

8) Diversity

The prevalence of white, Christian, male students, taught primarily by white, Christian male professors at most of America's universities and colleges, that began in the revolutionary era, remained largely intact until the early 20th century. But by that century's end, a more diverse faculty was educating a substantially diverse student body. Today, many colleges and universities regard racial, ethnic, gender, gender preference, national, religious and other forms of diversity as highly desirable, for several reasons. First, when students of different backgrounds learn about, from, and with one another, they discover a range of voices, experiences, and ideas that expand their outlooks. Second, this expansion provides important training for functioning in America's diverse society. Third, diversifying the student body can provide catch-up opportunities for groups such as Afro-Americans, who had previously attended college in very limited numbers. And fourth, with rapidly increasing global inter-dependence, understanding how best to communicate with those from cultures and nations around the world offers a huge political and economic payoff.

How has academia pursued the idea of developing a diverse campus, and how successful has it been? An important mechanism for increasing the percent of students from previously under-represented groups is affirmative action. Conceived during the Kennedy administration and implemented under Lyndon Johnson, affirmative action gives admissions or hiring preference to certain groups over others. In college admission, it mainly gives preference to Afro-Americans over whites. One can understand this by examining the data on college applications. On average, whites score significantly higher than blacks on SATs (Scholastic Aptitude Tests), by about 200 points out of a total of 1600. Yet black students make up 17 percent of the student bodies of the more distinguished universities and colleges—that's 7 percent higher than their numbers in the general population. At the less distinguished residential colleges and universities, the black student population is less, between 9 and 14 percent. As a measure of the degree of preference conferred by affirmative action, it has been calculated that if colleges were to judge all applicants strictly on the basis of scholastic success in high school, black admissions to distinguished universities and colleges would drop by 70 percent from their current levels. At the less distinguished schools, the drop would be about 50 percent.[19]

Black applicants are thus given a significant advantage. Whites who object to this often call it reverse discrimination. It should be noted, though, that traditionally other groups have been given a selective advantage in acceptance. One group is children of alumni, called legacy admissions, almost all of whom are white. A second group is skilled athletes. In contrast to the admission of minorities through affirmative action, it is difficult to find the moral imperative behind the special advantage provided these two latter groups.

Affirmative action has been a highly contentious issue since its establishment. In 2003, the Supreme Court handed down two important, related decisions. One decision upheld the principle of affirmative action in a case involving the admissions program of the University of Michigan Law School.[20] In the second, parallel case, whose decision was announced the same day and involved an undergraduate at the same university, a particular method used to evaluate minority applicants—adding "points" to their application scores—was banned as being too rigid in its support for minority applicants.[21]

These decisions affect all state colleges and universities in the USA, and are also likely to have a long-term spin-off effect on many private institutions. A 2005 legal over-view report by the AAUP stated: "We can expect the next decade to contain both legal and political challenges to affirmative action, as colleges and universities work towards implementing the details of the Court's decision, and as affirmative action opponents broaden the focus of their legal and political attacks."[22]

In Michigan's 2006 state elections, "Proposition 2" was voted in, amending the Michigan state constitution by barring affirmative action altogether in both student admissions and hiring policy at Michigan's state colleges and universities. Affirmative action had already been banned in two other states, California and Washington. When I visited the University of Michigan six months after the Proposition 2 vote, many faculty and administrators were still up in arms about the decision. I heard several comment that, had the state's universities been more successful in establishing relations and sharing their points of view with the public, Proposition 2 might well have been defeated.

The issue remains alive. In 2012, the Supreme Court agreed to hear yet another case, this one brought against the University of Texas, whose admissions practices adhered to the means of using affirmative action previously approved in the Michigan case. Predictions are for a close battle, with the possibility that the use of affirmative action in college admissions could be overturned.[23]

Diversity in university faculty hiring is a related issue. As one indicator, approximately 25 percent of faculty at research universities are female, and 9 percent are non-white.[24] These percentages show a slight rising trend from year to year. As for administrative leaders, over one quarter of America's institutions of higher learning have women presidents, including Brown, Harvard, MIT, RPI (Rensselaer), Princeton, and the Universities of California at San Diego, Michigan, and Pennsylvania. In recent years there has been a slowly increasing trend of hiring women presidents. There are, however, very few black presidents of colleges and universities outside of those that educate primarily black students. RPI, led by black and female Shirley Ann Jackson, is an exception.[25]

9) Excellence

Wanting to do the best possible work keeps some people busy until all hours. These people might include artists, architects, lawyers, CEOs, and professors.

Excellence as a value is not unique to academics, though widely held by them. Research universities are places where slipshod work is readily visible and rejected; long, hard hours of quality work are expected and respected. That's one reason why many university libraries don't close at dusk when many city libraries do, and why, late at night, things are often humming in research labs of major universities. It's why the written word, in research papers, grant applications, and books is usually checked, re-checked, and re-re-checked before being submitted. Excellence is also reflected in the system of hiring, evaluation for tenure and advancement of faculty—at each stage, serious attention is paid to the degree of excellence of the individual's work. Exceptions occur, but rarely.

Enough of the public is aware of academic excellence that advertisers, journalists and others make good use of it. Terms like "Harvard approved," or "As Stanford researchers have shown," or "University studies indicate" are sprinkled liberally around. It would be important to have this awareness backed up by a greater public understanding of just what Harvard, Stanford and other universities do that makes their imprimatur significant.

10) Service

It is often said that academic work is a service profession. Robert Young claims in his study of academic values that, aside from one's basic need to earn a living and thereby sustain oneself and one's family, a professor's work should consist primarily of altruistic service.[26]

Although I agree that service is an important academic value, I believe Young's statement is unrealistic. For one thing, until rather recently, service by a professor generally meant serving the university, not society. It meant taking part in academic committees, organizing a departmental seminar series, serving as department chairperson or dean, and the like. For instance, although I was a professor for 15 years at Cornell, New York State's land grant university, and was certainly expected to engage in service, I can't recall a single discussion about service beyond the campus. More recently, civic engagement activities have provided opportunities for academics to serve society, and some enthusiasts suggest that most research and teaching should be redirected toward helping to solve societal problems. However, it is still widely understood at research universities (as I feel is proper) that the highest work priority is research and the second is teaching, both organized around the subjects within a professor's academic discipline.

Surely a professor's research and educational activities constitute service to society. Whether one is teaching a course to 500 undergraduates or 5 graduate students, the purpose of the course is to serve the students. True, some self-serving aspect is also likely to be involved; the prof may like talking to a captive audience about a favorite subject, or may have a ball being a ham for an hour, and may hope that some of the students will be turned on and join an ongoing research project. Nevertheless, teaching mostly serves the students, engaging them in new interests, inspiring them with novel ideas, moving them toward a career. And this service includes a lot more than presenting those one hour lectures. There is writing or revising the lectures, finding creative ways to capture the students' interest, organizing the course mechanics (syllabus, reading lists, website), writing and grading exams, advising students, and coordinating the course with others in the curriculum. That's a lot of service.

University research also includes service, though it is less direct than teaching, where the recipients of the service are right there looking at the professor. Applied research creates improvements in many aspects of life, and basic research provides new ways of understanding our changing selves in our changing world.

Allan Bloom, in his classic, *The Closing of the American Mind*, referred to academia as America's "temple of the regime."[27] It is a temple, like many others, filled with treasures. These include libraries, museums, laboratories, lecture halls, campus grounds, faculty with their publications and lectures, and students. But the temple's most profound treasure—its Holy of Holies—is its reservoir of ideas, and perhaps most profound among these, its values.

In these first three chapters, we have explored three different types of ideas central to universities—the idea of a university, ideas from the disciplines, and value-based ideas. I have been claiming ever since the Introduction that universities are not very good at sharing these ideas with the public. It's now time to present my evidence for this claim, the subject of the next chapter.

Notes

1.   Cole, *Great American University*, 502.

2.   Derek Bok, *Beyond the Ivory Tower* (Cambridge, MA: Harvard University Press, 1982); Cole, *Great American University*; Robert B. Young, *No Neutral Ground: Standing by the Values We Prize in Higher Education* (San Francisco: Jossey-Bass, 1997).

3.   Freeman J. Dyson, *The Sun, The Genome, and the Internet: Tools of Scientific Revolutions* (New York: Oxford University Press, 1999), viii.

4.   Christopher Butler, *Postmodernism: A Very Short Introduction* (New York: Oxford University Press, 2002), 35.

5.   Anthony W. Marx, Inaugural Address as President of Amherst College, October 26, 2003, www.amherst.edu/-President/.

6.   Frank H. T. Rhodes, *The Creation of the Future* (Ithaca, NY: Cornell University Press, 2001), x.

7.   Preserved Smith, *The Enlightenment (1687-1776): Volume 2—A History of Modern Culture* (New York: Holt, Reinhart and Winston, Inc., 1934); John R. Thelin, *A History of American Higher Education* (Baltimore: Johns Hopkins Press, 2004). The list of colonial academic institutions that survive to this day is easily remembered by

anyone familiar with college sports, as it includes all the current Ivy League universities except Cornell (which was founded in 1865), plus Rutgers and William and Mary.

8. Thelin, *American Higher Education*, 24.

9. http://brattleborohistory.com/slavery/execution-sermon-sinners-in-the-hands-of-an-angry-god.html.

10. Thelin, *American Higher Education*.

11. Two particularly insightful treatments of academic freedom can be found in Chapter 1 of Bok, *Beyond the Ivory Tower*; and Chapter 11 of Cole, *Great American University*.

12. American Association of University Professors, http://www.aaup.org/AAUP/issues/contingent/contingentfacts.htm.

13. Candice Kant, "AAUP and Academic Freedom: A History," *The Alliance* 2004, no. 4 (December, 2004), 1. www.aaup.org/Com-a/Kantart.htm; Kennedy, Academic Duty, 124-5.

14. Jimmy Carter, *Our Endangered Values: America's Moral Crisis* (New York: Simon and Schuster, 2005), 8.

15. Alan Charles Kors and Harvey A. Silverglate, *The Shadow University: The Betrayal of Liberty on America's Campuses* (New York: The Free Press, 1998). Repr. New York: HarperCollins, 1999.

16. Sara Lawrence-Lightfoot, *Respect: An Exploration* (Cambridge, MA: Perseus Books, 2000).

17. Judith Rodin and Stephen P. Steinberg, eds., *Public Discourse in America: Conversation and Community in the Twenty-First Century* (Philadelphia: University of Pennsylvania Press, 2003).

18. Judith Rodin and Stephen P. Steinberg, "Introduction: Incivility and Public Discourse," in Rodin and Steinberg, *Public Discourse*, 21.

19. Alan B. Kruger, Jesse Rothstein, and Sarah Turner, "Was Justice O'Conner Right? Race and Highly Selective College Admissions in 25 Years," *in College Access: Opportunity or Privilege?* eds. Michael S. McPherson and Morton Owen Shapiro, (New York: The College Board, 2006).

20. Grutter v. Bollinger, 539 U.S. 306 (2003).

21. Gratz v. Bollinger, 539 U.S. 244 (2003).

22. American Association of University Professors, http://www.aaup.org/AAUP/protect/legal/topics/aff-ac-update.htm

23. Peter Schmidt, "Supreme Court Takes Up Challenge to Race-Conscious Admissions at U. of Texas," *The Chronicle of Higher Education*, February 21, 2012.

24. Cathy A. Trower and Richard P. Chait, "Faculty Diversity: Too Little for Too Long," *Harvard Magazine*, March-April, 2002.

25. Bryan Cook and Young Kim, *The American College President—2012* (Washington, DC: American Council on Education, 2012).

26. Young, *No Neutral Ground*, 12-13.

27. Allan Bloom, *The Closing of the American Mind* (New York: Simon and Schuster, 1987) 244-5.

Chapter 4. The Low Flow of Ideas

This chapter presents support for my claim that academic ideas are barely flowing from campus to society. I offer four different types of evidence. I begin with a case study, namely, Columbia University—and a comparison of this case with other universities—to see whether there is a history and a tradition of broadly sharing ideas from these campuses. Second, I examine various types of public service programs at universities to see how effectively they disperse academic ideas among the general public. Third, I analyze the writings of leading university presidents to determine their views on sharing ideas with the public. Finally, I present survey data I collected from a fairly well-educated segment of the population about the degree to which universities influence their lives.

Columbia Then and Now

Although each university has its own history, many were founded and developed in response to similar national needs and trends, and have faced similar pressures. Thus, we can gain insight from a specific case study, and I offer Columbia University, during slightly more than the past 100 years. "Columbia University in the City of New York," its official name, suggests a functional relationship with its urban surroundings. But has there been a long term flow of academic ideas to the public, or is this a recent development, or something not yet developed? These questions can be addressed by examining Columbia's effect on the adjacent Morningside Heights community, on the City of New York, on New York State, the nation, and even the world. Columbia's hymn, performed at its annual commencement ceremony, is *Stand Columbia*. We will examine where this university has stood, and stands today, vis-à-vis the public. As we will see, throughout much of its history, except for contacts with select, elite elements of society, Columbia has stood alone.

For a remarkable forty-three years beginning in 1902, one president, Nicholas Murray Butler, ran Columbia.[1] The keynote speaker at Butler's presidential inauguration was University of Chicago President William Rainet Harper, arguably the most civic-minded university president of that era. In his speech, Harper challenged Butler to make Columbia into "a university which will adapt itself to urban influence, which will undertake to serve as an expression of urban civilization, and which is compelled to meet the demands of an urban environment."[2] Harper's challenge was for Columbia to go far beyond educating its enrolled students.

Butler was a man able to make things happen. Brilliantly eloquent, efficient, businesslike and exacting, he was invited by both J. P. Morgan and Andrew Carnegie to leave academia and run their financial empires. But he was a Columbian through and through—undergraduate, graduate student and then junior faculty member in the Department of Philosophy, before becoming president.

Though of modest family origins, Butler's personal flair and driving personality drew to him men of great wealth and power, among whom he moved comfortably. A close friend and confidant of Theodore Roosevelt, he later fell out with TR, and in 1912 became the Republican candidate for US Vice President, with his eye on the US presidency. Although he never made it to Washington, he became President of the Carnegie Endowment for International Peace, was awarded the Nobel Peace Prize in 1931, and achieved close association with numerous heads of state throughout the world. All this during his Columbia University presidency!

Given his capabilities and contacts, did Butler lead Columbia to serve New York City as Harper had urged? Did the ideas of this university flow to the local neighborhood and outward? Things started out that way, even before he became university president. Notably, Butler applied himself to the improvement of the school-teaching profession, both founding and becoming the first president of Columbia Teachers College, initially an entity largely separate from the university.

But as university president, with his prestige, power, and geographical scope expanding, Butler devoted himself largely to increasing his own personal acclaim, disseminating his conservative views on politics and education, and promoting his ideas on world peace. Had he encouraged his faculty to share their ideas with the local or global public, they might have competed with his own public recognition. He was criticized for ignoring the New York public as he sought personal prestige nationally and internationally.[3]

Butler retired as Columbia's president in 1945 (after being strongly nudged out of office). As the era of his leadership came to a close, Columbia seemed the antithesis of Harper's 1902 vision. Butler had developed Columbia into a great research university, but its faculty offered little leadership of society, from local to global, and little sharing of its great ideas.[4]

Things did not change under Columbia's next president, future US President, Dwight D. Eisenhower. Ike, as he was popularly known, was a do-nothing university president; he did no fund raising, officiated at no faculty meetings, and was away from the campus for about seven of the nine semesters of his Columbia presidency.[5] This World War II hero was hired mainly for the acclaim he would bring to the university. He later recalled how the Columbia Board of Trustees had wooed him: "[They told me] I had a broad, varied experience in dealing with human beings and human problems..., that I knew at first hand many areas of the earth and their peoples."[6] Many areas, yes, but Morningside Heights? Harlem?

After Eisenhower came Grayson Kirk, President from 1953 to 1968. This shy, retiring professor of government involved himself in the State Department, the creation of the United Nations, and both New York City and Washington politics, but not in Morningside Heights, which he is said to have strongly disliked.[7]

Relations with the neighborhood turned particularly sour during this period. The university used what have been called heavy-handed tactics to buy up local property in neighboring Morningside Heights and Harlem. The goal was to provide for future campus expansion and, it was claimed, to limit the influx of "undesirables," mostly poor blacks and Puerto Ricans, to the neighborhood.[8] Years later, a former student reformer wrote, "For years Columbia Trustees had evicted tenants from their homes [and] taken land through city deals...."[9] Meanwhile, Columbia's student body included hardly any blacks or Puerto Ricans, although by 1960 these two groups comprised over a third of the city's population. This, it was said, bespoke a striking "indifference to the city's changing populations and political realities."[10]

Robert McCaughey, Columbia history professor and authority on the university's past, shared his view that, until the 1960s, Columbia showed "total indifference" to New York State and its capital, Albany, and to the nation and Washington DC. In the Butler tradition, the university was hardly involved with society at large, focusing more on the rich and powerful.[11]

Life on the Columbia campus then reflected the university's elitism, attracting many of the brightest students from the metropolitan area. It was said that "everyone was getting a PhD,"[12] and many who did, and undoubtedly absorbed Columbia's habits, would soon, as young faculty members, bring these to campuses across the country.

The Columbia faculty included a cosmopolitan, intellectual elite, primarily in the humanities and social sciences, many of whom felt detached from American society, except for its uppermost intelligentsia.[13] The campus was their haven. Among them was professor of history Richard Hofstadter.[14] In 1963, the most famous of his twelve books, *Anti-intellectualism in American Life*, won him a second Pulitzer Prize. In it he writes that as an intellectual (whom he defines as one who "examines, ponders, wonders, theorizes, criticizes, imagines," and is "playful" with ideas) he feels alienated from largely anti-intellectual American society. That society, he claims, thinks intellectuals are "pretentious, conceited, effeminate, and snobbish."[15] He concludes that, "Being used to rejection and having over the years forged a strong traditional response to society based upon the expectation that rejection would continue, many [intellectuals] have come to feel that alienation is the only appropriate and honorable stance for them to take."[16]

As such, what could one expect but a repudiation of the public at large? No wonder Hofstadter and most of his intellectual circle at Columbia have been described as "standoffish" toward American society.[17]

The main outlines of American campus history through the 1960s and 1970s are well-known;[18] the student protests at Columbia in 1968 and at other campuses across the country, the anti-Vietnam War, pro-civil rights and feminist movements, together with the wider struggle for social justice. Few campuses in America remained unaffected. Most responded, ultimately, by broadening their student admissions, and to some extent their faculty hiring, to include a more diverse range of applicants.

Yet, for the next two decades, in terms of sharing academic ideas with the general public, the changes at Columbia were modest. John Hildebrand, now at the University of Arizona, was a Columbia professor of biology in the 1980s. He recalls the campus as isolated from the community, with no encouragement of faculty, nor any easy mechanism, to engage in outreach activities. One exception, the evening school, was prohibitively expensive.[19] In my sabbatical year at Columbia in 1988-89, it was clear to me that this was the norm, at least among the biology faculty. My academic host that year was Eduardo Macagno, now at the University of California at San Diego. As he recently explained, things began to change very slightly during the 1990s, with more faculty becoming somewhat involved off campus.[20] This was during the Columbia presidency of George Rupp (1993-2002), who promoted some interaction with the public, especially in the social sciences.

The last few years have seen a visible increase in Columbia's involvement with New York, and particularly with City Hall. Some have wondered whether this has been motivated by the university's planning, and need for approval—subsequently received—to build a new satellite campus in the city's neighboring Manhattanville region. The university's acquisition of this land is based on the legal principle of eminent domain, which permits it to acquire an area designated as blighted, and to rejuvenate it for a public purpose, in this case, education. Although the planned campus, whose physical design is to be more open to the outside than the cloistered main campus, is clearly good for Columbia and probably also for New York, some people recall with suspicion the university's 1960s relationship to the city. It remains to be seen how fully the university and its current president, Lee Bollinger, will develop genuine academic sharing with the public this time around.

Today, campus attitudes remain mixed. I asked David Stone, the university's Executive Vice President for Communications, "Do you think that people in New York City, New York State, or even the USA look to Columbia University for ideas, inspiration or leadership?" Stone replied, "Why should this happen?

We're not the news media."[21] I was surprised by this reply from the man officially responsible for Columbia's communication with the outside world.

Recently, a few leading Columbia professors have become deeply involved with the public. In the sciences, Nobel Laureate Eric Kandel's book *In Search of Memory*, and physicist Brian Greene's several books, from *The Elegant Universe*, to *The Hidden Reality*, together with the broadcast appearances of these two scientists, are important contributions to public understanding. So is former Provost Jonathan Cole's book *The Great American University*. May they signal an upward trend. May *Columbia* truly *Stand* not only with those on, but also those off, the campus.

Although each university has its own story, there are often similarities among different campuses. The University of Chicago, despite president Harper's civic mindedness at earlier times, shares some elements with Columbia's history. As told by its president Robert Zimmer (interviewed by the author at the University of Chicago, February 12, 2009), Chicago has been introverted for some similar, and some different reasons, vis-à-vis Columbia. Only recently has Chicago begun some movement toward public involvement. The same is true of many other urban, suburban or rural universities.

A campus particularly involved with the public is that of the University of California at San Diego. Sociology Professor Mary Walshok, head of the university's Extension Program, is a national leader in the effort to connect campus to community. In *Knowledge Without Boundaries*, Walshok articulates her view as to whether universities share with the public: "It is the rare research university that includes the provision of institutionalized knowledge connections to off-campus publics as an important component of its central academic conversations or long-range institutional planning efforts.... On most campuses, the outreach, service, and linking issues only arise episodically and usually when faculty and administrators perceive a need for political support for a new research agenda or financial support for a new program initiative."[22] On the question of whether universities share with the public, we can take this as a no.

Since Walshok's book, published in 1996, there has not been a detailed treatment of the issue of universities sharing ideas with the public. Moreover, in *The Chronicle of Higher Education*, academia's self-analytical professional journal, articles on the subject are rare, except for those about online courses and other computer technologies.[23]

NYU historian Thomas Bender urges, "A democratic culture and polity invites and needs an open dialog on all questions pertaining to the human condition. Restoring a place for academic knowledge in the public culture and a role for public discussion in academic culture ought to be a high priority of both academia and public leaders."[24]

On one campus after another, I have encountered evidence of the public's suspicion and mistrust of academia. It will suffice to share the comments of four people I interviewed at the University of Michigan:[25]

- Cynthia Wilbanks, the university's Vice President for Government Relations and Director of the State Outreach office: "This university is regarded as elitist and arrogant by the state legislature and by the local community."

- Rebecca McGowan, member of the university's Board of Regents: "Most people around here don't give much of a thought to the university. And the legislature sees us as irrelevant to the needs of the state because it thinks our research subjects are theoretical and irrelevant. People think their kids should go instead to a community college so they can get a job, because the university can't really give them ideas that apply to their life."

- Marvin Parnes of the university's Community Relations Office: "The public doesn't feel the university's value to them."

- Doug Kelbaugh, Dean of Architecture and Urban Planning: "There's a feeling of elitism about this university among the surrounding communities."

It appears that the history of some major American universities during the past century has produced institutions distanced from, and barely interacting with, most of society. To now become truly interactive with the public will mean, not continuing a longstanding tradition, but rather developing new initiatives, or building upon currently incipient ones.

Service Programs

Until recently, a professor's "service" usually meant serving the university, and was rarely regarded as a major job component. The extent of service was barely considered in decisions on hiring, tenure or advancement. Today there are significant efforts to relate to the public. I discuss here four such efforts:

- *Civic Engagement* programs, which include teaching, research, consulting, and volunteering in conjunction with local agencies or other groups, usually to help solve local community problems;

- *Cooperative Extension* programs at land grant universities, which assist primarily farmers and their families, agri-businesses and related entities;

- *Continuing Education* programs for the public—primarily in-class and on-line courses;

- *Public History* and *Public Science* programs, which relate to society via these academic areas.

As we will see, the first two of these programs share with the public, but have little to do with ideas. The latter two share ideas, but their effectiveness is compromised by factors discussed below.

Civic engagement

I focus here on *community-based learning* or *service learning*, which consists of courses for regularly enrolled students taught by a professor; but there is extensive discussion and field work together with non-academic members of a local community agency or other organization. The goals are usually three-fold—to teach students how their academic knowledge can be implemented in solving practical civic problems, to develop in the students a life-long habit of civic involvement, and to actually solve real problems.

Although the professor may begin with a theoretical or historical overview of the types of problems addressed, the students usually spend most of the course time interacting with community organizations off campus. This might include information gathering, discussions to define problems and possible solutions and analyses, utilizing skills acquired in academic courses. It is generally agreed that the definition of problems and solutions should emerge from the joint discussions with the off-campus partners, reflecting the academics' respect for their partners and a desire to break the stereotype of know-it-all university people trying to solve problems for "less knowledgeable," off campus people.[26]

This type of teaching has been gaining adherents since the 1990s, and is part of the larger civic engagement movement in university education and scholarship. Ernest Boyer's book, *Scholarship Reconsidered* is regarded by many to be the first coherent statement of principles.[27] Some argue that this type of teaching should be greatly expanded in higher education,[28] while others argue it should be reduced.[29]

Community-based learning and other types of civic engagement activities are encouraged by a few dedicated national organizations, such as Campus Compact, a non-profit organization headquartered in Providence, RI, with affiliated offices in over 30 states. This organization helps more than 1100 member colleges and universities develop, among other programs, community-based learning courses.

To get a firsthand account of their work, I met with Campus Compact President Maureen Curley in Providence. The progress that Curley and her team have made in promoting campus civic engagement, including numerous publications, is impressive.[30] One of her comments resonated with a tension I had perceived on campuses: "The hardest places to convince [to join Campus Compact and become active] are the more distinguished institutions." These are the ones I'd been visiting. It's one thing for a university president to join Campus Compact, and another for that president's university to change its culture. Only 34 percent of institutions consider a professor's community-based teaching as part of the evaluation for tenure or advancement.[31] Such courses often raise eyebrows, largely because the students' learning is more experiential than intellectual, relatively unplanned rather curriculum-focused, and based on contact with community leaders more than with the professor.

Civic engagement in teaching, research and other activities is also promoted by Imagining America (IA), a consortium of universities with its main office at Syracuse University. IA encourages joint academic/public projects and promotes their wider acceptance within university and college cultures, including legitimizing such work for decisions about faculty tenure and advancement.[32]

How much dissemination of academic ideas to the public occurs through community-based learning? Not much, for three reasons:

- First, it is mostly the students, not the professor, who interact with those off campus. In some courses even the students' interaction is limited, focusing on data collection for a final course paper.

- Second, the students usually interact with the few people in the off-campus organization upon whom their work focuses. In a session I attended at the University of Pennsylvania, in which graduate students and their professors planned an education program with a local school, six university people and four school personnel were in the room. In other types of civic engagement, such as student volunteering (often one-on-one tutoring of school students or working with small groups) important help is given, but to very few people.

- Third, when the semester- or year-long course ends, or when the student graduates from college, contact with the local community terminates.

But community-based learning could provide a springboard for a broad sharing of ideas. Team members from the campus and the community could write articles in the local press, possibly a regular column, to keep the public informed of the joint civic engagement projects that are improving their community. Articles could include the sharing of academic ideas on which these projects are based, and ideas that emerge from the projects themselves. The public might be invited periodically to evening sessions to hear about the recent gains from the civic engagement projects. To promote the community's attendance, the event might best be held in a downtown venue, not on campus; I've been told several times that many local people feel uncomfortable attending events on campuses. Speakers might include the mayor or other leading civic official, the heads of the community and campus teams, and selected students and community leaders, including local people who have benefited from the program. Serving cookies from a local bakery wouldn't hurt. These activities can offer an opportunity for sharing ideas about what the university is, ideas from academic disciplines, and academic values.

It is worth examining one underlying concept of civic engagement. By bringing together civic organizations and university students, it is assumed that employees in the civic organizations don't have, and won't acquire, the students' skills. That's why they need the students—a continuing round of them, each year's influx replacing those in last year's course, or those who have graduated.

A different approach that I believe could provide more effective aid to the civic organizations is for colleges and universities to train these organizations' employees, through individual, purpose-designed courses, certificate programs, or whole degree programs. The employees would gain in empowerment and quality of work, and would likely develop life-long bonds with the university.

Their organizations would operate more effectively. This would decrease the future need for university students and faculty to partner with and assist these employees. The money saved by reducing the administrative infrastructure of civic engagement could go toward scholarships for the employees.

Cooperative extension

Cooperative extension is a type of public service of land grant universities. Established under the Morrill Act of 1862, today's land grant universities—at least one in each state—are generally state-sponsored, rather than private. A few of the better known are Michigan State, Ohio State, Pennsylvania State, Rutgers, and Texas A&M Universities, and the Universities of Arizona, Illinois, Minnesota, and Wisconsin. Cornell is the only land grant university that is partly private and partly state sponsored. MIT is the only fully private land grant university, though according to its provost, it no longer carries out the functions expected of a land grant university, such as maintaining cooperative extension programs.[33] With state support of universities declining precipitously in recent years, and these universities turning more to other sources of funding, the financial distinction between state-sponsored and private universities is dwindling.

Following the Morrill Act, two additional acts spread the influence of each land grant university throughout its state. The Hatch Act of 1887 led to the establishment, in nearly every county of each state, of an agricultural experiment station, administered by the land grant university. Here, researchers study matters of local agricultural concern and attempt to bring this knowledge to the farmers' attention in order to improve the state's produce. These agricultural experiment stations together have a federally supplied budget of over $1 billion.

The Smith-Lever Act of 1914 established the cooperative extension system, which authorizes a land grant university to hire and dispatch one or more agents (today, often someone with an MA degree, often in agriculture) to each county in the state. The agent's task is to increase the flow of information to the public about research developments in farming and related matters, as well as home, family and community issues, and youth-related subjects. Regarding youth, the cooperative extension service, under the direction of the US Department of Agriculture, runs the highly popular 4H youth agriculture program, which boasts over 6 million members, in elementary through high school. The cooperative extension system depends on federal, state, university and county funds, differently apportioned in different states.

America's land grant universities, then, oversee a remarkable outreach program that reaches way beyond the campus, and potentially, into every community in the nation—though in practice, much more to rural farming areas than to cities. The question I ask is, to what extent do these universities use this established network to bring *ideas* to the public? Yes, via this network, farmers can learn how to kill the potato beetle, and families can learn about health care. Both are important. But does a university's wide range of great ideas also flow through these channels?

Leaders of land grant institutions are asking similar questions. Here are some conclusions from a recent landmark study supported by the Kellogg Foundation on the Future of State and Land-Grant Universities:

> Our institutions are confusing to outsiders. We need to find ways to help inexperienced potential partners negotiate this complex structure so that what we have to offer is more readily available. Do we properly publicize our activities and resources? Have we made a concentrated effort to increase community awareness of the resources and programs available from us that might be useful? Above all, can we honestly say that our expertise is equally accessible to all the constituencies of concern within our states and communities, including minority constituents?[34]

To gain greater understanding of these issues, I visited four land grant universities and spoke with the leaders of cooperative extension programs—namely, the deans of agriculture schools, at the Universities of Arizona and of California at Riverside, North Carolina State University, and Cornell. I began at Cornell, with dean Susan Henry (interviewed by the author at Cornell University, September 13, 2007). She enthusiastically explained that the university's "Ag" school faculty feels its public mission deeply, and works intensively on its behalf, partly in cooperation with the extension agents distributed throughout the state. Much of this work is applied agricultural research and sharing its results with New York State farmers. But when I asked whether the wider range of university ideas flow through the cooperative extension network, she replied, "The public doesn't get the intellectual content of the university. I don't think we'll ever be able to explain to the public what a university does. We need to do more—good science writers, lecturers—but I don't think it's something that will be solved in the near future. It's been going on forever—an eternal problem." She added that some university faculty act "arrogantly" toward the public, something I'd heard occasionally during my interviews.

Susan Henry's words echoed at the other land grants I visited. University of Arizona's Dean of Agriculture, Gene Sander,[35] said that while Arizona is entirely a land grant university, it is mostly just the College of Agriculture and Life Sciences, one of fifteen different colleges at the university, that takes the land grant mission seriously. Some other colleges, departments within colleges, or individual professors, do engage with the public, but these activities are usually limited in scope and duration. Confirming this, Biology Professor John Hildebrand commented, "Most people here in Tucson, when they think about the University of Arizona, think about our medical school's hospitals if they're sick, or our sports teams if they're healthy."[36]

Gene Sander sounded both interested in, and despairing of, getting university ideas, as opposed to only technical know-how, out through the cooperative extension network. He was telling me that the idea flow doesn't really happen in Arizona. Then he stopped, looked up at the ceiling, smiled, and seemed to change subjects: "I grew up in a little farming community in Minnesota. My dad was the local cooperative extension agent. And the first time I ever heard a string quartet was when he arranged for a student group from the University of Minnesota to play an evening concert in my high school."

We looked at each other and both realized an idea was being born. He fleshed it out: "Each county in the state has its cooperative extension office that we administer from the university, run by an agent whom we hire. Their offices don't have large rooms for bringing public groups together. But public schools do. So let's see—the cooperative extension agent is there with his wide-ranging contacts among the public; the school auditorium is there, a non-threatening place for most people, usually empty at night; and the public is there. All that's needed is to plug some interesting and engaging university people into this already existing network. It's just a matter of using resources that we already have in place."

"Great idea," I said.

When I passed this idea by Agriculture Dean Johnny Wynne of North Carolina State,[37] he added that most people in the local communities respect and like the extension agents, who are hired not only for their technical know-how, but also for their personality and communication skills. "But we have no funds for such a program of idea extension," he demurred. Who needs funds? I asked myself. A student or faculty group with a creative program or a professor with an exciting public lecture might be happy to visit some communities around the state, stay overnight with local residents, and enjoy a home-cooked dinner.

Agriculture Dean Tom Baldwin at the University of California, Riverside saw things differently.[38] "This university's cooperative extension service is for practicality," he said. "It relates to the public regarding their practical problems, agricultural or urban." He did not see much possibility for broad idea sharing through California's network.

It appears, then, that cooperative extension services could potentially serve as an effective, inexpensive channel for sharing academic ideas, that would be favored by some deans. Seems there's some important work to be done here.

Continuing education

This term refers to adult learners, not "traditionally aged," undergraduates or graduate students. Adult learners are the fastest growing population at universities and colleges, whether taking courses in class or online.[39] Much of this growth is in courses on skills needed to compete in the growing global, knowledge-based marketplace. But as I have already stated, this book's concern is not with skills, but ideas; not competition but elucidation and inspiration; not market growth, but personal growth.

It seems likely that the greater the academic focus on skills for the global marketplace, the less educators will focus on ideas. There are already signs that this is occurring. In some liberal arts colleges, technical and career-oriented courses in professional subjects are showing up in the curricula in increasing numbers and drawing more and more student majors away from the humanities and other idea-rich subjects. Similar increases in technical and professional courses are occurring in continuing education programs for adult learners.[40]

Universities need to be vigilant that the movement toward the technical and practical remains balanced in relation to the humanities and other idea-rich subjects. Also, one can regard the interest of regular and continuing students in technical and practical subjects as an opportunity to introduce them, at least somewhat, to the wide world of ideas. Universities could encourage the teachers of these courses increasingly to present some of their material in the context of history, society, and the arts. If the teachers are uncomfortable doing so, they could invite their humanities colleagues for guest presentations.[41] This would use the students' career drive as a "hook" to introduce them to broader horizons. Probably most would not find the hook too painful. Some, perhaps many, may be inspired.

In this chapter, I focus on in-class courses for adults. (I discuss online courses in Chapter 9.) I begin with the University of Chicago's Graham School of General Studies, which teaches only in-class courses—as of this writing, the University of Chicago offers no online courses, and has no concrete plans to do so.

One Graham School program in the humanities, arts and sciences lists nearly 50 rather brief, non-credit courses. A second program with several liberal education offerings lasts four years and is taken one course at a time, on a non-credit basis. A third program is the Masters of Liberal Arts, three years, part time, taken one course each semester, plus the writing of a thesis or a special project; on completion of this third program, a student receives a Master of Liberal Arts degree from the University of Chicago. Quoting from the Masters Program's promotional brochure, this is a "multidisciplinary program that is all about exploring fundamental human questions and problems....Renowned scholars in the humanities, social sciences and natural sciences...will answer your questions, but also ask a few of their own. They will listen closely to your opinions and experiences. Sparks will fly."

Remarkably, anyone, irrespective of academic background, can take these courses and degree programs at Chicago, one of America's great universities. Costs are far lower than for regularly enrolled university students. As Cary Nathenson, Associate Dean of the Graham School, explained, many adult students want to really immerse themselves in the world of ideas and great books; and the university earns revenue from these programs, as the Graham School consistently runs in the black.[42]

Although these are excellent programs, I take the liberty of raising a few issues. First, hardly any of these classes are held on the University of Chicago campus, seven miles south of city center. Most are given at the university's Gleacher Center, a single large building located downtown. This is convenient for the adult students, as the campus would be, for most, a bit of a drive or bus ride. Also, some people feel a bit intimidated by a university campus. Moreover, there may be insufficient classroom space on campus during the weekdays, when some of the Gleacher classes are held. Yet other classes are given on week nights or weekends when this probably would not be a problem.

Given their limited presence on campus, the adult students are missing a lot. They miss the contact with the special university atmosphere, with students and faculty, campus activities, and various university resources, all attributes significant for the public experience with academia. Dean Nathenson agreed that the university is not well-branded to these adult learners, who generally say, "I'm taking courses at Gleacher," hardly realizing that Gleacher is part of the Graham School, which is part of the University of Chicago. Moreover, the courses in the first two programs described above are not taught by University of Chicago faculty, all the more reason for the students not to feel they're at the University of Chicago—which, in a sense, they are not. Despite these reservations, the courses surely enrich the lives of adult learners, as do the continuing education programs at schools such as Harvard and Princeton.

Harvard's continuing education program[43] differs from that of Chicago; classes are held on campus, in the evening. Like Chicago, the Harvard program has traditionally stressed liberal arts courses. But during the past decade, the number of professional, technical, or applied courses has tripled, and their attendance has soared, outstripping idea-oriented courses. Fewer than half the students in the Harvard program today are engaged in liberal arts studies, though for those who are, as in Chicago, the effect can be profound.[44] Although some of Harvard's senior faculty teach in the extension program, most courses are taught by junior faculty, faculty at other institutions, or non-faculty, something that the program's director, Michael Shinagel, admits can lead to a second-class status for continuing education students.[45] Nevertheless, many courses earn high marks in student evaluations. As at Chicago, anyone can take the extension courses, irrespective of educational background, with no admissions requirements, and at relatively low cost. Also as at Chicago, the program runs in the black.

Princeton's program takes yet a different approach. Called the Community Auditing Program (CAP), it invites adult learners to audit the university courses taught to its regularly enrolled undergraduates. At Princeton, I spoke with the program's director, Kristen Appelget, who beamed, "There's tremendous community interest in this program. We have so many applicants, we unfortunately have to turn many away because of lack of classroom space."[46] In spite of Princeton's rural location, about 600 adult learners per semester take CAP courses.

Kristen explained that community auditors can choose from approximately 200 courses taught for Princeton undergraduates. Auditors pay $120 for a one semester course, about 1/10 of what an undergraduate pays for the same course. Anyone who can't afford that is admitted for less, or for free.

Typically 10 percent of the seats in each participating course, which are hardly ever filled by enrolled undergrads, are reserved for CAP people. Priority goes to the regular students—auditors sit in the back of the class, may not ask questions of the lecturer during the class (although they can, and do, after class), do not take exams or attend labs or foreign language exercises, nor do they receive a grade or credit or a letter of recommendation. What they do get, Kristin explained, is "the chance to be part of the University experience." Popular courses for CAP auditors are in politics, bioethics, American history, English, psychology, and engineering.

I asked Kristin whether the tuition-paying students mind having the CAP people, mostly retirees, in class. "If they did, we would have heard about it," she said. "We sometimes see the enrolled students and the CAP students having lunch together, sharing cross-generationally, and that seems an added benefit of the program. A lot of our auditors are the age of the regular students' grandparents."

"And how is it for the professors?" I ask.

"Any prof who doesn't want CAP people in their course just doesn't sign up with us. But most really enjoy teaching these more mature people."

Many universities and colleges permit locals to audit courses, but few promote this with the vigor of the Princeton program. While visiting Cornell recently, in a morning phone call to a faculty friend, I mentioned my enthusiasm for the Princeton CAP program. He replied, with a sense of local pride, "Oh, we have a program like that at Cornell." I told him I was surprised, not having heard about it.

He and I met for dinner that evening. When we did, he looked frazzled. He had spent the previous two hours searching the fine print of the Cornell website and other documentation for mention of Cornell's CAP-like program. He finally found a brief statement that local residents can sign up to audit courses. A far cry from CAP, I realized. Glenn Altschuler, Cornell's Dean of Continuing Education, told me this type of program is not a priority for the university. In rural upstate New York, he claimed, few people would want it.[47] To me, though, the highly successful CAP program at equally rural Princeton suggests otherwise.

With reverse logic, David Stone, Vice President for Communications of Columbia University, told me that his university doesn't have, and wouldn't want, a CAP-like program because, in urban New York, such a program would be flooded with clients.[48] It seemed to me, though, that having people waiting in line is a sign of a not-to-be-abandoned idea.

The outlooks of administrators Altschuler and Stone appear fairly common. Heads of Continuing Education at numerous universities say it's difficult to convince their administrative superiors of their programs' value. Presidents and others watching the bottom line sometimes raise eyebrows about liberal arts courses for the masses.[49]

Continuing Education was given a significant boost through the remarkable philanthropy of Bernard Osher, who has so far established at 120 American colleges and universities "Osher Lifelong Learning Institutes." These offer in-class courses and other learning opportunities, especially for people over 50.

The good news about Continuing Education programs is that they offer adults the opportunity to experience new ideas through contact with academic experts, often in a university or college atmosphere, and some of these experts are also excellent teachers. The bad news is how few people take part in idea-based, in-class, Continuing Education courses. A massive survey reported by the National Center for Educational Statistics allows one to calculate that approximately one out of every 60 adults (that's 1.7 percent) are now taking such idea-based courses at America's colleges and universities.[50] This means that 59 out of 60 are not. If we restrict our analysis to the most distinguished schools— the roughly 100 top research universities, especially rich in ideas because they are the nation's main idea source—the figures change to about one out of every 1,200 adults (that's less than one tenth of one percent)! Given these low numbers, anyone who thinks that in-class, idea-based, Continuing Education courses are having a broad effect on society should think again. And anyone who thinks that *online* continuing education courses are doing any better has a big surprise coming in Chapter 9. Thus, although I hope these courses continue to grow, it is possible that few in the general public are prepared to commit to a semester long course with two to three meetings per week. Universities need to find alternative ways to reach a broad public.

Public history/Public science

When universities began listening more closely to the opinions of their students during the 1960s and 1970s, they also began listening to the public. Some faculties of humanities and social sciences, in particular, intentionally drew within earshot of those off campus. Out of this grew a few academic initiatives particularly tuned in, one way or another, to the public voice. I address here two initiatives that have continued to develop since that time—first, one in the humanities called "public history,"[51] and then a somewhat parallel development in the sciences, usually called "science, technology and society," or STS.

One cannot properly explain public history without first mentioning the closely related field of oral history. Oral historians record, transcribe, organize, interpret, and archive the personal experiences and recollections of ordinary people. As NYU history professor Jack Tchen explained, "Often the residents of a neighborhood offer their recollections unaware how rich they are in historical content about demography, politics, ethnicity, human interactions, and more."[52]

Whereas oral history involves primarily collecting data from the public, public history, in part, reflects these data and their interpretations back to the public. The public historian often utilizes oral recordings, along with other historical resources, not only for writing academic articles and books, but also in developing exhibits for museums and other public venues, interpretation at historic homes and monuments, documentaries for TV and cinema, civic celebrations, and popular books. Raw footage of recorded oral history is often incorporated into public presentations, and often comes across with compelling force.[53]

None of this recording, sharing back, or honoring the public was common prior to the 1970s. But by then, off-campus developments were encouraging greater public interest in history. There were popularly styled bestsellers such as Chicago radio personality Studs Terkel's Pulitzer Prize winning *The Good War* and others, based on his interviews of people from all walks of life. They demonstrated the richness of people's personal memories about significant periods in their life.[54] The American bicentennial celebrations engendered further historical interest, involving communities across the country in celebrating the nation's origins. Millions tuned in on TV. The genre of popular history on TV and in movie theaters received a boost with Alex Haley's wildly successful mini-series *Roots* in 1977, and later with Claude Lanzmann's 1985 film *Shoah* and Stephen Spielberg's 1993 film *Schindler's List*. In literature, the memoir genre caught on like wildfire. Later still, extensive historic and genealogical data bases on the Internet, notably Ellis Island's American Family Immigration History Center, opened for public use in 2005, have facilitated people's tracing their family histories.

Public history has grown in recent decades, supported by national organizations—the National Council on Public History (NCPH) and the Oral History Association. Many universities offer graduate training programs. In public history, 96 are listed in the NCPH website, though most offer MA but not PhD degrees.[55]

If all this sounds upbeat, there's also a down side. As NYU public history professor Daniel Walkowitz explained, "There's no teaching of public history at any of the elite universities. They just don't consider it a legitimate approach, which is infuriating. And even though some faculty at those schools may actually do a bit of public history research, they would never identify themselves as public historians."[56] Sheldon Rothblatt, former chair of the History Department at Berkeley, substantiated this, remarking that nobody in his department does public history, and adding, "Public history is not a serious or substantial part of the discipline of academic history."[57]

Since its inception, public history has had plenty of detractors within the profession—those who object to "generating from within [the public] the authority to explore and interpret their own experience, experience traditionally invisible in formal history because of predictable assumptions about who and what matters, interpretations more actively ignored or resisted by academic scholarship by virtue of their political content and implications."[58] Many academic historians simply do not accept people's memories of their lives and events they witnessed as a legitimate historical resource, nor do they regard the public at large as an appropriate audience for receiving the results of academic historical research, unless these are expressed in a formal, academic manner—which nearly guarantees that most people won't read them.

Let's walk across campus to the science side, and examine Science, Technology and Society (STS) programs. As with public history, considerable interest in science and society began in the 1960s. One result that I recall from my years at Cornell was the development in the late 1960s of a new undergraduate course called Biology and Society. We in the Division of Biology were invited to think about how our research related to society and give a lecture about it. (Mine didn't, so I didn't.) Thereafter, the course developed into a whole undergraduate major.

Today this major resides under the administrative umbrella of Cornell's inter-disciplinary Department of Science and Technology Studies. Its faculty carry out academic research and offer PhD degrees, along with their undergraduate major in Biology and Society. According to its lengthy newsletter, the department's star is rising—its faculty are landing big grants, publishing many books and journal articles, attracting the best graduate students, and winning awards. Its PhD graduates, out on the academic job market, are being snapped up by the likes of Harvard, the Universities of California, Illinois, and other distinguished institutions. However, nowhere is there mention of faculty engaging directly with the public. From the newsletter, this appears not to be part of the department's mission. Perhaps, I thought, this is appropriate, since in Cornell's STS department, the final S, unlike in most other universities, stands for Studies, not Society.

To check out how this Cornell department views itself vis-à-vis the public, I e-mailed several questions to the department chairperson, Stephen Hilgartner. I received a friendly reply with, however, no answers to my questions, rather a suggestion that I contact one department member, Bruce Lewenstein, apparently the only one out of seventeen who is substantially engaged with the public.

On to MIT's Program in STS, where the second S stands for "society". The chairman's polite reply to my e-mail included no answers to the same three questions, rather a referral (again) to one faculty member, John Durant, head of the MIT Museum, who is deeply engaged in public outreach. The website of MIT's Program states: "The primary activity of the STS program is research, which takes many forms: individual faculty members pursuing intellectual inquiry, teaching in our graduate program, organizing and hosting conferences, colloquia, and other types of publications."[59] Of the 26 books by the STS faculty listed on the website, all but two were published by university presses and have technical sounding titles.

Based on the above, I was not surprised to discover, based on further inquiries and explorations of STS websites around the country, that most present themselves primarily as undergraduate and/or graduate teaching and/or research programs having little or no involvement with the public.[60] But given the revolution that science and technology have created in the lives of nearly everyone, few subjects seem more relevant for the sharing of ideas with those off campus. It's disappointing that the word "Society" in the name of most STS programs represents a subject of study, and not a group of people with whom to engage. I suggest that STS programs and departments consider becoming more open to developing a genuine commitment to sharing scientific ideas with the public.

Two other types of academic programs in science are worth mentioning. University departments of Science Education generally are highly engaged with the public, but deal almost exclusively with school students and their teachers. Citizen Science programs create teams of volunteer assistants to help academics doing field research; the Citizen Science Program at Cornell's Laboratory of Ornithology, for instance, includes thousands of volunteer bird watchers who help track bird populations and learn some science in the process.

To summarize, public history is doing excellent work in sharing ideas with the public, but suffers from a lack of full acceptance by the academic history discipline. Most STS programs appear to function as traditional academic departments, teaching their courses and doing their research, with only the occasional faculty member substantially involved with the public.

Towers of Ivory

In this section I sample the statements of several outstanding university presidents on the university's connection to the public. Specifically, I ask whether they regard the university as something of an ivory tower. For present purposes, I define an ivory tower as an institution of higher learning separate and detached from, and somewhat standoffish toward, people who don't study or teach there. First, comments by four presidents show that for them, ivory is a thing of the past. Then, five presidents indicate that, for them, the ivory tower remains partly standing.

Clark Kerr, former President of the University of California, wrote in 1963, "We are just now perceiving that the university's invisible product, knowledge, may be the most powerful single element in our culture....The university has come to have a new centrality for all of us, as much for those who never see the ivied halls as for those who pass through them or reside there."[61]

For Kerr, a kind of open exchange was developing between campus and society. This, he explained, was a continuation of an ongoing trend that began with the opening of the land grant universities when, "The cloister and the ivory tower were destroyed by being thrown open to all qualified comers."[62] Yet he adds a note of uncertainty, stating, under the heading "Changes Still to Come," that "The great university is of necessity elitist—the elite of merit—but it operates in an environment dedicated to an egalitarian philosophy. How may the contribution of the elite be made clear to the egalitarians, and how may an aristocracy of intellect justify itself to a democracy of all...?"[63] These two questions go to the heart of the book you are now reading.

Nearly two decades later, Harvard's President Derek Bok stated his view that, "After World War II... the image of the ivory tower grew obsolete. Instead, a vast and intricate network of relationships arose linking universities to other major institutions in the society."[64] For Bok, it seems, it was primarily this network, mostly of professors and academic units interacting with corporations, foundations, and various branches of government, that signaled the end of ivory towerism. True, he also mentions the offering of services to the public by university medical schools and their teaching hospitals, and by law and other professional schools, as well as the university's economic value to the community (in spite of its tax-free status), its offering of assistance to community groups, opening access for the public to university facilities, and the offering of various types of courses for the public.[65] By and large, though, Bok stresses that the wrecking ball's strongest blow to the ivory tower has been the university's increased role in promoting America's economic competitiveness, productivity, and power, largely through its networking widely with various public and private institutions. He is less focused on sharing university ideas with a broad public.[66]

Similarly, former Cornell President Frank Rhodes writes in 2001 that the university is "no longer an ivory tower."[67] Like Bok, he emphasizes the university's networking with public and private bodies, as well as carrying out society-altering research.

For former MIT President Charles Vest in 2007, more than for Bok or Rhodes, what appears most essential for society from today's universities is their "strong interactions with business, industry, and government [which links them] to state, regional, and local industrial needs." He continues, "The new interactions between states and universities...are largely aimed at the role of modern technology in the economic development of the state."[68]

Yet a different voice is discernible from some academic presidents. Clark Kerr, in the 1995 revision of his original 1963 book, appears to have partly changed his mind: "At one time, the College[s] of Agriculture made contact with a majority of citizens in the state, and the borders of the campus really were the boundaries of the state. Many state universities, in more recent times, have concentrated mostly on the cultivation of governors and legislators, rather than on the public as a whole."[69]

Harold Shapiro, President of the University of Michigan and later of Princeton, asks, in 2005, to what extent the university is acting "not for ourselves alone," and concludes, "To my regret, this is one of those ideas that, while applauded in principle, is easily lost in the challenge of meeting one's day-to-day responsibilities. This makes it even more important to pause once in a while to adjust our sails and correct our course."[70] Consider the book you are reading an attempted heave-ho on the academic mainsail.

Former University of Pennsylvania President Judith Rodin, writing in 2003, concurs: "Rather than hiding in ivory towers, college and university leaders must keep relentlessly articulating the university as a marketplace of ideas…. From the intellectual heart of an issue…come creative solutions."[71] Rodin further states, "We cannot hope to cope with the complex threats and challenges we face today if we 'silo' our knowledge and faculty, or our students, inside carefully constructed and vigorously defended disciplinary, institutional and cultural walls."[72]

The presidents of the University of Chicago, Robert Zimmer, and Pomona College, David Oxtoby, both told me that some of the ivory still stands, and should, maintaining a campus elevated above the rough and tumble of everyday commerce to support contemplative work in peace and quiet.

In summary, there is no consensus among the presidents sampled as to continuing ivory towerism.

Ask the People

If we want to know whether the university is an ivory tower, we should ask people whose vantage point is off campus. That's because people inside a tower are in the only place from which the tower can't be seen. Thus, it's not enough to ask what university leaders think; we also need to determine what the public thinks.

For this, I developed a questionnaire for e-mailing to a sector of society all across America, each person to be greeted personally by name. My goal was to reach mature, working Americans with above average formal education but who are not an intellectual elite. I was interested in people who were living— to paraphrase Harold Shapiro—not for themselves alone—rather, whose work suggested a concern for others, and for the nation. I turned to staff workers of the American Red Cross (ARC). This organization's website lists more than 600 chapters throughout the 50 states, and more than 40 percent of these list the names and e-mail addresses of the chapter's staff (I did not write to the boards of directors or volunteers). These usually included the chapter's CEO and the heads of emergency services, volunteer services, educational outreach, and development. I sent out 2258 individual e-mails. Of those who responded,[73] a remarkable 77 percent have at least a bachelor's degree, compared to 27 percent of the American population over 25 years of age.[74] The ages range from 20s to 70s, with the greatest concentration in their 50s, and 83 percent are women.

The goal of the questionnaire was to determine the extent to which the respondents feel that colleges and universities play a useful role in their lives, particularly as regards access to ideas. Here are the main results. Unless otherwise stated, I list the answers to each question in the order of the percentages of respondents selecting particular answers, not the order in which they appeared on the survey.

1) Which of the following subjects would you be most interested to learn more about? (Respondents were asked, in this and the following two questions, to mark no more than two answers.)

70% Current events
27% Business trends
20% History
16% Religion, spiritual matters
15% Science
11% Entertainment
11% Literature, art
5%   Sports
4%   Environment
1%   Fashion

As you can see, "current events" was far and away the most frequent response.

2) Which of the following do you think would be most helpful to you in finding out about the subjects you marked in Question 1 above?

69% Internet
39% Newspapers or magazines
36% TV
24% Books
12% Radio
10% College or university—either on campus, or off-campus outreach
7%   Conversations with family, friends, or others
4%   Museums
2%   Other
1%   Just thinking about them

Here, the answer was the Internet almost 7 times as often as college or university.

3) Which of the following have most provided for you, in the last year or so, new information or ideas that you did not specifically seek out, but that you found interesting?

60% Internet
39% Newspapers or magazines
38% TV
24% Conversations with family, friends, or others
16% Books
14% Radio
4%   Museums
3%   Other
2%   College or university—either on campus or off-campus outreach
1%   Just thinking about things

The answer was the Internet 30 times more often than a college or university!

4) *Imagine that you could choose one of the following people to go out to dinner with, and speak with, either alone or together with a group of your friends. Which one would you choose?* (Respondents were asked to check one answer.)

28% A journalist
14% A business executive
13% A religious leader
12% A politician
10% A professor
8% A doctor
7% A musician
5% An athlete
2% An actor
1% A computer specialist

A journalist was chosen nearly 3 times as often as a professor.

5) *How much of a role would you say one or more colleges or universities are now playing in your life?* (Here I present the answers in the sequence that they appeared on the survey.)

23% None at all
17% Very little
36% Little
18% Much
8% Very much
0% Total involvement

On average, the respondents felt that the role of colleges or universities in their lives was between "very little" and "little." For only about a quarter (18 percent + 8 percent) of these highly educated people is academia playing what we could call a significant role.

6) *Would you say that America's colleges and universities generally are ivory tower institutions (that is, separate and detached from, and even standoffish toward, people who don't study or teach there)?*

28% Yes
44% No
30% No opinion

Although the responses to this question were mixed, it is interesting that 39 percent of those who expressed an opinion (28 divided by the sum of 28 plus 44) answered yes, that academia is an ivory tower.

7) *If colleges and universities were to increase their ways of relating to people other than their enrolled students, in which of the following ways do you think they could help American society, beyond what they are now doing?* (Respondents were invited to mark as many items as are relevant.)

92% Expose people more to new knowledge or ideas
70% Raise society's cultural level
63% Increase tolerance of one another in society
54% Encourage people to help each other more
52% Help people learn how to analyze problems
46% Encourage people to listen to each other more
42% Encourage people to respect each other more
33% Help people make decisions in their lives
29% Help increase truthfulness in society
19% Provide society with moral guidance

Remarkably, the average respondent checked five of these ten choices, suggesting they feel there is a lot more that colleges and universities could do to involve themselves with the public. The most frequently checked item was sharing knowledge and ideas.

A reasonable conclusion is that academia is pretty much irrelevant to the lives of most of these highly educated, mature, working Americans. They hardly consider a college or a university as a place from which to receive information or ideas of interest; hardly any said they had received interesting new information or ideas from these institutions in the year prior to the questionnaire; and few expressed interest in an informal meeting with a professor. Most said that colleges and universities play little or no role in their lives, and 39 percent of thosewho expressed an opinion stated that academia is an ivory tower. Moreover, a remarkable 92 percent claimed that colleges and universities could help Americans more by exposing them to new knowledge and ideas.

The sense of isolation from academia suggested in this survey parallels the experience of campus outreach expert Walshok, who states: "The general public...does not appear as convinced as academics, intellectuals, and journalists that research universities play such a vital and central role [in society]. They do not see these institutions as hubs of activity through which and out of which flows much of the knowledge essential to a complex modern society."[75]

To summarize this chapter, there is much to justify the claim I made in the Introduction, that "the sluice gates for ideas at most American campuses have long been nearly shut...." To the extent that Columbia and the other institutions mentioned are representative, there is not a longstanding academic tradition of deep idea sharing with the general public. Most types of service programs, while doing excellent work, share mostly career-oriented or technical know-how, or share ideas with a very small segment of the population. Opinions of university presidents are mixed on the ivory tower question. And the sampled American Red Cross workers reflect that academia is not especially there for them. It seems safe to assume that the majority of Americans, who have much less formal education on average than the Red Cross workers, would feel this as strongly, if not more so.

Notes

1. Michael Rosenthal, *Nicholas Miraculous: The Amazing Career of the Redoubtable Dr. Nicholas Murray Butler* (New York: Farrar, Straus, Giroux, 2006).

2. Quoted in: Lee Benson, Ira Harkavy and John Puckett, *Dewey's Dream: Universities and Democracies in an Age of Education Reform.* (Philadelphia: Temple University Press, 2007) 19.

3. Rosenthal, *Nicholas Miraculous*, 138.

4. There were exceptions, of course, to this lack of leadership, notably, three Columbia professors who attained national status when they were recruited by Franklin D. Roosevelt as members of his Brain Trust.

5. Robert McCaughey, *Stand Columbia: A History of Columbia University in the City of New York 1754-2004* (New York: Columbia University Press, 2003) 338.

6. Ashbel Green, ed., *My Columbia: Reminiscences of University Life* (New York: Columbia University Press, 2005) 364.

7. Ibid., 347.

8. Ibid., 409.

9. P. Rockwell, "The Columbia Statement," in *The University Crisis Reader. Vol. 1: The Liberal University Under Attack*, eds., Emanuel Wallerstein and Paul Starr (New York: Random House, 1971), 24.

10. McCaughey, *Stand Columbia*, 387-8.

11. Telephone interview by the author, May 8, 2008.

12. McCaughey, *Stand Columbia*, 389.

13. Ibid., 384.

14. David S. Brown, *Richard Hofstadter: An Intellectual Biography* (Chicago: University of Chicago Press, 2006), 120-121.

15. These three quotes are from Hofstadter, *Anti-intellectualism in American Life* (see Introduction, n. 3), 25, 30, 19.

16. Ibid., 393.

17. McCaughey, *Stand Columbia*, 384. McCaughey mentioned to me that two members of Columbia's intellectual circle at that time—Lionel Trilling and Jacques Barzun—were, more than the others, involved with "middle-brow" readers through their involvement with book clubs. Telephone interview by the author, May 8, 2008.

18. See, for instance, Jacoby, *Age of American Unreason*, 140-149.

19. Interviewed by the author at the University of Arizona, February 24, 2009.

20. Interviewed by the author at the University of California, San Diego, February 19, 2009.

21. Interviewed by the author at Columbia University, February 10, 2009.

22. Walshok, *Knowledge Without Boundaries* (see Introduction, n. 20), 272.

23. For a recent brief discussion of this subject, see Thomas A. Kazee, "Think Outside the Lunch Box," *The Chronicle of Higher Education* (January 19, 2012).

24. Thomas Bender, "Politics, Intellect, and the American University, 1945-1995," *Proc. Amer. Acad. Arts and Sciences* 126, no. 1 (1997): 31.

25. These four individuals were interviewed by the author at the University of Michigan between March 15-21, 2007.

26. Richard M. Battistoni, *Civic Engagement Across the Curriculum: A Resource Book for Service-learning Faculty in All Disciplines* (Providence, RI: Campus Compact, 2002); Kezar, Chambers, and Burkhardt, *Higher Education for Public Good* (see Introduction, n. 10).

27. Ernest L. Boyer, *Scholarship Reconsidered: Priorities of the Professoriate* (San Francisco: Carnegie Foundation for the Advancement of Teaching, 1990).

28. Kezar, Chambers, and Burkhardt, *Higher Education for Public Good.*

29. Fish, *Save the World* (see Introduction, n. 11).

30. Interviewed by the author, September 5, 2007. See Battistoni, Civic Engagement; Richard E. Cone, Abby Kiesa and Nicholas V. Longo, eds., *Raise Your Voice: A Student Guide to Making Positive Social Change* (Providence, RI: Campus Compact, 2006).

31. Campus Compact, www.Compact.org.

32. Imagining America, http://imaginingamerica.org/.

33. I thank MIT Professor Frank Levy for providing me with this information on MIT's land grant status.

34. Kellogg Commission on the Future of State and Land-Grant Universities, "Returning to Our Roots," www.aplu.org/NetCommunity/Document.Doc?id=187.

35. Interviewed by the author at the University of Arizona, February 23, 2009.

36. Interviewed by author at the University of Arizona, February 24, 2009.

37. Interviewed by the author at North Carolina State University, April 15, 2010.

38. Interviewed by the author at University of California, Riverside, February 17, 2009.

39. University Continuing Education Assoc., *New Face of Higher Education.*

40. Shinagel, *The Gates Unbarred* (see Introduction, n. 20); Michael Shinagel, "Informing Practice: What Every Good Continuing Educator Should Know," (lecture, Annual Conference, University Continuing Education Assoc., San Francisco, April 7-10, 2010).

41. A similar, though more general, suggestions was made by the American Association of Universities in their 2004 study of the place of the humanities in academia: Association of American Universities, *Reinvigorating the Humanities: Enhancing Research and Education on Campus and Beyond*, eds., Katherine Bailey

Mathae and Catherine Langrehr Birzer (2004), http://www.aau.edu/policy/article.aspx?id=7182.

42. Interviewed by the author at the University of Chicago, February 12, 2009.

43. Shinagel, *The Gates Unbarred.*

44. Suzanne Spradbury, "Liberal Learning and Working-class Adults: The Meaningfulness of Education," *Continuing Higher Ed. Rev.* 71 (2007): 71-89.

45. Shinagel, "Informing Practice".

46. Interviewed by the author at Princeton University, August 14, 2007.

47. Telephone interview by the author, September 13, 2007.

48. Interviewed by the author at Columbia University, February 10, 2009.

49. University Continuing Education Assoc., Annual Conference, San Francisco, April 7-10, 2010; Bilita S. Matges and Lareal L. Maguire, "The Self-directed Program Review: Demonstrating Value Added by Continuing Education," *Continuing Higher Ed. Rev.* 68 (2004): 67-77; Judy Ashcroft, "Flat World: Trends in Continuing Higher Education," *Continuing Higher Ed. Rev.* 70 (2006): 120-133.

50. National Center for Educational Statistics. National Household Educational Surveys Program of 2005: "Adult Education Participation in 2004-2005," Tables 1 and 12, multiply 21% x 18%, http://nces.ed.gov/pubsearch/pubsinfo.asp?pubid=2006077. The survey shows that 3.8 percent of adult Americans, in the academic year 2004-5, took at least one course "for personal interest." These probably included many idea-rich courses of the type I am discussing here. Let's estimate, generously, that 2/3 of these were courses of this type. This comes to 2.5 percent of adult Americans taking such courses. Of these people, about 1/3 took computer based courses, which I am not discussing here. The other two thirds, or 1.7 percent of adult Americans, took in-class courses. These were taught at the following types of institutions: "college/university, community/junior college, vocational/technical/occupational school." As I have stated, I am discussing here only courses taught at 400 major universities, which comprise about 1/10 of the total number of institutions of higher learning in the USA. Applying this 1/10 measure to our 1.7 percent of learners, we come up with a final, admittedly rough, estimate of just 0.17 percent of adult Americans. This equals one out of every 600 adult Americans.

51. Frisch, *Shared Authority* (see Introduction, n. 21).

52. Interviewed by the author at NYU, April 20, 2010.

53. Frisch, *Shared Authority.*

54. Ibid.; Rick Kogan, "Studs Terkel Dies," *Chicago Tribune*, October 31, 2008; Andre´ Schiffrin, *The Business of Books: How International Conglomerates Took Over Publishing and Changed the Way We Read* (London: Verso, 2000).

55. National Council on Public History, http://www.ncph.org.

56. Interviewed by the author at NYU, April 19, 2010

57. Interview by the author in Jerusalem, November 12, 2009.

58. Frisch, *Shared Authority*, xxi.

59. http://web.mit.edu/sts/.

60. The programs I sampled were those of Stanford, the Universities of Pennsylvania, California at San Diego, and North Carolina State, Virginia Polytechnic Institute, and the Claremont Colleges. One exception was Pennsylvania State University, whose STS chairperson emailed me, stating that several members of his program are in fact involved with the public, and that as a land grant university, "we take the mission of engagement with society seriously and strive to find ways to more effectively bridge academic scholarship and the public at large."

61. Clark Kerr, *Uses of the University* (Cambridge, MA: Harvard University Press, rev. ed. 2001), xii.

62. Ibid., 36.

63. Ibid., 91.

64. Bok, *Beyond the Ivory Tower*, 7.

65. Ibid., chap. 9.

66. Bok, *Universities and the Future*.

67. Rhodes, *Creation of the Future*, xi.

68. Charles M. Vest, *The American Research University From World War II to the World Wide Web* (Berkeley, CA: University of California Press, 2007), 9, 29.

69. Kerr, *Uses of the University*, 189.

70. Shapiro, *Larger Sense of Purpose*, 1.

71. Judith Rodin and Stephen P. Steinberg, "Introduction: Incivility and Public Discourse," in *Public Discourse in America*, Rodin and Steinberg, 21.

72. Judith Rodin. "The University as Discourse Community," in *Public Discourse in America*, Rodin and Steinberg, 233.

73. A limitation of this survey is that only 126 (about 6 percent of those contacted) replied. Of these, I removed from the pool 22 respondents who indicated, in answer to a question, that they are currently either studying or working at a college or university. The remaining 104 respondents comprise the informational pool of this survey. This sample size is radically smaller than those of such professional polls as Gallop or Harris, and some statisticians would disregard the survey. But I didn't because the answers to most of my questions showed overwhelmingly strong trends, far beyond their approximately 10 percent margin of error. This provided at least a glimpse, if not a fully accurate assessment, of the opinions of this relevant slice of the adult American population.

74. US Census Bureau, www.census.gov/population/www/socdemo/educ-attn.html (Data from 2007).

75. Walshok, *Knowledge Without Boundaries*, 9.

Part 2. Releasing the Flow of University Ideas

Part 2 of *A Dam in the River* examines four channels for the flow of academic ideas—visits by the public to universities and colleges, books written by academics, radio and TV broadcasts, and the Internet. In the coming chapters I point out major obstacles in these channels, and suggest how these could be overcome.

If you encounter suggestions that you would like to see implemented, or are stimulated to new thoughts, there's a lot to be done. If you are a college or university student, you can form a student organization to explore and develop ways to share off-campus the academic ideas you are acquiring. Propose to faculty and administrators that your institution become a national leader in this regard. Follow up!

If you are a faculty member, gather your colleagues to discuss sharing academic ideas with the public. Write a proposal for your deans and central administrators, perhaps suggesting that sharing academic ideas with the public should be included in the institution's mission statement. Follow through. Perhaps develop an inter-disciplinary center on campus to study university ideas, define best methods of sharing them, predict expected effects upon the public, and evaluate their impact. Consider developing a national academic society and an academic journal with these same goals.

If you are a college graduate, you can gather alumni to discuss sharing ideas from your alma mater with the public. Send a proposal to the central administration. Propose that your alma mater become a national leader in this regard. Hold your donations until you receive a satisfactory answer.

If you are not associated with a university or college, and would like to see these suggestions implemented for your own and your community's benefit, why not gather with like-minded neighbors to explore how to encourage your nearest college or university in this direction? Write a proposal; send it to the Dean of Arts and Sciences, the Provost, or the President—or all three. If you don't get a reply within a reasonable amount of time, pick up the phone and ask why. After all, whether this is a public or private institution, your taxes are directly or indirectly helping it stay in business. In this sense, those on campus work for you.

Whatever connection you do or don't have to academia, I suggest that you consider helping to establish a support organization for the sharing of academic ideas with the public—helping to place America's great universities and colleges in a position of leadership. I envision this movement as composed equally of on- and off-campus partners. I do not specify what form this movement should take, who should initiate it, or how it should function. Those who take up the challenge should define these things. There are, however, successful models for such movements, such as Campus Compact (Chapter 4) which, however, has different goals for academia than those proposed in *A Dam in the River*.

Part 2 brings us to the moment of truth for this book. Identifying a problem, as in Part 1, is relatively easy. Finding appropriate, cost-effective, and readily achievable solutions is more difficult. To the extent that the solutions presented here fill the bill—no big surprise, I believe they do—Part 2 becomes a moment of truth for academia as well. Will colleges and universities not only recognize the importance of sharing their ideas more fully with the public, but also act to effect substantial change? Perhaps they will find better solutions than those offered here, but at the very least, my suggestions may stimulate discussion and help point in useful new directions.

Chapter 5. Visiting Universities, I: A "Margaret Mead" on Campus

Even before academia opens its sluice gates more fully, let's jump into the reservoir, upstream from the dam, and see what ideas are floating around on campus. In this chapter, I share with you my explorations of two outstanding American institutions. One is a public (state-sponsored) research university—the University of Michigan, which I shall call, as they themselves do, U-M. The other is a private liberal arts college—Amherst. I visited each for a week to determine whether other people, were they to visit these campuses and jump into their reservoirs after me, would have a refreshing immersion in academic ideas.

I was impressed by the wealth of ideas I discovered on both campuses. I say "discovered," because neither campus had any procedure for sharing ideas with visitors like me. I found their wealth of ideas not *because of*, rather *in spite of*, these two institutions.

My explorations were guided by my experience with the "open-campus museum" at my home university. I had a general sense of what I was looking for. I had learned that a visit to a campus is—in the language of the tourism industry—a leisure activity. Most visitors come not to learn a subject formally, like the enrolled students, but rather seek a broader, more open experience, as in visits to museums, heritage homes, nature centers or botanical gardens. These leisure activities, often experienced when the mind is free of work and home concerns, can have profound and lasting impacts, cognitively and personally, on individuals and families.[1] Thus, a campus visit can be an important event in people's lives.

By calling these visits leisure activities, I don't mean that we want to turn campuses into Disney-type entertainment hotspots, with popcorn and cotton candy, disturbing the academic atmosphere. No huge hordes of gawking visitors like the 35 million attracted annually to Times Square. On my home campus, the visitation rate is modest and barely discernible in the hubbub of normal activity. The students or faculty who notice seem to appreciate the presence of guests, who perhaps convey a subtle but pleasing confirmation that this place is special and worth a visit.

In exploring the two campuses—in March, 2007—I thought of myself as a museum professional, a tourist, and an anthropologist searching out deep meanings. Join me now as I take off on these expeditions. My experiences at, and impressions of, both institutions were paralleled, at least generally, at most of the other 24 university and college campuses I explored.

U-M

U-M on the Web

Any good anthropologist studies the work site carefully prior to arrival. I did so as well. This is much easier today than it was for the famous early anthropologists. Unlike Margaret Mead, I have the Internet. This was important because, although I had always heard great things about both U-M and Amherst, I had never visited either.

On the Web I learned that U-M's main campus has over 26,000 undergraduates and 15,000 graduate and professional students, placing it in the large category, though about 40 percent smaller than Arizona State, with the largest enrollment of any residential US campus. Culturally, U-M dominates Ann Arbor, population 114,000, located about 45 miles west of Detroit. It is among the top five universities in the nation in overall financial support for research obtained from outside sources (about $750 million per year). It is ranked between first and fifteenth for its educational programs in most of its graduate and professional schools, and its undergraduate program ranks fifth among public (state-sponsored) institutions.[2] Its prestige worldwide in teaching and research is high. By all accounts, U-M is a university to be reckoned with—a place where visitors may well have a rich campus experience.

But as checked out on the U-M website what I might actually do there, and how I might encounter their great ideas, I realized that, from U-M's point of view, I, as a visitor, did not exist.[3] Scroll-down menus were available for prospective students, current students, faculty, alumni, donors and parents. FAQ's were from students, parents, staff, faculty and alumni. There were no menu items for a member of the general public who didn't fit these categories—nothing, that is, for over 99 percent of Americans. Yes, there were guided campus tours, but these are run by the Office of Undergraduate Admissions for prospective undergraduate students and their families. Although the tours were also open to other *visitors*—ah, here was that word at last—no tours are designed specifically for non-applicants.

Admittedly, from the U-M point of view, students, their parents, and the other categories mentioned are more important than I am. But I felt I was representing all Americans, and wondered if anyone had ever thought of "us."

When I clicked on the athletic department, everything changed. I should have guessed as much, as the Google snippet called U-M an "American institution of higher learning known for its research, academics and *athletics*...." (Italics added.) The athletics section of the website was shot through with rah-rah blurbs about sports, school spirit, and cheerleaders. U-M, of course, is a Big 10 sports university, and was the Big 10 football champion eight times in the years 1990-2005. The U-M football stadium seats an amazing 107,500 people, making it America's largest stadium, university or professional, except for car and horse racing venues. Nicknamed "The Big House," it fills up for all home games, irrespective of the weather.

It was becoming clear to me that U-M is sports wacky. Its website states, "Michigan Stadium has come to symbolize the pride, tradition and excellence of the University of Michigan." Oh, I get it—the stadium is their "Idea of a University" and I, as a visitor, was meant to catch a game. I can also catch twenty-six other types of inter-collegiate sports, in several of which U-M had placed third or higher during the season prior to my visit.

I was getting the impression that U-M is a major sports institution that also does some teaching and research. But it's not; it's a truly great university. It seemed, though, that I'd have a hard time contacting its great ideas.[4] So what was all this saying about how the university regards itself vis-à-vis the public?

About half of the research universities' websites I viewed resemble U-M's, with little or no obvious preparedness for potential visitors other than student applicants and their families. Most of the other half mention campus visitors, but not how they could have significant experiences with academic ideas, the central core of academia, as I defined it in Chapter 1.

Visiting U-M

Architecture and landscape design on college and university campuses are often strikingly attractive, an important part of the nation's heritage. As landscape architect Richard Dober writes, "Campuses will be centerpieces in our twenty-first-century culture, and greenery that serves and symbolizes colleges and universities a hallmark."[5] U-M is a fine example, with many beautiful buildings surrounding large, grassy spaces. But it is the palpable, bright spirit of youth that I find most exhilarating. This future in the making is, I believe, a major attraction. I follow a group of undergrads to a lecture hall to see whether sitting in on a class might hold interest for campus visitors.

As I approach the largest lecture hall on campus, capacity 530, the huge double doors burst open and Psych. 101 empties out. Standing amid the student outflow, I feel like a trout trying to hold its place in a rushing stream. Ultimately, I make my way in and take a seat in the back row.

A few minutes later, the professor enters with his laptop, sets up his Power Point projection on a large roll-down screen, and adjusts the microphone. The students drift in—about 110 of them—and distribute themselves throughout the large hall, making no discernible attempt to sit close to the lecturer.

The class is upper level undergraduate chemistry. Speaking clearly and in a highly organized manner, but with little enthusiasm and not a hint of humor, the professor analyzes graphs projected on the screen. The Margaret Mead in me notices that, while more than half of the students appear to be listening, none seem enraptured. Surprisingly few are jotting down more than occasional notes, and only a handful are taking notes on laptops. A substantial minority of the students do not appear to be listening at all. Some are gabbing, clearly not about chemistry. A few are doing crossword puzzles. After about 15 minutes, I get up and leave, apparently unnoticed.

The subject matter of this class was totally beyond what almost any non-chemist, myself included, would appreciate, and the teaching method, in my view, held little interest for visitors (perhaps also for students). If U-M were to invite visitors to lectures, they would need to select specific courses and professors the public might appreciate.

I sample several more lectures in different subjects, and things start looking up. For instance, a geology lecture about how fossils are formed, and an economics lecture about the correlation between the amounts of energy different nations consume and the level of social, educational and medical advancement of these nations are chock full of interesting ideas and eminently understandable, even without having heard the earlier classes—an important consideration for one-time visitors. Both lecturers speak enthusiastically and provide considerable comic relief, even if in a didactic, minimally interactive, style. Visitors with little or no background in these fields may well appreciate their lectures.

So my first conclusion is that at U-M, carefully selected lectures could hold visitors' interest. At the end of the chapter, I suggest how such single lecture experiences could be made available on a large scale.

Onward now, outside the lecture halls, to explore the U-M campus further for ideas. I begin at the impressive and beautiful "Michigan Union" (equivalent to the student union on many campuses), and head for the ground floor "Campus Information Center." On display are an impressive 50 or so different brochures for the taking—but alas, not one is for visitors; most are for students. "Do you have any brochures for visitors to campus?" I ask the on-duty student. He thinks for a moment and then pulls out from under the counter a *Campus Walking Tour* guide. It offers little information of interest, though—mostly the construction dates and names of buildings and of their donors, plus a few superficial statements, such as, "The 212-foot tower houses the Baird Carillon [musical bells], the third heaviest musical instrument in the world, with 55 bells ranging from 12 pounds to 12 tons." Did I come all this way to learn the their bells' weights? The student tells me that this isn't really a visitors center (which I had already gathered) and he suggests I try the Student Activities Building, also called the Huetwell Visitors Center. Sounds promising.

At Huetwell, there are not 50, but an amazing 70 brochures on display—but again, not one for visitors. When I inquire, the on-duty student pulls out from below the same *Campus Walking Tour* guide—they must be trained to do that. I ask what she recommends that I see.

"The football stadium." Big surprise.

"What else?" I ask.

"I really like the law school buildings; and Angell Hall is impressive."

"What else?"

"That's about it, I guess," she says, with a pleasant but helpless smile.

One of the world's great universities, and the person on duty at the Huetwell Visitors Center tells me, "That's about it." So why not print up a *good* walking tour guide, display it at both the Michigan Union and Huetwell, and have the on-duty students read it so that they can offer useful suggestions? And display it in Ann Arbor and Detroit hotels, visitor centers, and Chambers of Commerce. Send it out as an extra with the Sunday papers. Add it to the university website.

Getting frustrated, I sign up for the guided tour—you know, the one for 17-year-old applicants and their parents. The tour begins with an excellent, up-beat, ten minute DVD presentation on a large screen, beautifully narrated by U-M alumnus James Earl Jones. It presents lots of cheery students engaged in various academic and other activities, with a sound track backed up by Satchmo's "It's a Wonderful World," and an inspiring message from U-M President Mary Sue Coleman. It's well-suited to applicants and their families, so much so that, as we leave the screening area, the father of a visiting applicant and I agree that we, never mind his 17-year-old daughter, are ready to sign up for under-graduate degrees!

With just a little fine tuning, the DVD, so excellent for applicants and their parents, could be transformed into an excellent introduction to U-M for visitors like me—and the rest of America. I wonder why they haven't done so—but I am beginning to understand that U-M is hardly prepared for visitors and appears to be asking itself, "Why would anyone want to come and see us?"

The guide on the student-led tour is charming, well-informed, and tells the applicants and their parents what they want to hear—about the meal plan, dorm life and the faculty advising system. But she offers no insights about what this or any university is, does, or should be, not a single idea from a course, nor any research result from the faculty, nothing about the underlying values that make this place special. There is little for me on this tour.

This experience repeated itself at each of 12 tours I attended at other institutions. The guides, a self-selected group of students comfortable with public speaking, fit easily into the big brother/sister niche vis-à-vis the applicants, and enable parents to envision their child three or four years hence. When I asked about the guides' preparation, I found that none had received any professional training in guiding. I know from my museum experience that guiding is indeed a profession with much to learn besides the tour's content, with an extensive professional literature about best practices and other relevant matters.[6] (I know because I have studied guiding and, together with colleagues in education and communications, I teach the guiding course at our open-campus museum.) But student campus guides in training are usually overseen by more senior student guides, who themselves learned from yet more senior student guides. Although this is adequate, with room for improvement, for the college applicant tours, it just won't do for visitors coming to experience a great college or university.

Let me offer three suggestions for campus guiding programs:

- Universities and colleges should develop an academic course on guiding for undergraduates and graduate students, taught jointly by professionals in Communications, Museum Studies, and Education. Such training can serve students in many ways, including improved skills in public speaking, writing, leadership, and self-confidence. The guiding profession's best practices should be taught, and the course should be a prerequisite for becoming a campus guide.

- On campuses that only offer tours for applicants, develop separate tours—perhaps a range of tours on different subjects—for the general public.

- A specific suggestion—suppose the tour group is walking past a building in which the guide has taken an interesting course. The guide might say, "Let me share with you an interesting idea I learned from course X that Professor Y teaches in this building." (The guide might do well to schedule a meeting with ole Prof. Y beforehand and make sure to get the idea right, understand it in broad context, and be prepared to answer questions about it. A side benefit is that Prof. Y, whose ideas are thus shared with campus visitors, might become a stakeholder in campus guiding, and act as a valuable resource.) The guide could transmit two or three ideas learned from different courses or from other campus experiences. I have never encountered this or anything similar on any campus tour.

Following the U-M tour, I strike out on my own, looking for ideas on campus. To my surprise and delight, I find them staring me in the face. Yet I have the strange feeling that hardly anyone else sees them. Like Margaret Mead, discoverer of important ideas on Pacific islands, I feel I have made a great anthropological discovery on this academic island, right in America's heartland. And like those Pacific discoveries, it takes a visitor from afar—in this case, me—to make these "discoveries."

I find many university ideas literally spelled out all over the U-M campus. For instance, truth. The translation of U-M's Latin motto, *Artes Scientia Veritas*, is Arts, Science, Truth.[7] As this motto appears on a sign outside every campus building, you can't walk from one lecture hall to another without encountering the word *Veritas* perhaps five times, and another five on your way to the bus stop.

But when I presented a seminar to researchers at the U-M School of Education and asked the graduate students where, in the past week, they had seen any reference to the concept of truth, or the written word itself, no one had a clue.

What does it mean to have the word truth—one of the university values I discussed in Chapter 3—plastered all over the campus? It's just not possible that it means nothing. Truth is one of the most discussed, and most complex, topics in academia in our postmodern age. A simple sign with the seemingly innocent word *Veritas* could spark an important sharing of ideas by a properly trained tour guide—even if only by a brief explanation that the idea of truth, though a core value of academia, has become complicated, why it has, and how the university deals with the complications. I think that every guide on the U-M campus should be prepared for such a discussion.

Angell Hall, mentioned by the on-duty student at Huetwell Visitors Center, is a massive structure, but what I notice is the cumbersome sentence in huge letters carved deeply into its stone cornice: "Religion, morality and knowledge being necessary to good government and the happiness of mankind, schools and the means of education shall forever be encouraged." I would learn later that this is a direct quote from the Northwest Ordinance, which was passed by the US Congress in 1787, and which guided the settlement and future statehood of the Northwest Territory, including Michigan. This Ordinance prescribed the method by which new states were to join the union in America's westward expansion. Appropriate, then, that Angell Hall abuts State Street, and the scripted cornice faces west. True, American historians disagree about how this expansion should be viewed—as the bold taming of a wild land or an immoral displacement of Native Americans. But whatever one's perspective, westward expansion was to become a, if not *the*, dominant theme of 19th century America.[8] More specifically, the carved sentence constitutes the conceptual foundation for Michigan's system of public education, including, of course, U-M, on whose turf I was standing. The same sentence was restated as part of the 1862 Morrill Act that created the nation's land grant universities.

In short, someone officially inscribed that historic sentence, no doubt with a quill pen, into the Northwest Ordinance, and someone else inserted it into the Morrill Act. Someone else sculpted it deep into the cornice when Angell Hall was built in 1924. Ever since then, the sun has sailed across it daily, noon time rays angled to cast shadows deep into its letters, blackening them against the white stone. By afternoon, the rays penetrate the letters head-on, making them fade, only to disappear fully with the setting sun. Rewritten every sunny day for nearly a century, yet read by almost no one. But I feel, in this sentence, history's penetrating reflection. A properly trained guide could convey—I would say *must* convey—the many layers of meaning that radiate from the Angell Hall cornice.

Onward to the law library, where I find the carved inscriptions, "Free institutions, personal liberty," and "Liberty, equality, justice." And then to the William Clements Library with its two inscriptions extolling books: "Tradition fades but the written record remains ever fresh," and "In darkness dwells the people which knows its annals not." Carved alongside these inscriptions, and displayed on the sign outside every campus building, is the image of an oil lamp resting on a book, behind it the rays of the setting sun. The emblem's unwritten message is, "Read, day and night," and when tied to the motto included in the emblem—"Artes Scientia Veritas"—its meaning is, "Read day and night arts and sciences, and find truth." Nice idea, no?

Aside from the written word, unwritten ideas were all around. For instance, Angell Hall was built in the style of an ancient Greek temple, reflecting the ideas of classicism, stability, dignity and Greek democracy. The law school mimics the architecture of Harvard, Yale and Princeton, which mimic Oxford and Cambridge, which mimic the great cathedrals of Europe—each mimicry conveying its own historical and cultural ideas. Guarding the main entrance to Michigan Union are two stone-sculpted students, one in academic robes, the other in athletic garb, reflecting the idea of a sound mind and a sound body.

Hardly anyone notices building inscriptions, or sculptural and architectural messages. None are interpreted for the public—not in the DVD presentation, the student-led tour, the printed materials, or the website. Why not? Surely not because U-M no longer believes in the profound ideas these messages convey. Standing on campus, I want to call out to passersby, "Hey, did you notice this inscription, or that one?" Or call to the university administrators in their nearby building, "Hey, don't tell me about your stadium, or the weight of your bells. Tell me about your ideas—these ideas right here—and what they mean to you. Then tell it to all America!"

Amherst

Amherst on the Web

It's hard to imagine two academic campuses more different from one another than U-M and Amherst. As Amherst has just 1,640 students, it would take twenty-five Amhersts to equal U-M's enrollment. A liberal arts undergraduate college, Amherst's main priority is teaching. This is reflected on its website, where the blurbs about individual faculty members included a statement of their teaching interests, alongside their research interests. This is unusual. On the U-M website, as is typical, faculty blurbs make no mention of teaching.

Located among the rolling hills of Massachusetts, the college abuts Amherst's tiny, village-like commercial center, though its 35,000 population ranks it as a town. Smith, Mount Holyoke and Hampshire colleges are close by, plus the main campus of the University of Massachusetts, all of which, together with Amherst, constitute the Five Colleges Consortium, benefiting students and faculty. Amherst ranks each year among America's best liberal arts institutions. I came to see with my own Margaret Mead eyes what ideas lurk behind this high rank, and how these might be shared when the public comes calling.

Before proceeding, let me mention my surprise that the Amherst and U-M websites reflected a similar sports wackiness, even though Amherst is a sports David compared to the U-M Goliath. The Amherst website boasts that its athletic program is the oldest in the nation. (I presume the original players are no longer on the field.) An impressive 32 percent of students play on one of the many varsity teams, and 80 percent play in clubs or intramural sports. (Let's see, then, 112 percent of the students are athletes?) Fierce, war-like language describes these sports: Williams College is not just the rival team, but the "archrival."[9] Amherst claims to have "one of the top defenses in the nation," with a "fierce" passing "attack." (No *offense* intended, but isn't this a bit of *overkill*?) Two players earned the "Eastern College Athletic Conference Division III Northeast All-Star Honorable Mention." (One might have thought a *Conference* was where you sit and discuss things, *Division III* was an advanced math course, and *Honorable Mention* meant speaking about someone's moral virtues.) A student was named "NSSCFAC Football offensive player of the week." (What was his offense? I wondered. Had he perhaps uttered a swear word on the playing field?)

Visiting Amherst

The only campus tours, as at U-M, are student-run, operated by the Admissions Office, and intended for applicants and their families. The two guides of the tour—a male student and a female student—are charming, but they present an idea-free experience even in this enclave of liberal arts, replete with ideas.

Given Amherst's reputation as a teaching institution, I had e-mailed five professors whose courses, as described on the college's website, looked especially interesting. Explaining my project, I asked if I might sit in on their classes, and speak with them afterwards. Given the small class sizes, this request was necessary, whereas at huge U-M it was not. I received four gracious affirmatives, while the teacher of a course on gender respectfully declined.

So there I am on the peaceful Amherst campus, on my way to a class in Professor John Servos' course, *Science and Society in Modern America*. I arrive early at the small, light oak-paneled seminar room and introduce myself to Servos. (As we immediately establish a first-name relationship, I'll call him John.) Seven students slowly filter in—twelve are enrolled, but a bad flu has hit the campus.

John begins the class seated at the head of the table. After a few minutes, he is sitting atop the chair's back, his shoes resting on its seat, a position that looks dreadfully uncomfortable, but helps establish an informal atmosphere. Soon he is walking around the table, interacting directly with individuals or pairs of students, though audible to all. This enlivens the proceedings and de-focuses what might otherwise have been a more authoritarian, teacher-centered perspective reminiscent of a Renaissance painting. He asks engaging questions and receives excellent, thoughtful answers, mostly from three or four students. There's plenty of comic relief contributed by both John and the students. This is no lecture class, rather a highly interactive group exploration, guided by John's well-thought through lesson plan. He uses neither audio-visuals nor written notes; the framework for the 80-minute session is in his head.

Today's class revolves around a claim made by David Noble, in *America by Design: Science, Technology and the Rise of Corporate Capitalism*, part of which was required reading for the class. Noble's claim, about which John later reveals some reservations, is that by the late 19th and early 20th centuries, American industry had already established a measure of control over government, universities, and other institutions, to support its own commercial aims. John has the students imagine that they are living during that era and have established a factory for manufacturing an important new product. He has them strategize what kinds of control their company might wish to impose on the government, universities and other institutions to promote their company's success. They must take into account the types and locations of raw materials and markets, transport facilities, legal and constitutional constraints, technical issues, and more. Rather than giving a passive, frontal lecture, John has the students "discover" the motivations for the type of industrial influence they are considering. This resembles the "case method" of teaching, commonly used in business and law schools, but far less common in humanities courses. In John's class, this method encourages deep, reflective reading, analysis, and discussion.

As in the classes at U-M, I understand the material without having attended previous classes or read the assignment. The experience was engaging on the highest level, and I am certain other visitors would find it so. My interest is piqued not only by the subject, but also by John's excellent level of scholarship and the discovery teaching method he employed. John made me want to be an undergraduate again! (I'm getting used to this.) The excitement remains to this day, long after my visit to Amherst.

All four classes I attended at Amherst were excellent, but I'll describe just one more, *Introduction to Modern Astronomy* for non-science majors, taught by Professor George Greenstein. George phoned me at my motel to explain that he was sick, and that his associate, Dr. Arielle Philips, would be teaching the class. He mentioned an unusual teaching method he had developed, which Arielle would use.

This class is large by Amherst standards—45 students. Using an overhead projector, Arielle begins by screening two graphs. These graphs would clearly leave most non-science visitors, figuratively, in outer space. However, something special happens that changes my mind about this class and its relevance for non-science visitors.

Arielle briefly explains the information plotted in the top graph—it shows the movements of a certain star as it comes periodically a tiny bit closer to earth, then a tiny bit further away, then closer again, and so forth. Even though this star is very, very far away from earth, astronomers have detected that it wobbles ever so slightly toward us and away. But that's only a partial explanation of the way the star moves. Arielle asks the students to group in threes, and for each group to spend about five minutes discussing this graph, trying to figure out everything they can about the star's movements. She leaves the room for five minutes after clarifying that, upon her return, she will call on any trio of students for the answer. (As she later explained to me, George had discovered that leaving the room at such moments enhances the students' sense of free exploration.)

While Arielle is gone, I notice that nearly all 45 students are working on the problem, unlike the U-M chemistry class, where there was little active engagement. On returning, Arielle claims a particular fondness for the color orange, and calls on a girl wearing an orange T-shirt, together with her two partners. The group has not been able to come up with an answer, so Arielle, with no recriminations, says that her next favorite color is purple, and calls on a boy wearing purple stripes and his two partners. This group has gathered from the graph that the star moves in a circle—at one point its circular motion brings it a bit closer to the earth, and at the opposite part of its circle it is farther from the earth, and so forth in repeating cycles.

"Good," says Arielle. "Now, what would make a star move in a circle?"

The purple group again: "If something else near the star is also moving in a circle, its gravitational effect on the star could cause the star to circle as well." (They have learned about this type of effect earlier in the course.)

"Excellent. So now let's look at the second graph and see if we can get any idea about that 'something else,' as you call it, near the star, that might also be moving in a circle. What this second graph shows," she continues, "is an increase, then a decrease, then an increase, and so forth, in the light intensity coming to earth from this very star we've been discussing. Now spend five minutes in your groups trying to figure out when during the star's circular motion its light intensity brightens and dims." Again she leaves the room.

When she returns, she calls on the group sitting closest to me. They have figured out that the light intensity from the star decreases slightly for one brief period each time the star passes through a particular portion of its cyclic motion.

"Good. And what might cause the star's light, as seen on earth, to decrease once for each cycle?" Arielle asks.

"Maybe it's because that 'something else' that the purple guy over there [laughter] said moves in a circle is actually circling around the star. Maybe it is a pretty large object, a planet, say, that's big enough to block some of the light coming from the star to earth, whenever it cycles into a position between the star and the earth."

"Bravo!" cries Arielle.

"YES!" exclaims the trio's spokesperson, arms thrown up in victory, as though he'd just scored an Amherst touchdown.

Much more happens in this 50-minute session, but here's how Arielle concludes the class: "These two graphs were the actual evidence that astronomers used to demonstrate, for the first time ever, the existence of a planet outside our solar system. And you just figured it out!" She then projects on the screen the

NASA press release that announced this result to the world in 1995.[10] A broad communal smile of satisfaction passes across the students' faces as they pack up their books and start moving out of the class.

The story of this discovery could have been presented in standard lecture format in a few minutes. But the effect on the students could not have been as deep, satisfying, and memorable, had they not taken the original graphs and made their own "discovery." For one hour they were space scientists, doing what is referred to by educators as "learning by inquiry."[11] And recall, these are non-science majors!

Like most Americans, I've never had a course in either the history of science or astronomy. Yet these two classes, plucked out of a semester, provided me with very positive and engaging experiences based on new knowledge and ideas about intriguing subjects, and a sense that I had been privileged to experience brilliant teaching, excellent students, and the making of minds at a great teaching college. I came away with the *idea* of liberal arts education as I could not have appreciated it, had I not experienced it in person. As a cultural experience, it ranked up there with seeing a great play or hearing a great concert.[12]

A "VIP" on campus

Some universities and colleges open themselves up quite fully, albeit briefly, to the public, in a learning festival for one day or one weekend in the year. Berkeley has a successful weekend program that other universities might emulate. But positive as this is, there are 51 other weekends in the year. Although it would not be practical to hold such a festival throughout the year, considerably more year-long sharing of ideas with the public than currently occurs would certainly be possible.

Imagine if U-M, Amherst, and the many other fine institutions across the land had such programs. What a resource for public enlightenment this could be!

What might such a resource look like? Given my positive experiences sitting in on single lectures, I began to imagine how a program might be established that would offer this to campus visitors. As mentioned earlier, only a very small percentage of adult learners enroll in whole courses, many perhaps put off by regular class attendance, reading assignments and exams. For this population, something less demanding, though decidedly thought provoking, is called for. I believe that the opportunity to listen to selected lectures holds real promise.

Imagine, for instance, you are traveling, alone or with family or friends, for business or pleasure, to some location in the United States. You have half a day free of scheduled activities. What to do? Shopping? Museum? Zoo? Sleep? Imagine reading that the major college or university nearby has just opened up a new program. VIP, the Visitor Invitation Program, invites you to sit in on one or more course lectures. You check out the website, which might read something like this:

The University (or College) of (X) invites you to take part in a unique cultural/educational experience called VIP—Visitor Invitation Program. Anyone over 16 years of age can sit in on one or more course lectures, and choose from over 200 course options. In most courses, hearing an individual lecture, even without having heard the preceding lectures, should be fully, or nearly fully, understandable. We know, because we've tried it ourselves. So what's your passion? Plants? The Civil War? Jazz? Modern art? Politics? Classical literature? Philosophy? Whatever interests you most, you are likely to find a world expert on our faculty teaching a related course. We invite you to take part.

Come and hear the great ideas of our faculty, and enjoy not just the subject, but also the professor-student interaction. Enjoy the campus atmosphere. Spend an hour, a day, or a week soaking up ideas. Teaching is something The University (or College) of (X) is most committed to, and one of the things we do best. We are pleased to offer you entree to this core academic activity. Become a VIP (very important person) to us, by visiting our VIP.

Recall, this is all imaginary; it does not yet exist. Imagine that the announcement explains that the visitor selects from a course list (days and hours included) on the website. The visitor signs up and pays a modest fee on the Web by credit card and automatically receives an e-mail ticket to the lecture, along with the course syllabus and readings. Thus, the visitor can see where the particular lecture fits into the broader subject of the semester-long course, and can do any desired course reading before or after the lecture, though none is required or necessary to appreciate the lecture. A student in each course is appointed to check the attending visitors' tickets. The visitor can sign up for as many classes, in as many different subjects, on as many different days, as desired, each for a fee, as long as the computer notes a vacant seat in these classes.[13]

Now imagine that *every* major college and university in America had such a program. People would know that, on a campus near their home or wherever they travel in the country, they can always take advantage of a learning opportunity in America's outstanding universities and colleges. Going to Boston? Try out a lecture in or around the city—at Boston University, Brandeis, Harvard, MIT, Tufts, Wellesley, or many other options. Going to Austin? Chicago? LA? St. Louis? One needn't invest a whole semester—just an hour in a classroom, although probably many people would want more.

I believe VIP would bring people into closer contact with academia and its ideas. Visitors would be stimulated by the experience. Some may want to follow up with course readings. Some might be most interested in the information or ideas, others in the way the professor thinks through a problem and brings evidence to bear, perhaps others in the professor-student dynamics.

The good news is that it would be neither difficult nor expensive to develop the VIP, which could be operated by a small staff. The visitors' admission charges would cover part of the cost, more so as the number of visitors increases.

Coordination among institutions would be important. Website design, informational and reservations procedures ideally should be identical for all campuses. Otherwise, this program would quickly become a confusing, balkanized mess. Coordination also means that the individual institution would not have to create and pay for its own software for ticketing and payment, as this would be shared.

To me, empty seats in a university classroom are a wasted national resource. Shouldn't we let people who would appreciate the class fill those seats?

To determine how professors might feel about one-time visitors, I asked the four Amherst faculty whose classes I had attended for their feedback. Three responded that they would have no problem, and one said it would make him a bit uncomfortable to have different visitors in his class at different times. So presumably three out of the four sampled would agree to participate in such a program. Probably most teachers of large university courses would concur.

I asked Matthew Goldstein, Chancellor of the City University of New York, about the VIP plan. "Can you envision such a program at your institution?"

"Absolutely yes," he replied enthusiastically. "This could help break down the barrier between the public and academia."[14]

I am hardly alone in thinking that brief in-class experiences could attract many people. In 1975, Martin Knowlton, who had just returned from four years of hiking around Europe and staying in youth hostels, and David Bianco, Director of Residential Life at the University of New Hampshire, established the non-profit organization Elderhostel. It sponsored visits for the over 60 crowd to five New Hampshire colleges. The idea spread to other campuses and to many other, non-academic venues. Today the programs, renamed Exploritas in 2009, and again renamed Road Scholar in 2010, offer tours to over 100 countries, are not age restricted, and are attended by over a quarter million people annually. The original idea of visits to academic venues hardly remains, most of the tours now targeting nonacademic sites.

In 2007, New York entrepreneur Steven Schragis established the commercial venture, One Day University. On a Saturday or Sunday, visitors come to this traveling academy at a designated site, which could be an academic campus, a hotel, or a convention room in a mall. There they attend four or five lectures on different subjects presented by professors from the likes of Harvard, Princeton and Brown. The cost is approximately $250 per visitor, which includes lunch. The program won kudos from many of the more than 3,600 who attended the sessions during the first years. Having originated in the New York area, the program is expanding to other sites across the country.[15]

Positive as One Day University is, I have a few reservations:

- The price ($500 for a couple) surely excludes many people. It is far more expensive than I envision for a VIP program—approximately $10 per lecture per person. The cost difference derives partly from One Day University's having to pay travel, honorarium, and room and board to attract popular professors to the venue, and often rent the venue itself; and as a commercial concern, a profit must be earned. In contrast, lectures in the VIP program would be part of the university's business as usual. Faculty would not be compensated for VIP visitors in the lecture hall, and there are no travel, hotel or hall rental fees, and no profit.

- As One Day University is often held in a commercial venue, participants miss all the richness of visiting a university campus.

- Whereas One Day University offers a set menu of lectures, VIP permits the visitor to select from a wide variety of courses on campus, perhaps most of those offered to undergraduates.

Still, One Day University looks like a positive sharing of university ideas, albeit directed to a somewhat affluent, elite audience.

In the next chapter I invite you to my university campus, to experience another way of idea sharing with visitors—via the university's open-campus museum.

Notes

1. John H. Falk and Lynn D. Dierking, *Learning from Museums: Visitor Experiences and the Making of Meaning* (Walnut Creek, CA: Alta Mira Press, 2000); Douglas M. Knudsen, Ted T. Cable, and Larry Beck, *Interpretation of Cultural and Natural Resources* (State College, PA: Venture Publishing, 2003).

2. These points are corroborated year after year, with little variation, by the rankings published in *US News and World Report*.

3. Websites are updated regularly, so by the time this book is published, a very different text might appear on the web. However, my experience with the U-M website (http://www.umich.edu/) was an only slightly exaggerated version of what I have found on many other university sites.

4. Several university museums are located on or near the U-M campus. I visited three of these, and felt they were all quite good. But except for one small exhibit in the natural history museum that referred to some research on campus, they gave no real insight into the university or its ideas. Given the subject matter on display, these museums could have been located anywhere, on or off an academic campus.

5. Richard P. Dober, *Campus Landscape: Functions, Forms, Features* (New York: John Wiley and Sons, 2000), xi.

6. The field of guiding has an extensive professional literature going back nearly 100 years that includes books, journals and research reports about both the theory (yes, there is a theory) and the practice of guiding.

7. The three words are intended not as a connected phrase, but rather as three separate aspects of academia; Professor Francis F. Blouin Jr., Director of U-M's Bentley Historical Library, University of Michigan, pers. comm.

8. Michigan was the 26th state to join the union, in 1837. Ohio was the first from the Northwest Territory to join, as the 17th state of the union, in 1803. It was preceded by Vermont, Kentucky and Tennessee (not part of the Northwest Territory), and of course prior to these, the original 13 states.

9. I wonder how many "archrival" Amherst and Williams alumni are aware of the following act of 1824 of the Massachusetts legislature: "...if it shall hereafter appear to the Legislature of this Commonwealth lawful and expedient to remove Williams College to the town of Amherst, and the President and Trustees of Williams College shall agree to do so, the legislature shall have full power to unite Williams and Amherst Colleges into one University, at Amherst." (Charter of Amherst College, with Subsequent Legislation, 1991).

10. Since the discovery of the first planet outside our solar system, hundreds more have been revealed. The reason it took so long to find them is that planets, unlike stars, emit no light. Thus, they are not directly detectable, unless they happen to be so close to earth (that is, within our solar system) that we receive from them a reasonable intensity of light from our sun, reflected off their surface. For any planet outside our solar system, being so distant from us, an infinitesimally small percentage of the light reflected off its surface by its own sun (star) would reach the earth. Therefore, indirect means are required to detect planets outside our solar system, as the students in this class discovered.

11. Joseph J. Schwab, *The Teaching of Science as Enquiry* (Cambridge, MA: Harvard University Press, 1966).

12. Readers interested in experiencing vicariously some of this classroom excitement might appreciate Patrick Allitt, *I'm the Teacher, You're the Student: A Semester in the University Classroom* (Philadelphia: University of Pennsylvania Press, 2005). An award winning teacher of American history at Emory University, Allitt draws the reader engagingly into his highly interactive classroom.

13. The rules for in-class behavior would be like those of the Princeton CAP participants (Chapter 4). As in that program, up to 10 percent of the classroom seats could be filled by visitors.

14. Interviewed by the author at CUNY, July 24, 2007.

15. Patricia Cohen, "College is Quicker (1 day) the Second Time Around," *New York Times*, July 6, 2007.

CHAPTER 6. VISITING UNIVERSITIES, II: BLESSED BE THE GUESTS

In Hebrew, you welcome guests to your city, your home, or elsewhere, with the greeting "Bruchim ha-baim," which means literally, "Blessed be those who arrive." I wish this wonderful idea of blessing guests would underlie the relationships of college and university campuses toward the public. But as I commented earlier, I felt anything but blessed on the many American campuses I visited. Ignored would be more like it.

Let's imagine that you and I were to visit a university campus that made us feel blessed. What would such a visit be like? At Jerusalem's Hebrew University, we have attempted to create such a reality. Doing so was a new experience for us, so we proceeded gingerly, made some mistakes, made a few good decisions, and, I believe, established a positive way of welcoming our guests and sharing our campus and its ideas with the public. This chapter illustrates how.

They'll Laugh at You

Sunday is the first day of the workweek in Israel. It's 11:00 AM on Sunday, August 31, 2003, and the Nature Park & Galleries, the new open-campus museum at the Hebrew University's science campus, is celebrating its opening. On the central lawn, an impressive blue canvas tarp shades the hundred white plastic chairs facing the podium. Flags of the Hebrew University, of Jerusalem, and of Israel wave in the breeze. Blue table cloths cover the caterer's tables which offer assorted refreshments. Glossy, blue brochures propped on the chairs and blue signs all around announce the museum's opening. Officials from City Hall, university administrators, faculty colleagues, donors, and the press mill around, along with the museum's small administrative staff and its 15 student guides, T-shirted with the museum's logo.

The audience takes their seats. Having been privileged to develop this unusual museum, I approach the podium, lean toward the microphone, and begin to speak. But with some trepidation. Friends and colleagues have warned me that I was crazy to hold this celebration, to proclaim this museum open. "You've got nothing to show! No building. No exhibits. OK, you've got the geology gallery, but that's old and shows its age."

They were right about our utter nothingness. We had been working for over a year, spending mostly on staff salaries and program development the funds I had collected from donors. Although the funds were well-spent in developing our concept and educational goals and in training our guides, we had developed nothing tangible, nothing in brick and mortar. "They'll laugh at you," I was warned.

I heard the warnings. I understood the danger. But I had a different idea. I believed then—and believe even more strongly today—that any excellent university already *is* a museum—an "open-campus museum." It just doesn't know it.

It seemed clear to me that all the museum objects needed in order to activate an open-campus museum were already in place, some outdoors, others indoors. We simply had to remind ourselves of *The Idea of a University*, its *Ideas from the Disciplines*, and its *Value-Based Ideas*, and then look around the campus for how these could be, or already were, expressed. At the University of Michigan, some important ideas were permanently inscribed on buildings and signs. At the Hebrew University the expression of ideas would take a different form. What we needed was a system of interpretation to connect existing objects to important ideas, and to express these to visitors in an engaging manner. And that's what we had created. Our system of interpretation was our fifteen carefully trained, T-shirted guides.[1] Even though almost nothing had changed on campus, and not one brick had been laid, we had built our museum.

By no means was this the first museum without its own building. Note this definition by the widely recognized International Commission on Museums of UNESCO: "A museum is a non-profit, permanent institution in the service of society and its development, open to the public, which acquires, conserves, researches, communicates and exhibits the tangible and intangible heritage of humanity and its environment for the purposes of education, study and enjoyment."

This definition mentions nothing about a building. Thus, botanical gardens, arboreta, and many other visitor attractions not usually housed indoors are considered museums. Surely, then, if the elements of the above definition are fulfilled, a university campus can also become a museum.

Our plan worked. We opened to the public the next day, and our university campus instantly became that *plus* an added cultural/educational layer for the general public—an open-campus museum. It became one of the world's largest museums, the size of the entire campus, all holding the potential for our guides to point out meaning and ideas to visitors. And we had done it on a shoestring.

We prepared one hour guided presentations on ten different subjects—later we added five more—from which visitors could select. These included walking tours, sit-down interactive demonstrations, and workshops, such as behind-the-scenes tours of forefront research labs in action, interactive tours of Israel's National Collections of Natural History, tours of special collections in the National Library, and of the campus arboretum. Later we developed tours along the boardwalk of the campus' natural forest, and tours of the plant evolution garden and the bird sculpture garden.[2] All tours are on campus. We also developed a brochure, a guide book, and an audio-guide.

All this cost the University not one cent. The University President informed me at the outset that, although he was willing to approve the project, he would commit no funds. "Not now, not ever," were his stern words, uttered sternly. He has stuck to his word. I was permitted to raise the needed funds from donors, but under strictly regulated limitations—difficult, but doable.

King Solomon on Our Campus

Join me now on one of our museum's fifteen programs, the *Discovery Tree Walk*, which focuses on the campus-wide arboretum, with trees from six continents. Let's see how our guide, Rivka, interprets these trees to convey some important ideas.

When we arrive, Rivka has already introduced herself to a group of families with children, and has announced that the title of her tour is *Trees—The Largest Living Things on Earth*. (Each of our tours has a *title*, a single, clear *main theme*—this tour's theme is the grand scale of trees in overall size, the sizes of some of their parts, and the size of their impact on human life and culture—and a *story line* divided into themed sections. These features are regarded as best practices by America's leading professional guiding organizations,[3] yet they were absent from all the guided campus tours I attended at US colleges and universities.)

Rivka begins the tree tour at the tall cedar of Lebanon just inside the main campus gate. Through an interactive give-and-take with the visitors, she conveys the following points:

- In building the ancient Temple in Jerusalem, King Solomon used the wood of cedars of Lebanon, known for its tall, straight trunk, its strength, and its repellency to insects and fungi. Rivka highlights this historic connection with a brief passage from the Bible's Book of Kings.

- Solomon's Temple was the center of Jewish national, cultural and religious life. Symbolically, it is Israel's rough equivalent of the Washington Monument, and the Lincoln and Jefferson Memorials all rolled into one, though more than ten times as ancient.

- The university's designers selected the cedar of Lebanon for the entrance to symbolize that this campus was to be a "temple," though of modern, secular, pluralistic learning—a place central to Israel's culture. The creation, storage and dissemination of new knowledge and ideas on this campus would be essential to the nation's future. By bridging conceptually to the ancient Temple, this tree confers the highest honor upon this campus.

The cedar of Lebanon is the Hebrew University's museological equivalent of Angell Hall at the University of Michigan with its quote from the Northwest Ordinance. In museum parlance, these are examples of tangible objects (in Michigan an inscription, in Jerusalem a tree) invoking larger, intangible concepts (in Michigan, westward expansion and national aspirations, in Jerusalem the ancient Temple and the modern University, both as Israeli national focal points).

This is an example of an important type of work that museums do in interpreting objects—making these tangible-to-intangible connections for their visitors. Prior to my museum activities, I had worked at the Hebrew University for over 15 years, walking past that cedar twice a day, when entering and leaving the campus. I had scarcely noticed its tangibleness, let alone its intangibleness. The Hebrew University campus, like U-M and probably most major universities, is filled with objects symbolically imbued with ideas. But it takes interpretation to make these ideas known, felt, and appreciated. Not doing so is a major lost opportunity.

Let's do a little exercise. If you work or study, or have previously worked or studied, at a college or university, think what significant messages are to be found on its campus. Imagine yourself at the campus entrance. Is there a defined entrance? What's it like? Does it convey the idea of separation from its surroundings by means of a wall, a gate, a long entrance drive? Or does its suggest a connection to, and integration with, the surroundings? Does it hint that you're about to enter a significant place? How? What, if anything, is written at or on the entrance? In what language or languages? Why those? Is the University motto displayed? What does the motto signify; does it suggest any important university ideas? Perhaps a donor's name is inscribed, pointing to financial realities? If nothing is written, what might that suggest?

What would you write, if you could, at the entrance to your campus? How would you display it? What ideas might this express about your campus?

Step onto your campus. What do you see? Does the view suggest a special atmosphere, where special things happen? How do the buildings, lawns, walkways, trees, gardens, sculptures, and the people contribute to creating this atmosphere? Does the campus have a clear structural organization, or is it more amorphous? What might this say about how the institution was conceived when built, and even about its self-image today?

As you can see, many ideas about academia can be encountered even by taking just a few steps. The possibilities abound at my home university. Buildings, sculptures, trees, gardens, plaques, bulletin board announcements, exhibits, and people on campus are all part of the open-campus museum. A well trained guide can help the public explore many worlds.[4]

Why an Academic Campus is a Good Place for a Museum

Much of what I wrote in Chapters 1 through 3 about ideas from America's great universities applies to great museums, such as the Smithsonian National Air and Space Museum in Washington, DC, the Metropolitan Museum of Art in New York, and the Field Museum of Natural History in Chicago, to name just a few. Like universities, they *create knowledge* through the research of their curators and other scholars; they *store knowledge* in the form of their collections, catalogs, and the brains of their curators and other experts; and they *disseminate knowledge* through exhibits and other public programs, scholarly and popular publications, lecture series, films, and websites. Several values that universities hold dear, such as discovery, truth and progress (Chapter 3) are fundamental to museums as well. There is a parallel, and a potential synergy between these two types of institution.

Our open-campus museum in Jerusalem parallels the university in which it resides. Although this museum does not create new knowledge through original research, it synthesizes ideas based on the research of others; it is involved in the storage of knowledge, and particularly in disseminating knowledge through its various educational and cultural activities for the public. And our museum's parallel to the university extends to shared values. It is right at home on campus.

As I have not encountered, or heard of, an open-campus museum other than ours, I presume this concept will be new to most readers. Thus I offer a list of its potential advantages:

- Name and place recognition. If a new open-campus museum were developed at the University of Chicago, the University of Oregon, Swarthmore College, or any other major institution, it would automatically be stamped with the well-known name and location of its home institution.

- Reputation. It takes years to build a reputation for scholarship and authoritative knowledge. A major university or college already has this, and would confer it upon an open-campus museum.

- Landmark buildings. Much sought after by new museums, many universities already have landmark buildings, some historic, others contemporary. An open-campus museum wouldn't be housed in a building, landmark or otherwise. If it were, it wouldn't be an open-campus museum. Rather, such a museum would *include* the buildings on campus, both their facades and interiors, as part of its "collection" to be shown to the public as source material for ideas. The open-campus museum might include a visitors center (as of now, ours doesn't, though we are considering a modest version), and on-campus galleries that display or demonstrate treasures to the public.

- Attractive gardens and lawns. The gardens, lawns, and campus structures are the open-campus museum's environment, equivalent to the inside of a more traditional museum's building. Yet it costs our museum nothing to maintain these—the university does it. Compare this to a state-of-the-art museum building with all its hi-tech upkeep needs and its repairs of, say, a leaky roof. In our museum, the sky is our roof, and in arid Israel, the more it leaks the better.

- Maintenance. Question: How many open-campus museum staff does it take to change a light bulb? Answer: None; the university staff does that.

- Scholars. If you were building an independent museum, you would have to hire and pay for a scholarly staff. At an open-campus museum, these come with the territory, and in our experience, many are willing, even eager, to volunteer a modest amount of time.

- Guides.[5] University students, when professionally trained, can be excellent guides. Also, a student guide is, in a sense, a museum "object" of interest to visitors. "What are you studying? Where are you from? How do you like the studies here? What do you plan to do after graduation?" These are commonly asked questions.

- Flexible budgeting. With no building maintenance, no large permanent staff, and no other major fixed budget items, an open-campus museum can go with the cash flow. If there's little in the kitty at any given time, the museum can pull back on programming or advertising, and explain to the guides that, during the lull, they'll be guiding fewer groups. The guides won't disappear because they're university students, enthusiastic about the open-campus museum, and not overly dependent on their guiding income.

- Ethos. The great museums of the world develop their own ethos. The Exploratorium in San Francisco, the American Museum of Natural History in New York, and the Holocaust Museum in Washington, DC each has a different way of enveloping its visitors. Universities do too, and they would confer their ethos on an open-campus museum. Once, I asked a student at MIT for directions to the Electrical Engineering Department. He closed his eyes, thought for a moment, and answered, "Envision a trapezoid." He proceeded to explain the trapezoidal shape of the set of walkways, and how to navigate them. I never asked, down the road at Harvard, how to get to Electrical Engineering, but I imagine a different ethos, and maybe a different reply, such as, "Why would you want to go *there?*"

- Campus culture. This may include the school colors, motto, mascot, school song, and school pride. At the University of Michigan, I noticed that students sometimes greet one another with the words "Go Blue," a kind of football mini-cheer. During my student-led tour at Princeton, the guide pointed out a building designed by an architect who had graduated from Yale, well-known as one of Princeton's rival universities. In honor of his alma mater, the architect designed into one of the rain gutters a frieze image of a bulldog, the Yale mascot. The guide remarked, "On this campus, we think that's where Yale belongs. In the gutter." Cute.

As you can see, there is good harmony between a university campus and an open-campus museum. It's a short step, conceptually and financially, from the former to the latter. But in case you are thinking about establishing a new museum of *any* type associated with academia, let's consider some inherent cacophony.

Why an Academic Campus Is Not a Good Place for a Museum

Based on visitor questionnaires, most people come to our open-campus museum not for the purpose of academic learning, but for a broader type of experience. This is true of museums in general.[6] Some come looking for an enjoyable family outing, or an aesthetically, spiritually, and/or intellectually elevating experience, or because they've heard about a new project, or because Aunt Sarah is in town and they can't bear sitting around the house with her. Most people come to museums as a leisure time activity, with non-academic goals in mind. They don't come to learn the painting techniques of the Renaissance masters, or the sequence of biochemical steps in photosynthesis, or the details of China's political history. There are better ways to learn these things.

Many professors don't handle the concept of a leisure activity well. Renaissance painting techniques, the steps in photosynthesis, and Chinese political history are just the kinds of things they research, write about, and teach in their courses. Many faculty assume, incorrectly, that like their students, most museum visitors come to campus to gain this kind of knowledge.

Where do professors get such an idea? It's built into their work pattern. Professors have a kind of unwritten contract with students which, if written down, might look like this:

1) We the professors have important knowledge that you the students don't have.

2) You need this knowledge for your enlightenment, future employment possibilities, elevation of social status, or other reasons.

3) We assume you would also like to develop a world view more or less like ours, based on values such as rationality, the search for truth, creating progress in the world, and so forth.

4) We know how to transmit the knowledge and the world view that you want and need.

5) Given all the above, you should come to us, study hard, and learn by our proven methods.

I believe the above reflects the professoriate's majority view about students, and some students, at least, seem to concur, as they apply themselves intensively to learning.

Throughout most of the 20th century, most museum administrators and curators, whether at universities or not, regarded their visitors according to the five statements above. Visitors, they thought, recognized the need for exposure to the museums' expertise and authority in order to become cultured individuals. And so, museum workers thought, the visitors wanted to gain the curators' knowledge. They assumed the visitors would observe the objects on display, read the text, learn, and thereby improve their lives. This seemed to be the museum's proper role.[7]

However, research by forefront museums, especially by their Visitor Studies Departments—non-existent departments until a few decades ago—indicates that the five statements above are irrelevant to most of today's museum visitors.[8] Rather, one can easily imagine a visitor responding with five counter-statements like the ones below. Let's imagine a visitor to a tree walk:

1) You have knowledge about trees that I don't have? OK, but I also have knowledge about trees that you don't have. My mom used to read to me under a huge oak tree in our front garden. Soon I started drawing that tree. I drew it many times, in different lighting, weather, and seasons, until I knew that tree and the varieties of its beauty really well. Then I started drawing other kinds of trees. I doubt that you know trees in quite the way that I do.

2) I need your knowledge? What I really need is more of my own kind of knowledge about trees—a deeper insight into their beauty, for instance.

3) I need your world view? Actually, I've got my own, thanks.

4) You say you know how to pass on to me what I want and need. I wonder.

5) You say I should come to learn from you. But I don't care about the species' names and physiological processes. I care about the essence of trees, and being inspired by them. Can you offer me that?

I have reviewed proposals for new museums written by academic colleagues, some of whom are internationally renowned as experts in their fields. Often their museum proposals read like the syllabi of their university courses. They seem unaware that most museum visitors are not coming for academic learning. Upon encountering the claim that most visitors are looking for something different—a claim that has been amply validated by museum research—these colleagues see this as "dumbing down." Academics sometimes think any visitor who doesn't see the world through their eyes is a dummy. This kind of standoffishness, referred to earlier, tends to raise a barrier against the public.

Harvard sociologist Sara Lawrence-Lightfoot has written persuasively of the varied purposes and styles of learning that people engage in during the second half of their lives, compared to more goal-directed learning in their youth.[9] I propose that academics should take seriously, and accommodate themselves to, the public's diverse interests, learning styles and purposes, as Lawrence-Lightfoot suggests. Rather than dumbing down, this can lead to broadening out. This has been my experience in my museum work.

We mustn't ignore visitors who want more academically oriented learning. For instance, in a program about trees, the steps in photosynthesis, species names, and geographical distributions would likely interest some visitors. That's why some good exhibits have "more information" stations that interested visitors can approach, while most others pass by. And it's why our guides are trained to answer diverse types of questions.

In the next section, I suggest how an open-campus museum can connect with individual visitors about the objects on display and ideas about them, by taking into account the visitors' prior experience with similar objects and ideas.

Doing a "4PM"

Most museums see themselves as serving the visiting public, and consequently have progressed further than universities in knowing how to communicate their ideas with a general audience. Many of the more advanced museums, when developing a new exhibit, invest time, energy and money to discover how best to connect the exhibit's subject and content to its potential visitors. Early in the planning stage, there is a "front-end evaluation," which surveys how a sample of the expected visitors relate, in terms of their knowledge, interest, experience, memories, and emotions to the exhibit's subject, display objects, and interpretation. This information is vital in creating the exhibit. During the displays' construction, there is a "formative evaluation," assessing the public's response to exhibit mock-ups. This can lead to important modifications. After opening day, there is a "summative evaluation," which examines the public's response to the completed exhibit. This information is used to fine tune the completed exhibit and make it work even better.[10] (Imagine a university professor carrying out such a complex self-evaluative process in developing a new course!)

Praiseworthy as this process is, and successful in improving museum exhibits, the museum can't know in advance who will come to the new exhibit. Rather, the front end and formative stages, at least, involve statistical sampling. But our open-campus museum is based not on exhibits, but on tours, demonstrations and workshops, led by guides. This provides a golden opportunity to learn something about our visitors, and to then use this knowledge to enrich their tour experiences. None of the many professional books or journal articles about guiding techniques suggested how a guide might do this. So my graduate student Dina and I tried to find a way to make this happen.[11] Here is a brief description of Dina's research which shows a new way to obtain and use knowledge about the visitors so as to engage them more fully on the tours.

Dina used Rivka's *Discovery Tree Walks* in her studies. Rivka agreed to conduct her tree walk using the four-part method we devised. Dina evaluated the effect of this method on the visitors' experience. Let's join Rivka once again, this time along with Dina and a group of visitors, as they embark on a tree walk that was part of Dina's study.

The first part of our four-part method: Rivka first says to the group, "Before we begin, I'd like to invite you all to jot down a few things." Dina hands out clipboards and pencils, one to each family or one to each person, as the visitors wish. On each clipboard is a piece of paper with a circle in the middle. Inside the circle is the word "Trees." Radiating from the circle are eight sun-ray lines. "Jot down whatever comes to mind when you think about trees—maybe something you remember from the past, even the distant past, or something you like or dislike about trees. Or maybe you want to draw something. Let's take just a few minutes for this."[12] You would think they had all taken happy pills. They love it!

The method's second part: After a few minutes, Rivka asks if anyone would like to share briefly something they've written down. Several do.

The third part: Rivka responds to several comments. Here is her response to a comment from a 12-year-old boy, who was with his parents and sister: "You say that you and your parents and sister built a tree house. Wow! What does it feel like up there? [Rivka waits for an answer and pursues briefly the boy's feeling of being in the tree house.] Great. Well, as we're walking along, maybe you and your family would like to see if you can find any trees that would be good for building tree houses—let us know. Also, do you see that tree way down in the corner there? That's a sequoia. In California, its native home, it grows to be the tallest tree in the world. When we get there, have I got a story for you! [Of course, it's for everyone.] Please remind me when we're there—I could forget—to tell you about a young woman who climbed up 80 meters high in a sequoia tree—that's about three times as tall as this four-story building here. There she stepped into a simple tree house, not much more than a platform with walls and a cover, and she stayed there for—guess how long—two years! Without coming down once! She had good reason. Wait till you hear.

The fourth and final part: During the tour, Rivka relates back to the visitors' comments and her responses in parts 2 and 3 of the method. For instance, when the group arrives at the sequoia, she addresses the boy and his family, as well as the whole group, and tells the amazing story of the woman who lived in the tree to help dramatize the fight against the cutting down of ancient sequoia forests by lumber companies.[13]

Several things transpired in this four-part interaction. Rivka honored the visitors by including their personal experiences in the university's tree walk. Moreover, by getting them to think about what it feels like in their tree house, she brought their emotions into the tour. She also transferred partial authority to the boy and his family by having them decide, on the basis of their experience, which trees would be good for tree houses. And she gave them the gift of the Sequoia story.

Rivka had her own story, which she told, but enriched with the visitors' personal experiences. She motivated them to grasp the particular messages she wanted to convey, including ideas about botany, such as what makes a tree strong enough to hold up a tree house, and ideas about nature protection, via the Sequoia story.

Our four-part method created a bridge between the visitor's life and tree ideas. As I had told Dina, Rivka, and the other students in my guiding course, the life of each museum visitor is divided into three equally important periods. The first period is from the moment of birth until they show up at your tour. The third period is from the end of your tour until the end of their lives. The second, "equally important period" is your one-hour tour, during which you connect the first period of their lives with, and thereby enrich, the third period.

Here in brief summary is Dina's four-part method:

1) Visitors jot down thoughts.

2) Some visitors share their thoughts with Rivka and the group.

3) Rivka states a connection between visitors' thoughts and something they will see during the tour (this is usually, but not always, possible).

4) Upon arriving at the relevant object, Rivka expands on its relevance to the personal thoughts of the visitor.

Though simple, this method relates conceptually to at least two larger ideas discussed earlier. One is constructivism in education, which posits that a person will absorb an idea best if it can be hung on a conceptual hook that is part of the individual's unique "mental skeleton." The boy's tree house was his, and probably his family's, hook. The other idea is Multiple Intelligences, which identifies eight different types of cognitive, aesthetic, kinetic and other personal abilities, reminding us that different people can have very different ways of relating to the subject and the objects of a guided tour.

Does Dina's method make any difference to the visitors' experience during the tour? To test this, she quantified the visitors' experiences, using two methods. One method was checking off on a prepared checklist every time any visitor carried out an action that reflected involvement in the tour's subject, such as picking up a pine cone, asking the guide a question about a tree, or answering a question the guide has asked. Dina's second method was a questionnaires that visitors were asked to complete immediately after the tree walk.

Dina used the data she acquired to compare two different types of tours. Tours like the one I described above, which included the four-part method, were the "experimental" tours. The other tours were "control" tours, in which Rivka did not carry out the four-part method. Instead, she spent the same amount of time prior to setting off for the first tree, chatting with the visitors in a similarly friendly way, about museums, how the visitors arrived and where they parked, but not about trees.

Dina found that every single item on both the checklist and the questionnaire indicated, to a statistically significant extent, that the people on the experimental tours were more engaged and/or had more positive experiences than those on the control tours. Dina later discovered that this was also true if, on the experimental tours, Rivka replaced the first of the method's four parts (the visitors' writing down their associations with trees) by simply asking them, "When you think about trees, what comes to mind?" and then followed up with the other three parts of the method.

We were convinced that we had discovered an important way to relate to our visitors, and called this four-part method the "4PM." I would go around to our other guides and suggest, "You know, you really ought to think about doing a 4PM." At first they thought I meant going out for afternoon tea, so I needed to explain.

It's all about attitude, about academics recognizing, moving toward, and honoring the public in order to draw them in and facilitate communication, rather than expecting only that the public honor them. Simple as this attitude is, it's foreign to many academics. Yes, the university is filled with experts who know all kinds of things about their areas of expertise that most visitors don't know. But academia needs a bridge to the public. Dina's 4PM builds that bridge. As we'll see later, universities ought to be doing 4PMs all over the place for the public, in all sorts of different ways.

University Museums and the Open Campus Approach

I conclude this chapter by comparing the opportunity of a university to share its ideas with the public via a traditional museum, in a building—which I call a "museum"—versus an "open-campus museum." Since the year 2000, several universities have planned, begun building, or actually opened major new museums. These include Duke University's Nasher Museum of Art (at a cost of $23 million), The University of Oklahoma's Sam Noble Museum of Natural History ($45 million), The University of Texas' Blanton Museum of Art ($83 million), Harvard's planned unification, renovation and expansion of its art museums (estimated at $100 million), plus a new museum planned for Harvard's new Allston campus in downtown Boston. Few major museums at major universities have gone the way of Princeton's Natural History Museum, which actually closed during this same period. It would seem, then, that overall, the museum environment on American campuses is on the upswing.

Not really. For instance, with university operating costs constantly rising, academic museums are receiving less and less of their home institutions' budget, both percentage-wise, and in absolute terms. In a 2001 survey of 36 art museums at American universities, none received from its home institution full funding for the annual budget, the average being 41%, down from 76% fifteen years previously. The situation has worsened since the economic downturn.

Moreover, the cost of running a modern museum is rising steadily. Visitors to academic museums increasingly expect, but do not often find, the amenities offered in off-campus museums—quality restaurants, upscale gift shops, full disabilities access, and sophisticated, interactive, hi tech exhibits. To place this in perspective, the cost of producing a single permanent exhibit in an already existing gallery of a natural history museum runs an average of $500 per square foot of floor space. For an exhibit of substantial, but not unusual, size, say 5,000 square feet, that's $2.5 million. For one exhibit! Note that this is an *average* cost, which can easily triple if the exhibit is built with lots of "bells and whistles." This does not include renovations to the gallery itself which, if required, would skyrocket the cost. Then there's financing the museum's research facilities, staff salaries, and more.

Few universities are prepared for such expenses. The lack of adequate funds keeps many existing university museums, especially of natural history, archaeology, and anthropology—museums whose exhibits are more complicated than pictures on the wall or sculptures on the floor—looking dowdy. Some people are charmed by the classic oak display case with its slightly dusty, rare fossil that was discovered by the nearly fossilized, retired professor. Most people are not.

As much as I love museums, I would question whether the funds required to build and maintain them are the best use of dwindling academic dollars. I'm sure many presidents of leading universities would love to receive a museum-sized donation for a new research building, renovated lecture halls, graduate student fellowships, or other aspects of the institution's core mission.

All this ought to increase a university's interest in considering an open-campus museum, which can operate on a minimal budget, and promote public understanding of, and interest in, the university, something existing campus museums rarely do. But I predict it would take a lot of convincing to move a university in this direction.

I invite you now to listen in on a hypothetical conversation between a hypothetical university president and myself that I suspect is close to how a real conversation might go. (Although I have interviewed several college and university presidents for this book, who are listed in the Appendix, I did not have this particular conversation, as it would take most of the interview time to explain what I mean by an open-campus museum.)

Me: "...and so, I suggest you consider an open-campus museum to share your great institution's great ideas with the public."

President: "But we're already doing that. We invite the public in all the time. We have museums, concerts, theatrical performances, public lectures, sporting events, and guided tours of the campus. We have in-class and online courses for adults, and civic engagement and volunteer programs. And we publish bulletins and books, and then there's our informative website. What more do you want from me?"

Me: "I guess I want you to read my book; I hope it will convince you that, in spite of all the great things you just mentioned, little of it reaches the general public.

President: "Sorry, but I can't agree to expand our activities any further."

Me: "Why not? Compared to the museums you already operate, an open-campus museum would cost very little, and would tie together many of the ongoing campus activities into a coherent program with greater impact and more depth. It would make all your parts work better than they do now.

President: "What's wrong with the way my parts work?"

Me: "You have no consistent set of goals or strategies for dealing with the public. The director of your art museum reports to the provost, the director of your natural history museum reports to the arts and sciences dean, and the director of your botanical garden reports to the biology chairperson. None of these entities know what the others are doing, or what is happening in your other galleries or libraries, bookstore, university press, publications office, faculty club, admissions office, public relations office, outreach/extension office, athletics program, restaurants, or any other campus offices and venues relevant to the public. There are no tours for the general public, only for student applicants and their families. Visitors to your campus get either mixed messages or no messages, and go home missing the deeply moving experiences you could provide. Why not open the public's eyes to the fact that your campus is one of America's treasures? Just as they go to see the national parks and the nation's great museums, why not visit campuses like yours—which, together with you, could become a national leader in public education. Oh, and there are no signs on campus pointing to the toilets."

President: "You don't say. But we can't afford to get into all this now. Do you have any idea how hard it is to raise money from donors these days?"

Me: "I do, actually. But an open-campus museum will cost you very little, and might even turn a profit. It could even bring in some big donors."

President: "We can't start changing the whole campus around with renovations and constructions for visitors."

Me: "You don't need to change anything on campus. When you read my book (did I mention I've written a book?), you'll see that we didn't make any physical changes in order to start our open-campus museum. Those came later, as donors came forward."

President: "All those visitors you want to invite, families milling around, kids running all over the place—it would disturb the campus atmosphere and activities."

Me: "In our experience this hasn't happened."

President: "Another thing—I can't ask our professors to start hosting visitors—they would object to doing this, and to the time it would involve, and rightfully so."

Me: "Agreed. The open-campus museum and its student guides would do the 'hosting.' Only professors who want to spend an hour here or there, showing their labs or leading a discussion, would do so. In our experience, many professors want to take part and request that we enlist their help."

President: "I guess you think you're starting to convince me about this, eh?"
Me: "Am I?"
President: "Let me think about it."

Quiet please—the President is thinking. Meanwhile, let's slip into the campus book store and thumb through some writing by academics for the general public. Academics are good at writing, correct? Not quite, as we'll soon see.

Notes

1. To train the museum guides, I developed, with input from colleagues in several fields, a masters level course in museum guiding. Students wishing to guide in our museum must pass this course, in which they prepare their own sample guided tour. They must then refine their tour, which usually requires much additional work, before being accepted as museum guides.

2. The last three items—forest boardwalk, plant evolution garden, and bird sculpture gardens, are among the projects built on the campus by the open-campus museum, in the years since its opening.

3. Two US organizations are widely recognized as the most advanced in developing and promoting effective guiding methods: The National Association for Interpretation (which offers a variety of training workshops), and the National Parks Authority.

4. Many of the messages available on campus need to be discovered from a variety of resources. Often one faculty member is appointed as the institution's historian, and there is usually an institutional archive. At least one, and in some cases many, books may have been written about the institution. The public relations office or other administrative office may maintain useful banks of information. Elderly faculty and staff members hold many significant memories.

5. As of 2012, the museum has decided to reduce the number of its guided tours and increase the signage and other forms of interpretation, permitting visitors to traverse the museum in a self-guided manner.

6. Zahava D. Doering, "Strangers, Guests or Clients? Visitor Experiences in Museums," *Curator, The Museum Journal* 42/2 (1999), 74-87; Andrew J. Pekarik, "From Knowing to Not Knowing: Moving Beyond 'Outcomes,'" *Curator, The Museum Journal* 53/1 (2010), 105-115.

7. Marjorie Schwarzer, *Riches, Rivals and Radicals: 100 Years of Museums in America* (Washington, DC: American Association of Museums, 2006).

8. Doering, "Strangers, Guests or Clients?"

9. Lawrence-Lightfoot, *The Third Chapter* (see Introduction, n. 13).

10. Samuel Taylor, *Try It! Improving Exhibits Through Formative Evaluation* (Washington, DC: Association of Science-technology Centers, 1991); Lynn D. Dierking and Wendy Pollock, *Questioning Assumptions: An Introduction to Front-end Studies in Museums* (Washington, DC: Association of Science-technology Centers, 1998); Judy Diamond, *Practical Evaluation Guide: Tools for Museums and Other Informal Educational Settings* (Walnut Creek, CA, AltaMira Press, 1999).

11. Dina Tsybulskaya and Jeff Camhi, "Accessing and Incorporating Visitors' Entrance Narratives in Guided Museum Tours," *Curator, The Museum Journal* 52/1 (2009): 81-100.

12. We derived the idea of having visitors write their personal thoughts about trees from a prior study that used a similar approach but for different purposes: John H. Falk, "Personal Meaning Mapping," in *Museums and Creativity: A Study Into the Role of Museums in Design Education*, eds., G. Caban and others (Sydney, AU: Powerhouse Publishing, 2003).

13. Julia Butterfly Hill, *The Legacy of Luna* (New York: Harper-Collins, 2000).

CHAPTER 7. BOOKS, "THE GREATEST THINGS WE HAVE"

Recently, I watched on the Internet a lecture by Yale professor of history David Blight.[1] It was the introductory session of his course on the Civil War. He mentioned that, as the lecture was on January 15—Martin Luther King's birthday—he would begin by reading (appropriately, given the course's subject) a section of King's famous "I have a dream" speech, delivered in Washington on August 28, 1963. Picking up a book, he read with quiet dignity but underlying passion, the passage containing what he called the speech's central metaphor, "the promissory note in the bank of justice."

Reading from the lectern, he reminded me of King himself, standing on the steps of the Lincoln Memorial and drawing upon phrases from both Lincoln and the Bible. If any students had doubted the relevance of Lincoln and the Civil War to modern America, this brief reading surely dashed those doubts.

Professor Blight then put that book aside, picked up another, and before opening it, he began an impassioned plea for the students to honor books:

> We live in a world where all of us take books for granted. We throw books on the floor, we load them in our backpacks...we lose them, we write all over them. It's only a few generations ago that there weren't any book stores to go to. Your great grandparents couldn't meander through a book store.... Books are precious things....Think of a book, just for a moment, one of your all-time favorite books, as a newborn child brought into the world. [Here he caresses the book he's been holding.] Probably a lot more planning and thought and design and construction, at least intellectually, goes into that book than goes into most babies [laughter].... They're somebody's dream. Somebody's creation....In some ways they're the greatest things we

have....I want to quote to you from the oldest history book in western civilization.

He turned to a pre-marked page of the book he'd been caressing, Herodotus' *The History*, and read a passage that defines the study of history.

This chapter is about books, "in some ways...the greatest things we have," to re-quote Professor Blight. Books that, like the two from which he had read, transmit the human experience. But specifically it's about books written by today's academics. There are additional formats for written academic work—professional journals, magazines, newspapers, and the Internet. But a book gives the academic writer the opportunity to expand on his or her area of expertise, and to develop a narrative that invites the reader on an extended journey of ideas. In a book, the journey can be long enough and the ideas deep enough to change forever the way the reader thinks about the subject.

In this chapter, we will ask how effectively academics transmit their ideas, through the books they write, not just to other academics, and not just to an elite upper crust of society, but to a broader public. My comments will be based largely on what writing experts say, but will also include my own exploration of books.

Writing experts had warned that academics don't usually write well for the public, and I might therefore be disappointed. Reed Malcolm, an editor at the University of California Press, commented, "the authors we typically work with—academics—have difficulty writing for a trade [that is, public] audience. To retrain them to write for a wider audience can be quite excruciating."[2] William Germano, former editor-in-chief of Columbia University Press, wrote, "Academic writers must often struggle to find the 'trade voice.' Though it may sound perverse to say so, most scholars know too much to write well for a trade readership."[3] Janice Goldklang, former editor of Pantheon Books at Random House, was more blunt: "The writing of most professors is just so boring!"[4] Mostly, though, I would like to share with you the comments of a most interesting writing expert.

Nicholas Lemann

I first encountered Nicholas Lemann through an LA Times piece he wrote, a kind of review, some 50 years late, of a George Orwell essay about writing. Reflecting on Orwell's essay, Lemann proclaimed that "...better writing can engender a better society [and] can improve not just our readers' experience of our work but the lives of everybody."

Amen. And I thought to myself, academics are positioned to do this, given their collectively held knowledge and wide-ranging ideas on just about everything. But Lemann highlighted a particularly egregious example of bad writing, "the kind of fancy, pretentious, imprecise prose usually purveyed by intellectuals [including, he seemed to imply, professors]....Nobody who has read [Orwell's] essay can ever use a formulation such as 'not unlike' again with a clear conscience."[5] I imagined Lemann might also disapprove of "no less important," "not infrequently," "as it were," "indeed," (oops, I tend to use that one not infrequently), and referring to oneself as "this author" and the reader as "the reader." I also wondered which kinds of sentences he would allow dangling prepositions to dangle from.

Lemann knows—umm—whereof he speaks. President of the Harvard Crimson, the student newspaper, during his undergraduate years, he has held high editorial positions with the Washington Post, Atlantic Monthly, and The New Yorker. He has written five books, plus numerous articles—for the New York Times, the New York Review of Books, and other magazines for the cognoscenti. In 2003, with no academic degree higher than a BA, and no prior full time employment at any university, but with a list of credentials an arm's length long, he was hired as not just professor, but Dean of America's premier school of journalism, at Columbia University—the school founded by Joseph Pulitzer. (Yes, that's *the* Pulitzer.) Surely this guy could tell me a thing or two about academics as writers, so I went to meet him at his place of work.[6]

In the lobby of Columbia's Journalism Building is a bronze bust of Pulitzer and his words: "The power to mold the future of the republic will be in the hands of the journalists of future generations." Nice, but I would say that "in the hands of the universities" makes at least as much sense. Eager to hear what journalist and university dean Lemann would have to say about this, I stepped into the elevator, and headed for his top-floor office.

In our conversation, which turned quickly to academic writers, Lemann pointed proudly to a trio of paperbacks on his desk. "I just managed to get a young assistant professor of journalism, author of these three books, approved for tenure," he said. "And they're all trade books—you know, the kind journalists write—intended for the general public, not just for academics, and all published by commercial houses, not university presses."

Surprised, I asked, "Does Columbia now reward tenure and job advancement for this type of publishing also in, say, the Department of Sociology, or Anthropology, or Political Science?"

"God no!" he exclaimed. "The Journalism School is different. We're viewed as a professional school, not so academic. So for us it's possible. For them, never. Even so, it was a huge battle for me to get this approved."

I explained my interest in the quality of academic writing for the general public and asked for his thoughts on the subject. Turned out he had plenty. He spoke about personalizing one's writing, being present in it, and creating a relationship with the reader. (I liked that—sounded a bit like "doing a 4PM," at our open-campus museum.) He explained that creating a relationship implies respect for the reader, since it's likely a writer would want to relate to readers he or she respects. "And a writer needs to develop a story line, or narrative, with richly descriptive scenes, realistic dialogue, and a build up and resolution of tension," he said. He added that writing with emotion and a judicious touch of humor are important skills. "Most university faculty haven't a clue about these things," he said, pounding the table lightly on the word "clue".[7]

Makes sense, I thought. For most academics just starting out, the biggest thing they write is their PhD thesis, which they submit to their faculty advisor first for comments and later for approval. The advisor, though, gained his or her writing skills in the same way, by submitting a thesis to some faculty advisor one generation back, and so forth all the way back to Socrates, who never wrote a PhD thesis.

Lemann continued, "Every so often a colleague in psychology or physics or whatever invites me to lunch and says, 'I want to write something for the public. Can you give me a few pointers?' I tell them, 'No way—it's not about pointers! Writing for the public is a craft, and learning it takes a tremendous amount of time and hard work. It's like the violin—while you're learning it you have to practice hard every day, and after you've learned it, you need to keep practicing, or you lose it.'"

The violin? OK, this was making sense to me, though I was feeling a bit baffled by the breadth and depth of negativity I was hearing. I recalled many books by academics—some by friends and colleagues—that I had enjoyed very much over the years. True, I hadn't then been wearing my museological hat and wondering whether the general public would appreciate these books. Yet I was left feeling uncertain whether these experts could be right, and totally unclear what my own exploration of academic books would reveal.

Tricks and Treats

I proceeded to read, or re-read, lots of books, mostly in physics and biology, written by academics who stated explicitly that their target audience included people with no formal knowledge of the book's field. As I plowed through one book after another, I began, grudgingly, to agree with the writing experts that much of this material, while suitable—and often fascinating—for someone with years of science background, would be far less suited to the non-scientific, or minimally scientific public. Based on comments in their prefaces, some authors seemed to believe that if they just left out the math and the technical jargon, their work would automatically become understandable and engaging. Others hailed their own writing precision as sufficient for attracting and holding a wide audience. A few commented that they were unwilling to pander to the general public, and one well-known writer on evolution seems to specialize in insulting his public.

Missing from most of these books were the stylistic features Lemann had recommended—personalizing the writing and making the writer present, creating a relationship with the reader, respecting the reader, developing a narrative with a story line, tension, rich description, dialog, humor. Although the authors were brilliant in their fields, it seemed they had never taken Lemann's version of "violin lessons," or at least had not continued to practice.

I recognize that it is difficult to make complex concepts, such as those in modern physics, clear to the uninitiated reader. Here's an illustration: Two individuals traveled through the USA in 1921 to raise funds for the newly established Hebrew University of Jerusalem—my current employer. The travelers were Chaim Weizmann—research chemist, international Zionist leader, and later Israel's first President—and Albert Einstein who, that year, won the Nobel Prize in physics. The two were to become co-chairs of the Hebrew University's first Board of Governors. The story goes that every evening during the trip, over dinner, Einstein would explain his theory of relativity to Weizmann. By the end of the summer, Weizmann summed up the result of all this explanation—he was convinced *Einstein* understood relativity.

This story aside, I believe that any subject can be successfully explained, not only to the likes of Weizmann, but to most people. But the explainer needs to employ at least two tricks. One trick, mentioned earlier, is to discover any points of contact that can form a link between the text and the interests, experiences, memories and emotions of potential readers. In Lemann's language, this is part of creating a relationship with the reader, and it's a bit like doing a 4PM in our open-campus museum.

The second trick is to stop the explanation at the right moment. To illustrate, imagine you are presenting a slide show about your newly built house to a gathering of friends. An initial long distance photo shows the house exterior and part of the garden. Anyone can appreciate this picture. The next photo, taken from just inside the front door, shows parts of the living and dining rooms. So far so good. Then there's a series of photos from different angles of different rooms, ending with the rumpus room. Viewers might need some orientation, but most will more or less understand. Then come the architect's drawings—the floor plans and the elevations of several rooms. You begin losing the folks who didn't do so well in high school geometry. Photos of the house's wiring and plumbing diagrams elicit audible snores. Bottom line—the rumpus room was the place to stop, the architect's plans belonged in the question period, and the wiring and plumbing belonged in your desk drawer.

Both tricks—creating a relationship and knowing where to stop the slide show are about knowing and respecting one's audience. Judiciously balancing the interests of both expert- and general-reader can produce writing suited to both. Not easy, I'm sure, but doable.

Let me share with you the writing of a distinguished astrophysicist who, in my view, got it just right. This man taught at Cornell during the years I was there, 1967 to 1982. I first encountered him indirectly when my family and I spent the academic year 1973-74 overseas on a sabbatical leave. That year, we rented out our house near Cornell, exactly as it was, even down to our Scrabble game, to a young professor of astronomy and his wife—Joe and Joy. They returned the house to us in pristine condition, with one interesting addition. In the Scrabble box were telltale score cards of a great many games by four players—Joy, Joe,

Linda and Carl. Poor Carl had not won a single game all year long. Who would have guessed, then, that Scrabblisticly challenged Carl—the late Carl Sagan, that is—would include, among his many extra-ordinary talents, using Scrabble's 26 letters to write winning books for the general public?

The last of the 20 books Sagan authored or co-authored was *Billions and Billions*, published in 1997. True, this book, a series of essays, treats some subjects that are not among the most abstractly difficult in physics. Nevertheless, Sagan deserves billions of kudos for a conversational and friendly style that reaches out to readers. There are many references to everyday experiences, and Sagan knows how much to say and never takes the reader too far. He stops the slide show in the rumpus room. Also, his writing is respectful of other religious or life orientations, something not overwhelmingly common among academics.

In his 1980 book *Cosmos*, which accompanied his wildly successful PBS TV series *Cosmos—A Personal Voyage*, Sagan effectively connects the book's subject with the reader, stating, "...[W]e are, in a very real and profound sense, a part of [the] Cosmos, born from it, our fate deeply connected with it."[8] He becomes our personal tour guide through the universe in space and time. He made me feel like an astronaut traveling on Viking I, and landing on Mars, just sixteen days too late to mark America's bicentennial (the landing occurred on July 20, 1976). Reviewing the history of space travel, he connects the reader to the entirety of the cosmos:

> The Cosmos was discovered only yesterday. For a million years it was clear to everyone that there were no other places than the Earth. Then in the last tenth of a percent of the lifetime of our species...we reluctantly noticed that we were not the center and purpose of the Universe, but rather lived on a tiny and fragile world lost in immensity and eternity, drifting in a great cosmic ocean dotted here and there with a hundred billion galaxies and a billion trillion stars. We have bravely tested the waters and have found the ocean to our liking, resonant with our nature. Something in us recognizes the Cosmos as home. We are made of stellar ash. Our origin and evolution have been tied to distant cosmic events. The exploration of the Cosmos is a voyage of self-discovery.

And continuing with a touch of humanity and humor: "National boundaries are not evident when we view the Earth from space. Fanatical ethnic or religious or national chauvinisms are a little difficult to maintain when we see our planet as a fragile blue crescent fading to become an inconspicuous point of light against the bastion and citadel of the stars. Travel is broadening."[9]

Nicholas Lemann, no doubt, would really like this stuff. Me, too. Star explorer Sagan certainly deserved a gold star for his communication with the public. But such writing is rare, which indicates the difficulty many academics face in hitting the mark when addressing the general public—especially, it seemed to me, on scientific subjects.

Shakespeare On His Team

Recently I mentioned over coffee to the director of an Ivy League university press that I believed professors in the social sciences and humanities were better, on average, than scientists at writing for the general public. Lowering his coffee cup, he pursed his lips, tightened his gaze, and proclaimed, "Academics, as a rule, can't write, period."

I said to myself (only to myself, not wanting to sound naïve), "Gee, I thought those guys across campus were really good at this stuff." And even if this director's proclamation was right, he slipped in the phrase "as a rule," leaving room for exceptions. Let me share with you one exception.

Enter, stage left, Harvard's Shakespeare whiz Stephen Greenblatt. He describes how he wrote a book chapter honoring his friend, Stanford professor of comparative literature Sepp Gumbrecht.[10] The chapter appeared in a festschrift celebrating Gumbrecht's 60th birthday.

Festschrifts, Greenblatt comments, are "honorific books that are almost never read, even by the person who is being honored." Greenblatt wanted to write his essay in a non-academic, popular style that might lead a reader who happened upon the essay's first sentence, to move on to the second, and perhaps even to the last.

Gumbrecht had recently researched the aesthetics of sports. Here's how Greenblatt began his un-festschrift-like contribution: "Sepp Gumbrecht's *In Praise of Athletic Beauty* (2006) came along about fifty years too late for it to have had the practical effect on my life that it might have had: namely, to have gotten me into Harvard." Greenblatt proceeds to write a highly personal account of *his own*—not Gumbrecht's—life, centered around televised sports as an important element in the culture of his Jewish immigrant family in Boston. He writes about the great Ted Williams, and Fenway Park, and about how his father tried to convince him that the Harvard interviewer would want to know that he was a well-rounded kid (which he wasn't), and not an egghead (which he was), as demonstrated by the fact that he could talk sports (which he couldn't).

Aside from Greenblatt's first sentence, he does not mention Gumbrecht again until the article's final paragraph. But in all that comes before that paragraph, in the stories about the Red Sox and his father's hours of watching televised sports as his ticket to American identity, he is preparing the reader for the Gumbrechtian crescendo of that final paragraph. It's as though, throughout the essay, Greenblatt is holding a kaleidoscope, and rotating it ever so gently, just a degree or two of turning at a time so that hardly anything changes in its composite image. And then finally, he gives it just a tiny extra tweak and all the pieces about Gumbrecht and athletic beauty that had been poised to shift position do so instantly, readily finding their place in the reader's mind.

Using his own life story, Greenblatt makes Gumbrecht's scholarly work come alive. A writer can hardly be more personal with readers than inviting them into his own life, as Greenblatt does here. He comments, "I am certainly not afraid of the personal voice and not averse to personal anecdotes, provided that they are good and that I can make good on them...." To me, he's a writer ahead of most others, one from whom we academics can learn. But then again, he's got Shakespeare on his team.

What can be done to elevate academic writers toward the level of a Sagan or a Greenblatt? Some academics would claim that nothing need be done because they and their colleagues write just fine, thank you—anyone not engaged by their prose will just have to try a little harder. But we've already encountered this "we're OK" attitude and found it wanting. As we'll see presently, the resources and skills needed to create a significant improvement in academic writing for the public are right there on university and college campuses. All that's needed is the will, commitment, and organization to make it happen. But before discussing this, let's take a broad look at the types of books academics write, and the types of publishers who produce them.

Kinds of Books

Here are four main types of books that academics write:

- College text books. These are intended for the classroom, not the general public, whom I define for present purposes as all those not currently studying or teaching at a college or university.

- Monographs. These are written mainly for colleagues and graduate students in an academic author's professional field, readers expected to have a fairly detailed knowledge of the subject area. Like text books, monographs are usually not intended for the general public. Authored primarily by scholars in the social sciences or humanities, they consist largely of reports on research findings and/or interpretations, typically within a narrow subject area. Research in the natural sciences is rarely published in monographs, but rather in articles (typically called "papers") in scholarly journals. Monographs and scholarly papers are generally peer reviewed. The writing style is often formal and dry. To quote a former president of the University of Florida, monographs are "books that university faculty members like to read and write."[11] Here's a recent example: *Cassirer's Metaphysics of Symbolic Form: A Philosophical Commentary.* I doubt you're going to snap this one up at the airport.

- Academic trade books. These are intended for a wider demographic spectrum of readers. Their readers often include colleagues and their students in the author's sub-specialty as well as academics outside this sub-specialty, and segments of the general public inclined toward somewhat brainy reading. The word "trade" indicates that these books have some commercial value, as distinct from monographs. The book you are now reading is intended for this category.

- Trade books (without the word "academic"). Although these books, fiction and non-fiction, are by far the most commonly written and sold, few academics write them. Most books on the front tables at Barnes and Noble are in this category. Their authors include novelists, journalists and other professional writers, politicians, TV and movie stars, business executives, and life improvement coaches.

Suppose you're a professor thinking of writing a book. Which of these four types would you be most inclined to write, and why? While I was at Cornell, I wrote a textbook in my field, neural mechanisms of animal behavior.[12] Why? To make a statement that I hoped would be read by students and colleagues in my field, defining what I saw as the field's most important issues, findings, and future directions. This being a rather small field, I expected to make very little money from this book, and this expectation was admirably fulfilled. Also at Cornell, a colleague, Bill Keeton, published a textbook for introductory biology courses.[13] His was the first introductory college text that, in its time, was regarded as reflecting modern biology. It swept the older, more classically oriented texts off the shelves. I never asked Keeton, who unfortunately died at age 47, about his motivation for writing this textbook, but he certainly made both a statement and a fortune.

The motivation for writing an academic monograph would be different. Money? Forget it; typically, no more than a few hundred to (rarely) a few thousand copies are printed. Making a statement to be read by colleagues and graduate students in one's field? Definitely. General public? Hardly. Yet in spite of these very low sales and the highly focused readership, monographs are the main output of the academic social sciences and humanities. Many monographs are modified PhD dissertations, whose publication gives a PhD recipient a chance at an academic job. Once hired, without publishing yet more monographs, this individual would not likely receive tenure or later advancements at a highly regarded university or college.

What about the motivation for writing an academic trade book, such as *A Dam in the River*? As you must have noticed, I have a message that I feel should be widely circulated—that academics need to share their ideas far more widely with society, for the good of both society and academia. My motivation is the desire for this message to be heard and to influence events. I believe that many authors of academic trade books feel similarly.

The border between academic trade and trade books is fuzzy. Strictly trade books often are written for those seeking a more entertaining, less deeply thoughtful read. Mostly, this is where the money is. Some university writers shy away from strictly trade writing. But the fuzzy zone on the border with academic trade has real potential for academics able to write engagingly and share their ideas with a broad readership.

Publishers

Both non-profit university presses and commercial presses publish books by academics intended for the public. Let's look at these two options.

A university press is usually owned by its home institution and housed in offices on or near the campus. As most universities are non-profit institutions, they confer this non-profit status on the press. There are over 80 university presses in the United States. As a group, they publish mostly monographs, some academic trade books, and few textbooks or trade books.

Commercial presses are profit making businesses, generally having no formal association with any college or university. They publish trade books, college textbooks and some academic trade books, but practically no monographs.

The frequent mergers, buyouts, deal-making and deal-breaking in the world of commercial publishers are the stuff of headlines. Take the grand old firm of Random House. Established in the 1920s primarily by the much admired Bennett Cerf, the firm gained a distinguished reputation as a publisher of classic and contemporary literary greats as well as a near "random" variety—hence the firm's name—of other quality books. Recently, Random House has been bought out three times by media and entertainment conglomerates for which books are just one of many commercial interests—RCA in 1966, S. I. Newhouse in 1980 and the German firm Bertelsmann in 1998. Other firms not specializing in books but now looming large in commercial publishing are the entertainment and media giants Disney, AOL-Time Warner, Viacom, and Rupert Murdoch's News Corp.

One outcome of these developments is that marketing and sales executives of commercial firms exercise a strong and increasing influence on publishing decisions. Thus, a manuscript profoundly important to only a small population segment, even if beautifully written, is becoming less and less likely to find a willing commercial publisher.

Another outcome of conglomerate publishing is a new, semi-covert form of censorship; for instance, if your manuscript drops a negative hint about Murdoch's Fox News, or you mention that you didn't enjoy your family trip to Disneyland, don't even think about submitting it for publication to Murdoch or Disney Books. With more than 80 percent of today's book sales controlled by a handful of conglomerates, the types of books on the market are becoming—on average—more "correct," entertaining, and vapid.[14]

True, some conglomerates have imprints, or divisions, specializing in high quality books, including some authored by academics; and some commercial, though mostly small, firms independent of the conglomerates also publish such works. But all these together account for less than 1 percent of all book sales.[15] Given all this, university presses could, in principle, expand their role with the general public by publishing more academic trade and fuzzy zone books. Let's see, in the next section, whether they are up for this role expansion.

University Presses

We begin by looking back in time. When Daniel Coit Gilman established Johns Hopkins, America's first research university, in 1876, he recognized the need for a scholarly publishing house to disseminate its research findings. The University Publication Agency opened two years later, and in 1891 it became the Johns Hopkins Press. Within two years, three additional universities opened presses—the newly established Universities of Chicago (1891) and California (1893), as well as the already existing Columbia University, also in 1893. It was a while before additional university presses opened in America, but several did before World War I, including Harvard, Princeton and Yale.

America's first university presses were strongly influenced by the academic establishment in Germany, either directly, or indirectly by way of Gilman and Johns Hopkins. Gilman had been inspired by the university presses he had encountered in Germany. Columbia's press was started at the suggestion of Nicholas Murray Butler, who had studied in Berlin, and whose uncle headed the press at Johns Hopkins. At the University of California, the press was started at the urging primarily of a young geology professor, Andrew C. Lawson, who had received his PhD from Johns Hopkins. And the University of Chicago, following the model of Johns Hopkins, focused on developing its graduate school, and consequently generated a research orientation and a press to publish research results.[16]

Gilman stated that the purpose of a university press was to "diffuse [knowledge] not merely among those who can attend the daily lectures—but far and wide."[17] The University of Chicago's President Harper was of like mind, claiming that through the university press, "the usefulness of the University would be immensely enlarged and carried to the ends of the earth."[18] And Yale's President George Parmly Day quoted French philosopher Henri Bergson: "Yale University I do not yet know; but the Yale University Press I know. It is a very important publishing enterprise."[19] Clearly, for these early leaders, a university press was to be a voice to the public, calling out far beyond the campus gate. These presses helped build their universities' reputations throughout the world.

To what extent are today's university presses a "voice to the public?" Do they convey academic ideas well beyond their gates, "far and wide," as Gilman proposed? If not, are they sufficiently flexible to expand their public role?

To answer this question, let's first consider the overall output of America's university presses. All told, they publish approximately 10,000 titles—that is, different books—per year. This amounts to approximately 6 percent of all titles published in the USA. But their actual sales revenues amount to less than 2 percent of all American book revenues, with the commercial presses gaining the lion's share of the sales.[20] Thus, one can estimate that about two out of every hundred books bought in the US are published by a university press.

In attempting a "quick and dirty" verification of these figures, I surveyed all the books displayed on the four large front tables that you almost can't help bumping into in the Barnes and Noble store at New York's Union Square (under the watchful gaze of the store's security guard). The first table, labeled "New Non-fiction" displayed 70 books, of which the largest number, 20, were about current affairs; not one of the 70 was from a university press. At the second table, "New Fiction," none of the 65 were from university presses. At the third table, "Biography," the numbers were 1 out of 83. In "History," though, on the fourth table, university presses did better, with 5 out of 72 books. The survey totals were 6 out of 290 (or just about 2 percent) of the displayed books from university presses—a remarkable parallel to the 2 percent figure noted in the previous paragraph.

To dig deeper, I developed and e-mailed a questionnaire to the heads of eighty university presses.[21] Approximately 90 percent of the books published by the 17 presses that answered my questionnaire were written by university or college professors. Most were monographs. On average, academic trade books amounted to 28 percent of their publications, and purely trade books close to zero percent.

The academic trade percentage was lower, just 18 percent, for the largest of the presses that answered the questionnaire—the ones that publish the largest number of books overall. Thus, the percentage of academic trade books published by university presses as a group is likely to hover somewhere above 18 percent. It is mainly this fairly low percentage that university presses intend to be of some interest to the non-university public. I didn't ask on the questionnaire how many of their books are within the fuzzy zone between academic trade and pure trade, but my sense is that most university press books are pretty clean-shaven, even if many of their authors are not.

Surely, I thought, some of these university press books do very well on the market. How often does one reach a bestseller list, I wondered. Silly me. I sampled the bestseller lists of *Publishers Weekly* once per month for a 6 month period during 2007, with 360 bestseller listings.[22] None were from university presses.

Finally, in my questionnaire, I requested from each university press the sales data on their three bestselling books in the past five years. Four of the presses, including two of the largest, refused to answer. Of the 13 that did, only four presses had any books at all with sales above 30,000 copies. Two of these four had a few books with sales of over 100,000 copies, and one book about the history of the university's home state sold a remarkable 455,000 copies. For each of five other presses, the single best seller reached between 20,000 and 30,000 copies. In short, for most university presses, a few tens of thousands are about the most that any book sells—and sales of this level are rare for all university presses. By contrast, the major commercial presses tend to see a book with these sales numbers as a mild failure, and they focus their energy on marketing their authors who can sell a million copies.

How can one explain American university presses' relatively low output of academic trade books? Three economic factors explain a lot.

First, being tied since their inception to the publication of low-selling monographs placed university presses in an economic stranglehold. Although the market for monographs has always been small, it is now even smaller. Research libraries, by far the largest buyers of monographs, have been decreasing these purchases since the 1970s.[23] Between 1987 and 2001, this drop amounted to more than 25%. Research libraries now spend approximately 75% of their acquisitions budget on scholarly journals, mostly very pricey scientific ones published by commercial firms. This includes the cost of site licenses so that university libraries can make journals available on the Internet to those on their campus. Moreover, the acquisitions budgets of research libraries have been dwindling for some time. Given all this, monograph purchases and university presses are suffering more than ever.[24]

Second, most university presses, from the beginning, received little financial backing from their home universities, and many have always operated on a shoestring. Today, on average, they receive just 10% of their revenues from their universities, and this is decreasing. About 85% of their income is from sales which, as we have seen, suffer distinct limits and growing threats.

And third, the public's reading of academic trade and other books is impacted by the Internet. Some people who would have read this type of book for enlightenment are now surfing for knowledge on the Web which, however, rarely adheres to the same standards as university publishing. People buy hand held devices for downloading books, and soon Google's immense downloadable book library will be accessible. The ready availability of information through these sources brings into question, at least for some people, the need for purchasing academic press books.[25]

And yet, book reading continues, and even seems to be increasing. According to the Association of American Publishers, in 2010, Americans spent $11.7 billion on books, up 3.6 percent from 2009. Americans claim they read more books now than they used to, an average of 5 books a year according to one survey, or 5 for men and 9 for women, according to another. (Women read mostly novels, men mostly history and biography.) Adult Americans spend an average of 108 hours per year with books, not too far off, one might say, from the 181 hours they spend on the Internet. In spite of these encouraging figures, university press sales of hardcover books dropped from 2009 to 2010 by 0.5 percent, while paperback sales increased by just 1.3 percent.[26] University presses must be saying to themselves, "It's not that people aren't buying books. They're just not buying *our* books."

Given these problems, many university presses, especially the smaller ones, have been stuck and are feeling a real crunch. Some have cut out certain fields of coverage. Others face the prospect of closing altogether.[27] University presidents are increasingly questioning the significance of their presses for their core mission. For many of these presses, the future is uncertain. Peter Dougherty, Director of Princeton University Press, commented, "...university presses should be publishing more books [and] we should publish them better...."[28]

The current situation is enough to give America's university presses one giant, coast-to-coast headache. But there are pills for headaches. Although I am not a physician, I would like to prescribe two pills, to be taken together. I believe they can help solve these two intertwined problems—the tenuous situation of many university presses, and more central to this book's main theme, the inadequacy of academic writing for a broad public.

Pill No. 1

This first pill has been "on the market" for some time, and I am by no means the first person to prescribe it. Yet for many university presses, it is a hard pill to swallow. Its medical indications are low sales, its expected result is heightened sales, and its mechanism of action is the publication of more academic trade books, more books in the fuzzy zone between academic trade and trade, and even some more trade books. This could enhance the communication of academic writers with the general public; by bringing in more revenue, still more of these types of books could be published to further enhance this communication. But this pill can have some complicating side effects new to academic publishers. So if you work at a university press, ask your doctor if this medicine is right for you.

Here comes the small print about side effects. A potentially big selling trade book requires investing a larger financial advance to an outstanding, or at least very popular, author—if such a person can even be encouraged to write for a university press—as well as covering the high costs of intensive editorial development of text and illustrations, fancy production, a large initial print run, extensive promotion, marketing, storage and distribution. A press may also have to retrain staff or hire new staff because issues specific to trade books will likely arise. Everyone would cross their fingers and hope that all this leads to enhanced sales. But it could just as well lead to the loss of the small fortune already invested in the book.

Most university presses don't have the resources to invest on this scale, nor can they afford the financial risks involved. Here are two suggestions that may help reduce both the requirement of resources and the risks involved: 1) Take pill number 1 in the form of a time-release capsule and let it work gradually—first print a few more academic trade books, then a few fuzzy zone books, and then one or more strictly trade books. 2) Make full use of market research (not the case at university presses) to judge in advance what subjects and which authors will sell among the general public, and then focus on what this research shows.

I interviewed the heads of several university presses, and I learned about the hard work they do in scouting out the very best authors. William Germano, former head of Columbia University Press, sums things up: "Editors [at university presses] take advice, study the competition, read journals, absorb topical material from the mass media, attend conferences, surf the 'Net, lunch with agents."[29]

Yes, but how much do they talk to their potential clients—their potential readers? In most businesses, that would be the priority when launching a new product. But in response to the question, "Does your press carry out an ongoing program of market research?" 9 presses answered no, 6 said yes, and 2 said they weren't quite sure what I meant. Of the 6 presses that answered yes, 5 answered no to the question, "Has your press utilized the expertise of your university's academic departments, such as Business, Sociology or Communications, in developing and carrying out market research?" From the added comments written by some presses, it was clear they had confused market research (receiving information from the public) with advertising (sending information to the public). All this does not indicate overwhelming marketing-savvy among at least some university presses.

Here's a down-to-earth statement about marketing, from a book published by the Harvard Business School: "The market orientation holds that a company must understand what customers want, need, and value and then must organize itself to produce and deliver the products and services customers truly value."[30]

Seems pretty obvious, right? This was a paraphrase of what Alfred Sloan, Chairman of the Board of General Motors, told GM's stockholders in 1933. For over three quarters of a century since then, successful business people have been drinking in this idea with their mothers' milk. (As I write this, in January, 2011, GM, along with Ford and Chrysler, are scrambling to recover from deep financial troubles, with the aid of huge federal handouts. Did their troubles result, in part, from forgetting Sloan's advice?) Marketing, of course, has become enormously important in the business world, and any firm expecting to succeed needs marketing experts either on staff or as consultants. But a strong marketing approach has so far not meshed with the tweedy non-profit ethos of university presses, many of which have been slow to adopt this strategy.[31] Perhaps it's time they de-tweed.

In case you're thinking I'm trying to nudge university presses too far out of their comfort zone, here is a blockbuster product I am definitely *not* suggesting for them. A Bible recently published by a commercial firm comes with a DVD that was described as having a "400-member cast [that] includes Forest Whitaker as Moses, Angela Bassett as Esther and the eternally slinky Eartha Kitt as the serpent in the Garden of Eden." Samuel Jackson was the voice of God.[32] Although many a university press editor might cotton to the idea of signing a DVD contract with the Lord himself, the universities should leave Moses, Esther, and God to the world of commercial publishing, along with their first six months' sales of 325,000 copies!

Pill No. 2

This second pill is new on the market. That is, I have never encountered this idea before. Its medical indications are an inadequately small number of academics who excel at writing for the general public. Its expected result is a major improvement in their writing. The pill's mechanism of action emerged in part from my conversation with Nicholas Lemann, who commented that most academics don't realize how hard it is to learn to write well for the public—like learning to play the violin and then continuing to practice regularly.

"You mean there's no hope for people trained, say, in science who want to learn popular writing?" I asked.

"I didn't say that," he replied. "Most senior faculty members simply have no idea how much there is to learn in this, and when I tell them, they realize they have neither the time nor the inclination. But give me a twenty-something, show me three pages this person has written, and I'll know whether the potential is there. Next, give me that person's life for a full year, during which they do nothing else—nothing!—but learn writing. And after that year they'd have to remember to 'practice the violin' every day." He paused thoughtfully, closed his eyes for a moment, and then barely whispered, "Could we do this? Yeah, we could do this."

I was excited by Lemann's idea, and started to imagine the training process. I envisioned a course in popular writing for university scholars. Recalling how Lemann had railed against the phrase, "not unlike" in academic writing, I thought to honor him by calling the course "Not Unlike Good Writing."

Every university has people skilled at teaching and coaching writers, whether in the department of journalism, communications, English, fine arts, or the editors at a university press. So the teaching side of the equation seems pretty easy. It would be a plus to have the editors at the university press play a prominent role in the course, as I explain below.

Who would take this course? Graduate students, postdocs and professors. It might make sense to enroll mainly professors, though, because the postdocs, and especially the students, will not all end up on university or college faculties, whereas the goal of the course is to enhance the writing excellence of the professoriate.

The problem is, almost no professor (or grad student or postdoc) is going to give up a whole year—as Lemann had insisted—to become a better public writer. Doing so would almost certainly be a bad career move, as these people would fall behind in their academic fields. So we're going to have to compromise. Here's one type of compromise—by no means the only type imaginable—that I believe could work.

"Not Unlike Good Writing" could be a course that meets one night a week for two years. It would require writing homework. The course could cover the writing of letters to the editor, op-ed pieces, newspaper and magazine articles, blogs, books for the public, as well as writing for radio, TV, and film. The course could take responsibility for a column in the local newspaper, and/or a blog, about new ideas from the university. The column or blog could serve as outlets for the best weekly writing by the course's enrollees.

Although I had never heard of such a course, especially for faculty, I decided to check whether I was re-inventing the wheel. I selected 5 major universities with highly regarded writing programs (Cornell, Stanford, Yale, and the Universities of Iowa and North Carolina) and sent personalized e-mails to every faculty member in their English, Fine Arts and Writing Departments—people well connected with university writing programs throughout the country—to ask if they knew of any such course. Of the 53 respondents, no one knew of such a course at any university, yet many praised the idea. Yes, there are campus writing centers for students, and postdocs can use their services, primarily for transforming their PhD theses into scholarly monographs, and faculty who wish to can drop in at these student writing centers and pick up some pointers. But recall Lemann's comment that it's not about pointers. So far I have come across no equivalent of intensive "violin lessons" for faculty writers in American universities.

One e-mail respondent commented, "Universities tend to assume that faculty no longer need help with writing, or perhaps that no one outside their fields is qualified to provide such help." Another wrote, "My gut instinct is that if I were to suggest that any professor of whatever discipline could benefit by having his prose improved, it would spatter all over the fan!" I had become accustomed to this attitude that everything is fine, no change needed.

Recently, I came across the Writing Centre for Scholars and Researchers at the University of Melbourne in Australia.[33] I e-mailed Simon Clews, head of the Centre, and his reply revealed the closest thing I've seen to the as yet non-existent course "Not Unlike Good Writing." The Centre offers PhD students, postdocs and faculty a series of workshops on writing non-fiction for the non-academic public. Upon completing these workshops, participants may apply for sponsorship during the preparation of a book manuscript for publication. The sponsorship includes mentoring, advocacy and liaison with publishers and agents, and financial support. Between 2005 and 2009, the program trained over 300 participants and awarded 44 sponsorships. Amazingly, as Clews described, the entire Centre consists of a single room staffed by him (he teaches the workshops) and an administrative assistant. "The rest," he said, "is all smoke and mirrors."

Closer to home, the US Congress' Scientific Communications Act of 2007 proposed tackling a different but related problem. The bill recognized that "graduate training programs in science and engineering often lack opportunities for students to develop communications skills that will enable them to effectively explain technical topics to nonscientific audiences."[34] The bill was to direct the National Science Foundation to fund grants for science graduate students to improve their communication with policy makers and business leaders. A promising idea, until Congress voted it down.

An interesting variation on the theme, at the University of Missouri, is a training program in journalistic skills for *undergraduates* working in research labs. The biology and journalism faculty running this program report being "shocked by the size of [the] cultural gap" between professional scientists and journalists, and surprised 'how difficult it is for even brand-new 'scientists' [the program's undergraduate trainees] to step outside their isolated disciplinary world...." The program claims some genuine success in developing, among the science under-grads, skills for communicating with the public.[35]

How effective could Pill No. 2 be in curing the epidemic of mediocre academic writing for the public? Imagine if every major American university had a "Not Unlike..." course, or a Simon Clews. Now let's rein in our imagination and suppose that just twenty of America's major research universities were to teach such a course. Let's say that each registers twenty new people annually (far fewer than in Clews' courses), from all the academic disciplines, in a two-year writing course. That's 400 people each year signing up for these courses, or 4,000 in a decade. Say that just half of these actually do significantly more and better writing than they otherwise would have. That's 2000 academics, within a decade, writing for the public significantly better than now. Suppose that each writes just one book selling 10,000 copies. That would put twenty million im-proved books in the hands of the public! And these "Not Unlike..." courses would cost each of these universities almost nothing, other than assigning a few good writing teachers, already on campus, to teach this course.

If we want to encourage excellent writing on academic subjects for the public—as I believe we should—how can we expect this to happen effectively without providing the relevant training? Would we deprive, say, our medical students of professional training, hoping that some really good neurosurgeons and cardiologists would spring out of thin air? Surely there are potentially great writers on America's campuses waiting to be found.

As mentioned earlier, university presses might do well to help teach the course "Not Unlike...." This would enable them to develop mutually beneficial, ongoing relationships with professors on their campus. Perhaps those taking the course would confer on the university press the right of first refusal to publish their next book. This could save the press money, relieving it of the need to bid against competitors with a high advance on royalties for what one can expect will be a fine book. This seems a fair arrangement, given that the university press would already have contributed via the course to the writing prowess of the academic author. (In fact, commercial presses sometimes include a first refusal statement—called an "option clause"—in their contracts with authors.)[36] Au-thors could continue to build on their training from the press' editors, while the press carries out market research for the book. Proximity and strong personal relationships could be considerable attractions for both author and press.

A recent document, *The Value of University Presses*, co-authored by the heads of three academic presses, lists 24 ways they contribute to society, scholarship, and the university community. The 24 ways do not include helping to improve anyone's writing (beyond the standard process of editing books accepted for publication).[37] I suggest rounding out the list to 25 ways.

All this is a different means of operating than is common among university presses and authors today. Very few books published by these presses are written by the professors of their home university; according to my questionnaire, the figure is around 5 percent. Some universities don't have a press, but even at those that do, faculty generally prefer a different press—one more focused on their subject area, or with a stronger reputation. Some faculty don't want to be regarded as relying on a "home team advantage" in having their manuscript accepted for publication.

Where the questionnaire asked whether the university presses "actively seek out desired authors for trade books," 15 out of the 17 presses replied that they seek out "some, but by no means all"; and where it asked whether they give priority to authors from their own university, 11 of the 15 replied, "no."

There are unfortunate consequences of primarily publishing works of faculty from other universities. Academic administrators of a press' own institution must wonder how effectively their press is fulfilling their institution's mission. This is one likely reason that universities offer their presses so little financial support. To cite a recent report, "...universities do not treat the publishing function as an important, mission-centric endeavor. Publishing generally receives little attention from senior leadership at universities and the result has been a scholarly publishing industry that many in the university community find to be increasingly out of step with the important values of the academy."[38] If a university's press were to publish more books by its home campus faculty, including more academic trade, fuzzy zone, and even trade books, and were to work at improving the writing of its campus faculty, an expected result would be an increase in both the impact and the world renown of these authors, and of their home university, whose administrators would likely see the press as more in step with the institution's goals. This in turn would benefit the university press.

To help a university press build these deepening relationships with the scholars on campus, I suggest that the university administrators re-locate the press centrally on campus, and not in some far flung office. Of the 17 university presses I surveyed, just 2 are housed centrally on the main campus, while 3 are in a peripheral part of campus, 1 is on a secondary campus, and 11 are off campus—7 of these within, and 4 beyond, walking distance. Placing its press away from the center of the main campus activity hints that a university does not see it as central to the campus mission, and does not intend a close faculty-press relationship. The same university wouldn't place, say, its organic chemists and biochemists, two groups that require extensive interaction, on opposite sides of campus, or of town.

Finally, there's one more thing university administrators might consider doing—begin judiciously accepting a wider range of books by their faculty as acceptable forms of university work relevant for tenure and academic advancement. I am referring to the most thoughtful, professional and profound academic trade, fuzzy zone, and even trade books. The best of these can create important new syntheses of ideas, generate new understanding, and impact strongly on both academia and the public. Administrators should welcome the best of this kind of writing.

Why not request that applicants for faculty jobs comment on their intention to do some of this type of writing? Why not request published, or at least completed written examples? Why not ask applicants to deliver, besides an academic seminar, a popular lecture to a general audience? Why not look for, and promote, the next Carl Sagan or Stephen Greenblatt?

I hope my two pills haven't given you indigestion. I hope they stimulate thinking and action to improve academic writing for the public, and help get university ideas flowing throughout the land.

Most Americans spend much more time with TV and radio than with books. To what extent do these media broadcast ideas from academia? Among the wide selection of rock music on radio, and sports on TV, is academia on the airwaves, attempting to touch the mind, heart, and soul of the public? And if so, do the mind, heart and soul tune in? These are among the questions I discuss next.

Notes

1. http//www.academicearth.org/speakers/david-w-blight-1,

2. Kimberly Winston, "The Evolution of Scholarly Publishing: Academics are Learning a New Language to Reach a More Diverse Audience," *Publishers Weekly*, November 11, 2002.

3. William Germano, *Getting it Published*, 2nd ed. (Chicago: University of Chicago Press, 2008), 35.

4. Interviewed by the author at Random House, New York, August 27, 2007.

5. Nicholas Lemann, "The Limits of Language," *Los Angeles Times*, November 4, 2007.

6. Interviewed by the author at Columbia University, August 30, 2007.

7. A parallel discussion about presenting academic subjects, but in film, using a personalized approach and a story line with emotion, humor and other engaging features is presented by academic biologist turned film maker, Randy Olson, in *Don't Be Such a Scientist* (see Introduction n. 24).

8. Carl Sagan, *Cosmos*, (New York: Random House, 1980), xii-xiii.

9. Ibid., 318.

10. Stephen Greenblatt, "Writing as Performance," *Harvard Magazine* (September-October, 2007), 40-47.

11.   John V. Lombardi, "Elegant Artifact or Auxiliary Enterprise: University Presses," *Scholarly Publishing: A Journal for Authors and Publishers* (January, 1992), 67.

12.   Jeffrey M. Camhi, *Neuroetholgy: Nerve Cells and the Natural Behavior of Animals* (Sunderland, MA: Sinauer, 1984).

13.   William T. Keeton, *Biological Science* (New York: Norton, 1967).

14.   Schiffrin, *Business of Books* (see Chapt. 4, n. 54).

15.   Ibid., 170.

16.   Seth H. Dubin, *The Emergence of American University Publishing in the Late Nineteenth Century*, MA thesis, The City University of New York, 2006; Thomas Wakefield Goodspeed, *A History of the University of Chicago* (Chicago: University of Chicago Press, 1916); Johns Hopkins University, *Daniel Coit Gilman* (Baltimore, MD: Johns Hopkins University, 2009); Kerr, *Uses of the University* (see Chapt. 4, n. 61); Rosenthal, *Nicholas Miraculous* (see Chapt. 4, n. 1).

17.   http://www.press.jhu.edu/about/index.html.

18.   Goodspeed, *University of Chicago*, 137.

19.   George Parmly Day, *The New Era of Publishing at Yale* (New Haven: Yale University Press, 1914), 14-15.

20.   Association of American Publishers, http://pujblishers.org/press/24; John B. Thompson, *Books in the Digital Age* (Cambridge, UK: Polity Press, 2005).

21.   I carried out this survey between December, 2007 and February, 2008. In most cases, I sent it to a press' Director, in a few cases to the Chief Editor, and in a few others, where these names and addresses were not available, to the press' general e-mail address. I received 17 replies (21 percent of those I had e-mailed), which included a wide range of press sizes, over a wide geographic distribution. In all, 8 were from state, and 9 from private, universities.

22.   These *Publishers Weekly* lists did not actually include 360 *different* books, because some—roughly a third—remain on the lists for more than a month. The categories I examined were hardcover nonfiction, paperback trade, paperback mass market, and hardcover fiction.

23.   Peter Givler, "University Press Publishing in the United States," in *Scholarly Publishing; Books, Journals, Publishers and Libraries in the Twentieth Century*, eds. Richard E. Abel and Lyman W. Newman. (New York: Wiley, 2002). Also available at http://ww.aaupnet.org/resources/upusa.html.

24.   Raym Crow, "Publishing Cooperatives: An Alternative for Non-profit Publishers," *First Monday* 11, no. 9 (September, 2006), also available at http:firstmonday.org/issues/issue11_9/crow/index.html; Robert B. Townsend, "History and the Future of Scholarly Publishing," *Perspectives Online: American Historical Association* 41, no. 7 (October, 2003), also available at http://historians.org/perspectives/isues/203/0310/0310vie3.htm.

25. Andrew Keen, *The Cult of the Amateur: How Today's Internet is Killing Our Culture* (New York: Doubleday, 2007).

26. Sarah Nelson, "Who's Reading What?" *Publishers Weekly* (October 27, 2007); Association of American Publishers, http://publishers.org/press.24; Jim Milliot, "Reading Time Picked Up in '06," *Publishers Weekly* (August 20, 2007); Putnam, *Bowling Alone* (see Introduction, n. 23), 239; http://productivewriters.com/2011/02/16/book-e-book-sales-data-united-states-2010/.

27. Peter Givler, "Universities and Their Presses in Hard Economic Times," http://www.aaupnet.org/aboutup/hardtimes.html.

28. Peter J. Dougherty, "A University Press in a University Town: The Public Role of the University Press," Speech delivered to the Friends of the Princeton Library, December 4, 2005; Personal communication by Mr. Dougherty.

29. Germano, *Getting it Published*, 71.

30. Harvard Business Essentials, *Marketer's Toolkit: The 10 Strategies You need to Succeed* (Boston: Harvard Business School Publishing Corp., 2006), xiii.

31. Schiffrin, *Business of Books*, 136; Thompson, *Books in the Digital Age*, 149.

32. Juli Cragg Hilliard, "Scripture With Sizzle: Bible Publishers Entice Across Generations with Color, Sound, Graphics and Video," *Publishers Weekly* (October 14, 2007).

33. http://gradresearch.unimelb.edu.au/writingcentre/contactus.html.

34. http://www.govtrack.us/congress/bill.xpd?bill=h110-1453).

35. Jack C. Schultz and Jon T. Stemmle, "Teaching Future Scientists to Talk," *The Chronicle of Higher Education* (April 5, 2012).

36. Schiffrin, *Business of Books*, 82.

37. American Association of University Presses, http://www.aaupnet.org/news/value.html.

38. Laura Brown, Rebecca Griffiths and Matthew Rascoff, *Ithaka Report: University Publishing in a Digital Age* (New York: Ithaka, 2007), 3.

Chapter 8. Public Radio and TV: A "Broad Casting" of University Ideas?

The digital world is altering not only how books are published and read, but also how television and radio broadcast their programs. In 2009, the FCC (Federal Communications Commission) required TV stations to switch from their traditional "analog," to the contemporary digital, broadcasting format, capable of delivering programs over the Internet. Radio broadcasting, though lagging behind, is also making the digital switch.[1] As a result, more and more of what is heard and seen on radio and TV is available on the Internet, via computers or hand-held devices. To quote a recent study, we are now in a period of transition "to a multimedia world where audio, video, still images and text may be available to you anytime, anywhere, on any device."[2] Some communications experts are claiming that TV and radio are rapidly disappearing as distinct forms of communication, to become just two nodes in a multi-nodal, digital communications environment.

Despite these trends, this chapter is devoted to radio and TV and the extent to which they share university ideas with a broad public. I discuss the Internet and university ideas separately in the next chapter, because most people still relate to radio and TV differently than they do to the Internet. You can turn on and tune in the radio or TV, lean back, and enjoy. But the Internet is interactive—lean back and nothing much happens.

Radio and TV offer entertainment first and foremost. The big commercial broadcasters adjust program content and style to maximize earnings. Nothing else influences their programs anywhere near as strongly as this one factor. Thus, they try to entertain the largest possible audience, whom their advertisers hope will buy the largest possible number of products. And nowadays, cable and satellite companies try to enlist the largest number of paying viewers.

Who doesn't like entertainment? But aside from entertainment shows on commercial stations, who is working to provide thoughtful, stimulating, inspiring, aesthetic, uplifting broadcasts? Answer—non-commercial, or "public" broadcasting stations.

To what extent do the non-commercial stations share ideas from academia with the public? As we will see, this is very limited; even the nation's most thoughtful broadcasters are not very effective in communicating the thoughts of the nation's greatest thought generators—the universities. Why? What, if anything, can be done about it? I will focus on non-commercial, which I will contrast with commercial, broadcasting. We'll begin with TV, and later switch it off and tune in to radio.

TV

The dichotomy between commercial and non-commercial broadcasting resembles the dichotomy between commercial and university presses. While the major commercial broadcasters, like commercial publishers, are led by economic incentives to reach the largest possible audience, non-commercial broadcasters, like university presses, try to fill the less popular, and less remunerative, thoughtfulness gap. As with book publishing, commercial TV networks are selling out to huge conglomerates. For instance, Disney owns not only its own film studio, theme parks, and book publishing house, but also ABC Television Studios—which produce *Gray's Anatomy*, *Ugly Betty*, and *Lost*—as well as the ABC Network, whose affiliated stations broadcast these shows. Disney also owns ESPN, America's premier national sports broadcaster. We're talking very big money. For instance, ESPN (read "Disney") pays the NFL a spanking $1.1 billion per year for football broadcasting rights.[3] With slight variations, it's like that at the other major commercial TV networks as well.

With all their resources, commercial broadcasters know how to produce slick, professionally executed and highly entertaining programs with broad appeal. As a recent evaluation showed, the 54 top rated TV shows—those with the largest viewing audiences—are all on commercial, not public, TV.[4]

There's lots of watching going on. A remarkable 99 percent of American households have TV sets, and 66 percent of homes have three or more sets. The average American watches the tube for 4 hours and 38 minutes a day, which equals more than two months per year of continuous watching, day and night, or an entire decade of continuous day and night watching out of a 75 year lifetime! Adults watch more than children or teenagers, and year by year, TV watching is increasing.[5] In case you don't see enough TV at home, you can sometimes catch it in taxis, elevators, bars, restaurants, airports, and on hand-held devices.

Three different varieties of non-commercial, or public, TV stations are relevant to this discussion:[6]

- PBS non-university stations. These are affiliated with the national Public Broadcasting System (PBS) and are not formally connected with academic institutions. This most common type includes about 2/3 of the 357 PBS stations.[7] Among the best known examples, all in major urban centers, are WGBH in Boston, WNET in New York, WETA in Washington, DC, and KQED in San Francisco. These and several other major stations own advanced production studios and produce many of the most watched public programs, aired on all PBS stations. (Many other programs seen on PBS stations are produced by private production firms, sometimes in association with a given PBS station.)

- PBS university stations. These stations are affiliated with PBS but are usually located at, and often owned by, universities. These transmit to an extensive local area surrounding the campus, or even state-wide. About a third of PBS stations belong to this group. Most are not located in large urban centers; prominent examples are the Universities of Illinois, Indiana, North Carolina and Ohio.

- Independent university stations. Generally located at and owned by a university, these are not affiliated with PBS. They rarely show PBS programs. They transmit to an extensive local area surrounding the campus, or state-wide. Less than a dozen of these exist; two prominent examples are at the University of California at San Diego, and the City University of New York.

To understand the present and possible future roles of public TV in sharing academic ideas, let us consider their history.[8] (In this discussion, I will use the term "non-commercial" TV when referring to the period prior to 1967, when the current national system was created. For the subsequent period I will use the term "public" TV.)

From the outset, American television developed primarily as a commercial enterprise. This differed from TV's development in Britain and much of Europe, as well as in Japan, Australia, and Canada, all of which placed non-commercial TV at the center of their broadcasting enterprise. Americans, though, favored the free market opportunities whereby both broadcasters and advertisers could accumulate great wealth. Many Americans were also suspicious of possible state domination of the airwaves in a public system.

The NBC network began commercial TV broadcasting in 1947, with CBS and ABC following by 1948. Watching TV caught on like wildfire. Already by 1955, 75 percent of American homes had a television set. TV spread more rapidly than any other newly invented domestic device—about three times faster than the refrigerator, seven times faster than the automobile, and nine times faster than the telephone.[9]

Non-commercial TV existed, but was a slow starter. In 1948, with the three main commercial stations already established, the non-commercials had not yet built a strong following or a robust Washington lobby. They were about to lose out to commercial stations in the competition for FCC broadcast licenses. Therefore, it was good news for the non-commercials when the FCC ceased licensing new broadcast stations from 1948 to 1952. It would take these four years, and the dedicated work mostly of a few key individuals, for non-commercial TV to gain a foothold and the prize of its own broadcast stations. The key individuals were from three different workplaces—the Ford Foundation, the FCC and, important for this discussion, universities.

- *Ford Foundation.* In 1951, the Ford Foundation hired C. Scott Fletcher to head its new Fund for Adult Education. Having directed the national Committee for Economic Development, Encyclopedia Britannica Films, and international sales for Studebaker cars, Fletcher knew money, culture, and people. He implemented Ford grants of over $11 million, a huge sum at the time, for developing non-commercial TV. Early on, he drew several national university leaders into the planning of the nation's non-commercial television.

- *FCC.* The commission's Frieda Hennock, like Fletcher, was a true believer in non-commercial TV. Foreign-born, female, Jewish, progressive, and often abrasive—very different from the other FCC members—she was somewhat shunned by them. Yet her intensity of purpose wore them down. Thus, the FCC in 1952 reserved 242 stations across the country for non-commercial "education" television, which later morphed into "public television." In 1953, Hennock appeared on the first show broadcast by the first of these new stations, KUHR at the University of Houston. The next two non-commercial stations also began broadcasting at universities—The University of Southern California, and Michigan State.

- *Universities.* The role of universities in non-commercial TV was soon to blossom. Taking on positions of responsibility in key national committees and organizations were the presidents of NYU, MIT, Penn State, and the Universities of Illinois and Oregon, as well as senior administrators from Case Western Reserve, Columbia, Illinois Tech, and Wesleyan, and numerous professors from various institutions. It seemed that academia was to play a significant leadership role in non-commercial television. This role, however, was short-lived.

The year 1967 was a watershed for non-commercial television. In January of that year, the Carnegie Commission on Educational Television released a high profile report, later called the Carnegie I Report. It distinguished between "instructional," or "educational," TV—which I have been calling "non-commercial," mostly airing professors lecturing on camera—and "public TV," which would incorporate a wider range of more appealing formats. The Carnegie I Report focused on the latter of these options, and recommended the creation of a "federally chartered, nonprofit, nongovernmental corporation." Ten months later, following Congressional deliberations, President Lyndon Johnson signed into law the Public Broadcasting Act, which created the Corporation for Public Broadcasting (CPB), as the Carnegie I Report had proposed. CPB's first task would be to create a coherently functioning national system of public TV. Funding, which would come from federal, private, foundation and other sources, would support the creation and distribution of suitable television programs to the licensed non-commercial (now called "public") stations around the country. It would also provide upgrading and support for these stations.

In his comments, President Johnson pointed out that, "...we want most of all to enrich man's spirit. That is the purpose of this act." Public broadcasting "...will be free, and it will be independent—and it will belong to all of our people." He stressed a parallel between universities and public broadcasting: "In 1862, the Morrill Act set aside lands in every State—lands which belonged to the people— and it set them aside in order to build the land-grant colleges of the Nation. So today we rededicate a part of the airwaves—which belong to all the people— and we dedicate them for the enlightenment of all the people."[10]

But as we will see, Johnson's wish for public broadcasting to enlighten "all the people" has not been fulfilled. Not even close.

Between 1967 and 1970, this newly created system grew into its current structure, with three main components. First is CPB, the national level corporation. Second is a pair of national level organizations established by CPB, one for television (the Public Broadcasting Service, or PBS), the other for radio (National Public Radio, or NPR, which I discuss later in this chapter). Third is the constellation of public broadcasting stations spread throughout the nation, some for TV (affiliated with PBS), some for radio (affiliated with NPR), some for both (affiliated with both). Recall, about one third of the public TV stations are situated at universities.

PBS does not own its affiliated stations, though it exercises considerable influence over them. Not only does PBS provide most of the programs for its affiliates, but also—important for this discussion—it specifies approximately when they will be aired. It does so through its "common carriage" policy, which specifies that certain children's PBS programs will be aired in the morning hours, and certain adult PBS programs during primetime—from 7:00 to 11:00 PM. Programs that a local PBS station may produce, geared specifically for its own local audience, are shown outside these two time slots. To know how extensively PBS stations share university ideas with the adult public, we should focus on primetime, when adults are most likely to watch, and examine the common carriage programs.

Who's Watching?

Viewer statistics gathered by PBS in 2009 indicate that, on an average evening, a mere one half to one percent of Americans watched PBS stations during primetime. A Neilson study gave the slightly higher figure of 1.6 percent, but showed that the percent of PBS viewers in the population had decreased fairly regularly over the previous seven years. With the average American adult watching over four and a half hours of TV daily, there's much watching of commercial, though little of public, TV.[11] This contrasts with the situation in many European countries and Japan, where public TV attracts up to half the viewers during primetime, in spite of competition from private, commercial channels.[12]

With America's TV culture built on a commercial infrastructure, public TV had to find its own niche by filling in the gaps left by the major networks. Most PBS insiders regard their niche audience as an affluent, highly educated segment of society. Public TV insider James Day states that, "Because PBS was created as an 'alternative' to mainstream television, it has been exiled into the ghetto of high-minded educational fare."[13] As another analyst observes, "While PBS has tried to shed its schoolmarm image [of earlier educational TV], it has not strayed *too* far from its upscale professional niche. As market strategy, this makeover is less about making PBS accountable to broad popular demand than it is about catching up with the tastes and desires of upper-middle class lifestyle clusters and positioning PBS more securely within them."[14]

One reason for this strategy is that PBS and its affiliate stations depend for approximately 25 percent of their annual revenues on public donations, and for a further 15 percent on corporate underwriting.[15] Therefore, public television "has not courted new constituencies who 'don't count' on business spreadsheets or whose tastes and desires might jeopardize its claims to provide a 'quality environment for a corporation's brand recognition.'"[16] Given all this, public TV doesn't try very hard to reach the audience that President Johnson envisioned, namely, "all the people."

This analysis is not universally agreed upon. PBS President and CEO Paula Kerger told me straight out, "It's not an elite audience at all."[17] She handed me an internal working document which, based on Nielsen ratings, shows that with regard to race, ethnicity, educational level, and income, the percentages of PBS viewers closely match their percentages in the overall population. But these figures are strongly influenced by the kids watching morning programs like *Sesame Street*. The demographic range of kids watching this program is likely to be far broader than the range of adults attracted by erudite evening programs. Most PBS professionals and analysts appear to agree that PSB does indeed target a somewhat elite adult viewing audience.

For further insight, I spoke with a major producer of PBS programs, Lowell Bergman. A former New York Times correspondent and producer of CBS news' magazine program *60 Minutes*, Bergman is now Professor of Journalism at Berkeley and a producer of the PBS investigative journalism program *Frontline*.[18] He asked:

> Am I interested in reaching more people? Sure. I went into broadcasting because potentially it has a much wider reach than print, which is where I used to work. But the problem is, getting in-depth information to people is very difficult. For *60 Minutes* it's easier. Their investigative pieces each last just 12 minutes, down from 15 minutes because of increased advertising. So their pieces are less nuanced,

less deep, and in some ways less honest. Lots of people will watch 12 minutes of superficial analysis. But *Frontline's* hour, that takes you deep into the subject, just isn't what most folks want to hear about.

"So are you saying that *Frontline* is not for most Americans, rather, just for an elite few?" I asked.

"Exactly," he replied.

PBS Programs and University Ideas

Does the PBS audience, though small, experience academic ideas of the types discussed earlier, namely, *the idea of a university, ideas from the disciplines, and value-based ideas*? True, sharing academic ideas with the public is not specifically included in public TV's mission. Nevertheless, as a non-commercial source of thoughtful programming, PBS's interests and point of view clearly overlap those of academia.

In this section I sample some key primetime programs to see whether they share with the public any of the above trio of university ideas, and whether they enhance public awareness that many of these ideas derive from universities. A key criterion I use is the frequency with which academics appear on screen, discussing or demonstrating something in their area of expertise. Although many academics are notoriously bad at this, some are excellent.

We'll look at four primetime shows. Two are current affairs programs with a magazine format, *Frontline* and *Need to Know*. The third is the history program *American Experience*, and the fourth is the science show *NOVA*. Although the producers frequently use academics as resource people for program development, this does not necessarily mean that academics appear on screen, that their academic ideas are broadcast, or that viewers realize that the ideas often originate from universities.

Take the *Frontline* production by Lowell Bergman called *The Card Game*, which exposes the excesses of the credit card industry. This industry earns most of its income from late payment fines and compounded interest collected from those least able to pay. To the exceedingly wealthy execs running the industry, squeezing the poor in this way is just good business—finding and exploiting a market. The show made my blood boil, which is a major purpose of investigative reporting. I noticed that, although this show included numerous on-screen speakers ("talking heads"), only one of these heads was academic. It belonged to Elizabeth Warren of the Harvard Law School (elected in 2012 as US senator from Massachusetts). She appeared for a total of 75 seconds out of the show's 55 minutes. Where were the academic experts in economics, business, psychology, sociology, history or other fields, whose insights might have added considerable enrichment? Likewise for most other *Frontline* productions, which rarely give voice to academics on the TV screen.

The program *Need to Know* screens academic talking heads fairly frequently. A striking example was an insightful interview with Boston University Professor Andrew Bacevich. Behind Bacevich was a printed backdrop with the words "Boston University" appearing over and over, like a department store's gift wrap paper. In case anyone forgot Bacevich's academic affiliation, a second's glance at the screen would restore the memory. Perhaps more PBS interviews should include backdrops showing the speaker's affiliation (though a single printing of the university's name might suffice).

The PBS show *American Experience* goes to the opposite extreme. This excellent history program does not even identify its on-screen academics as academics, or give their university affiliation. They are identified according to their field of interest, as "scientist," or "historian," or by some other generic designation. Thus, although the viewers encounter ideas from academia, they wouldn't know that academia is the source, or that they are being exposed to academic expertise. After all, a "scientist" could be someone who writes about science but has little or no research experience. A "historian" could be a member of a local historical society, rather than—as in the case of Daniel Vickers, a talking head on an *American Experience* program about the history of whaling—chair of the History Department at the University of British Columbia, and a research specialist in maritime history. Viewers would only know he's some kind of historian.

I wondered why WGBH, producer of *American Experience*, did not share with the public the credentials and home base of their talking head experts. So I e-mailed them to ask. Here's their reply:[19] "There are two standard reasons: 1) The longer the title, the harder to read, especially on a limited time span; and 2) The "Historian" title is used only [for] those with a Ph.D degree."

Really, now. Reading a caption of a few words would not stress the average ten-year-old. And although it is interesting that the "historian" designation is only for those with a PhD, how would a viewer know this? All this seems beside the point, which is that a caption such as, "History Professor, University of British Columbia" would convey several important messages, such as:

- We of WGBH and *American Experience* recognize the significance of expertise in the subject area;

- The speaker is a high level expert, and thus worth listening to;

- This is the kind of expertise found at universities;

- Not all professors are boring. Vickers sure isn't.

NOVA, by contrast, gets academic credentialing right. Outstandingly produced, like the other programs mentioned here, *NOVA* also provides clear recognition of academics and universities as sources of forefront ideas. Take *Lord of the Ants*, that traces the scientific career of Harvard's Edward O. Wilson. I took particular delight in this program, not only because it reminded me of Wilson's lifelong contributions to science and nature conservation, and his extensive sharing of his ideas with the public, but also because it brought me back to my first personal encounter with him.

I had just entered graduate school, and Wilson had just been hired as a Harvard assistant professor. He was appointed as a member of my advisory committee, and I may have been the first graduate student for whom he ever served in that capacity (at least I like to imagine so). Wilson's subject was ants, a field whose scientific name is myrmecology. There were not then, nor are there now, a lot of myrmecologists in the world. Wilson was to become one of the greats among this small but dedicated cadre. His own specialization within myrmecology was ant behavior, and since the subject of animal behavior and its mechanisms had already captured my interest, I sat for a semester in the front row of his animal behavior course. I also wandered frequently into his lab, which was filled with ant colonies from all around the world, the ants running around inside glass containers. You'd walk into that lab and feel a strong urge to scratch.

NOVA's *Lord of the Ants* begins with this statement narrated by Hollywood's Harrison Ford: "Every so often, a giant emerges on the stage of science.... Ed Wilson is such a man...." (I hoped, in vain, that Ford would mention the eager young graduate student in the front row.) The entire show makes it clear that Wilson the "giant" is actually a gentle, cuddly man with a quiet sense of humor, who speaks easily and comfortably with anyone. In following Wilson's life from child naturalist to world leader in natural science, Harrison Ford explains that, as a student, "He came to study at Harvard's Museum of Comparative Zoology, and he's been there ever since....For Ed Wilson this was paradise." BBC naturalist David Attenborough comments that Wilson was able to take "several steps back to see the widest picture" of life on earth, and help establish the now thriving research field of Sociobiology. As a prelude to becoming perhaps the world's leading, and most visible promoter of saving biodiversity, Wilson explains, "I learned that [to help save life on earth] I had to become more public."

Wilson's combination of academic and public excellence presents a model for which more academics might well strive. And *NOVA* offers a model of how PBS can provide an appropriate means of communication. In its many programs on a diversity of scientific subjects, *NOVA* presents the great ideas from academic research, recognizes and honors the academics and their universities as the source of these ideas, no doubt inspiring among viewers a healthy respect for academia. Given the full range of public broadcasting, this level of university exposure is rare.

Finally, there are PBS's special projects. In 2009, renowned documentary film maker Ken Burns produced *The National Parks: America's Best Idea.* This 12-hour series, overwhelmingly beautiful in its still and moving imagery and musical score, fascinating in its story line, includes numerous talking heads who add depth to the story. They are identified generically, which appears to be a Burns signature. William Cronon, who returns repeatedly to the screen, is identified as "historian," though I discovered he is Professor of History, Geography and

Environmental Studies at the University of Wisconsin, and formerly Professor of History at Yale, with two multiple-award winning books and a host of other publications to his credit. "Historian?" Like Ken Burns is a camera buff.

The National Parks: America's Best Idea mentions that in 1864, President Lincoln signed into law the preservation of Yosemite Valley and the Mariposa Grove of Sequoia trees, both of which would later become parts of Yosemite National Park. This was the first time the nation had set aside treasures of nature to be saved from private development and preserved for the common good. Although not mentioned in the film, this was just two years after Lincoln had signed the Morrill Act, paving the way for establishing America's land grant universities. While the national parks were to provide general access to nature's greatest creations, the land grant universities were to provide general access to humanity's greatest creations—the accumulated knowledge in all fields of inquiry. I am waiting for Burns, or some other outstanding film producer, to make a similarly beautiful and fascinating film for public broadcasting that might be titled *The American University: Our Nation's Other Best Idea*.

Clearly, most of PBS primetime is not sharing robustly with its viewers the university ideas listed earlier, or an awareness that universities spawn these ideas. *NOVA* is a wonderful exception, an example that other programs could follow.[20]

What could academia do to help make this happen? Unfortunately, although university figures were among the early leaders of public TV, that relationship has long since withered away. Only one of the 27 current PBS board members holds an academic position, namely former Nebraska Senator Charles (Chuck) Hagel. (Though not traditionally trained academically, Hagel was appointed by Georgetown University in the field of "national governance," obviously owing to his extensive political experience.) None of PBS's 14 member senior executive staff are academics. And PBS has 10 "partner" organizations, of which nine are media organizations and one is a media program of the Annenberg Foundation. None are academic. Shouldn't academia restore some of its former involvement in public TV, in part to influence PBS to communicate to the public about academia's contributions to the world of knowledge?

Re-establishing an academic influence in public TV may be an uphill battle. Journalists, who largely run PBS, tend to attract other journalists, and some hold academics in mild disdain regarding broadcasting. For instance, in his detailed book about PBS, journalist James Day never suggests putting academics on camera; rather when serious ideas are called for, he calls for more journalists: "Needed in today's complex world of mass-mediated information is an ongoing analysis of the issues by those who are most informed and least involved: the experienced journalists who cover the day-by-day developments." He continues: "The smell of chalk dust still clings to [public television's] skirts, a legacy from its earlier incarnation as educational television." And he bemoans "those gaseous explorations of cosmic abstractions...or tedious illustrated lectures rationalized as adult education [that] sound more like graduate seminars than the fare that might attract us to television at the end of a trying day." Public TV must "discard its earnest 'good for you' image, and lighten up without yielding an inch of ground to its primary mission of high quality programming."[21] For Day, lightening up means, in part, keeping academia out of PBS.

While many journalists fear that academics are boring on the air (some are, some aren't, but being good at it is a learnable skill), academics tend to fear that journalists present their ideas inaccurately (some do, some don't, and some could learn to do better). But this divide will not be bridged by journalists, who have little motivation to do so. Rather, it is up to academia to recognize the benefits of greater involvement in public broadcasting, learn the necessary skills, and begin to make a difference.

Alternatives?

So far, this discussion has centered on some of the greatest PBS productions, broadcast through common carriage agreements by virtually all PBS stations. Two alternative program sources potentially rich in university ideas are *PBS university stations* (those usually located at, and often owned by, a university) and *independent university stations* (those usually located at and owned by a university, but not affiliated with PBS). These draw about the same percentage of the local viewing audience as PBS non-university stations. Being associated with a campus, both are well positioned to draw upon academic resources and create idea-rich programming. But do they?

The PBS university stations would need to show any such programming outside of primetime, owing to PBS' common carriage agreements. I asked Beth Welsh, Director of Research at PBS, whether these stations effectively present programming with ideas from their home universities. "The extent of their locally produced programming is minimal," she said, "as such stations typically fill the majority of their schedule with PBS-distributed programs."[22]

To gain my own sense of a PBS university station, I visited the University of North Carolina's UNC-TV. The station is located far off campus. In fact, Steve Volstad, UNC-TV Director of Communications, explained, "People in the general university administration see the TV station as separate, not an integral part of the university.... Faculty sometimes appear on broadcasts, but few ever have their own show."[23] Tom Linden, Professor of Journalism at the UNC, who does produce and engagingly host occasional UNC-TV programs, added that many viewers are probably not sure whether UNC-TV actually is connected to UNC. He explained that the university discourages public recognition of this connection, so that donors to UNC-TV will not think they're off the hook regarding donations to the university. "Academia is not a subject often presented on UNC-TV," he said.[24] This station appears to fit PBS President Paula Kerger's description of PBS university stations: "The university people wouldn't even know their campus has a station."[25]

Turning now to independent (non-PBS) university stations, as these can show their own programming during primetime, do they share university ideas more effectively? Less than a dozen independent university stations dot the national map, so together they reach only a minuscule percentage of the public. Nevertheless, I visited two of these, UCSD-TV (at University of California San Diego) and CUNY TV at the City University of New York.

Lynn Burnstan, UCSD-TV's Managing Director proudly stated, "We have the freedom to show our faculty on screen during primetime. Our programs [show] our experts talking, not a narrator. So the experts have much time on camera. This contrasts with a PBS station on a university campus, which rarely represents the university itself. There is often a wall between a PBS station and its home university."[26] In fact, UCSD-TV broadcasts lectures, interviews, panel discussions, and workshops, throughout the day, as well as concerts and plays originating largely from the University of California's several campuses. CUNY TV produces less of its own programming, but when it does, as Executive Director Robert Isaacson told me, "With our open mike, nothing is out of bounds for discussion, and we never know what's going to come up. It's no-holds-barred TV. Academic freedom is alive and well on our station." [27] These program's conversations come across as open and fresh, not pre-staged, or pre-digested. Often I'm aware of watching people think through their points, rather than spouting sound bites.

The budgets of even the most active independent university stations are tiny compared to the major PBS university stations. For instance, the annual operating budget of UCSD-TV is about a million dollars (UCSD providing about $300,000, and the rest coming mostly from donors and corporate underwriters). By contrast, UNC TV's annual budget is $25 million, and that of WGBH Boston is $200 million. (For perspective, commercial network TV typically spends about $3 million to produce a *single hour* of a dramatic series;[28] that one hour costs three times the entire annual UCSD-TV budget!)

Thus, the independent university stations are particularly constrained to a modest type of broadcasting—a type that comes in below the PBS radar, so to speak. However, a camera turned on for a lecture or a panel discussion may well catch some remarkable academic ideas. It's almost as though the low budget creates this type of programming, which would otherwise be unavailable on TV.

There's a down side, of course. Seldom does one encounter on an independent university station a trained professional broadcaster with a proper broadcast voice. A lecturer may be camera shy, or have an irritating or nervous tick or awkward body language. The camera's view may be somewhat static, and may not effectively catch the Power Point slides. And the studio or lecture hall may be less than beautiful.

Imagining how to add just a bit of pizzazz, I asked Burnstan, "Do you offer on-camera training to your faculty?"

"We help them a bit," she answered. "Sometimes the way you ask a question can help."

But just as I suggested in Chapter 7 that universities should train interested faculty in writing for the public, shouldn't they also train some professors in media presentation? Wouldn't this be good for these professors, the university, and the public? Surely, many universities have the expertise to carry out such training in their communications or journalism departments.

I wondered, though, why there is just a handful of independent university stations across the nation. Isaacson gave me the answer—money. Building and outfitting a modern broadcast station, let alone running it, could seriously drain university finances.

However, it seemed to me that some universities and colleges could hitch a ride on local public or even commercial TV stations, sharing university ideas without the cost of building or running a station. This way, there may be opportunities for many colleges and universities to reach a wider audience. The University of California has recently entered into a partnership with YouTube to create and present on a new Internet channel called UCTV Prime, featuring U. Cal. and other researchers. This first-of-its-kind YouTube agreement with a university takes advantage of the flexibility inherent in U. Cal's independent (non-PBS) university station.[29]

And Now a Word From—Whom?

People in the TV biz told me to delete this section, which is about commercial, not public, TV. This section's central proposal wouldn't work, they said. Worse, by leaving my proposal in, I would embarrass myself.

So here's my proposal. It begins by noting that weekly Saturday broadcasts of college football commonly draw between 4 and 11 million TV viewers per game. And the 2010 Rose Bowl, with Ohio State taking on the University of Oregon, drew nearly 20 million. These are among the largest audiences ever "assembled" on earth, for anything! And they are broadcasting what? Universities. Hmmm. Do I sense an opportunity?

Let me share my experience of viewing on TV a very ordinary Saturday football game between Berkeley (called Cal in the sports world) and the University of Tennessee. The game was played at Cal's Memorial Stadium.

In the pre-game warm-up, three throaty sports "analysts" explain the experience that I, along with several million other viewers, am about to have: "We'll be keeping an eye on colleges all around the country." (Oh good, I think to myself, this will be a national academic experience.) "We'll put the day in perspective." (I expect nothing less of academia.) "We'll compare this year's stats to last year's records and to all-time records." (Excellent! I have great respect for archiving.)

But then, "Cal will be working really hard this week getting ready for next week's LSU game." This was my first surprise. I had thought Cal would be working really hard this week on forward looking technology research, not its forward pass; on running important experiments, not its running game; on astrophysics, not Astroturf.

Don't get me wrong; I enjoy TV football. And an exciting game it was, with some amazing running plays. Also, there was one moment, a very unfortunate one, actually, with a serious-looking injury that produced heart-wrenching drama. A Tennessee player is down and totally immobile. Doctors, coaches, and other attendants surround him, kneeling. His teammates, standing at a distance, fix their gaze on him. Then suddenly, as if choreographed in advance, his whole team kneels together in prayer. The Cal players look on. The fans hush. The TV announcers, a lot less throaty now, air an instant re-play showing this young man taking a sharp knock to his helmeted head. There is clear concern of a possible broken neck and a lifetime of quadriplegia. His limp, motionless body is placed on a stretcher and lifted onto an open van that drives him toward the exit gate. Then, just before reaching the gate, he raises one hand and waves. No broken neck. Instant relief for all. Seventy thousand fans, released from tension, heartily cheer him off the field. The game resumes.

Drama like this you don't get from a televised lecture on Kant.

Yes, this is university football. But it's all about football, not universities. The game is totally divorced from the campus surrounding Memorial Stadium, divorced from all the reasons that the Berkeley (that is, Cal) campus exists, none of which have anything to do with football. Grandiose images cross the screen at a dizzying pace—bright uniforms and flashing helmets give a group of 20-year-olds the look of national heroes, not college students; cheerleaders and screaming fans, wave their arms in unison like extremists at a political rally; televised views from the Goodyear blimp render Memorial Stadium as a monument of cosmic significance; the fast-talking trio of football "analysts," two of them former college football stars, seem to know the "score"—that what really matters to America about universities is who wins on Saturday. Then there's the intense determination written across the faces of the two opposing coaches, each wired with space age communication systems, and each knowing that his sky high salary—many times more than the highest paid professor on campus—depends on the performances of a 20-year-old college student who happens to be his quarterback, and this young man's classmates who make up the rest of the team.

As you may know, on some sports channels, the competing universities project messages to the public through a brief video that is played during time outs or half time. The Cal video lasted just 30 seconds, half of which was devoted to Cal sports other than football. The remaining 15 seconds presented everything else about Cal, which I remind you is the University of California at Berkeley, one of the world's most outstanding and distinguished institutions of higher learning.

So what's to be done? Let's begin with the "Big 10," (actually, now 11) universities, which include some of the strongest football teams, some from fine academic institutions, like the Universities of Illinois, Michigan, Minnesota, and Wisconsin, as well as Northwestern and Penn State. Recognizing that commercial broadcasters need these schools as much as the schools need them, I suggest that the Big 10 schools make an important group decision. (Although the words "group decision" seems an oxymoron for many universities, the Big 10 are already united by a Committee on Institutional Cooperation that could facilitate this process.) I suggest they decide to demand not thirty seconds between plays, but 5 minutes of the 20 minute halftime, with the broadcaster having no control over content. This will surely go against the broadcasters' profit-driven policy of using halftime to analyze the first half of play, and to keep "an eye on colleges around the country," updating the public with the latest scores. But 5 minutes of halftime could be made part of the huge rights payout the broadcasters fork over to universities for coverage of their sporting events, placing these universities in a strong bargaining position.

The universities might get Ken Burns to film the stunning video I suggested above, about the American university, perhaps in ten five-minute installments, each shown on a different Saturday of the season. The whole series could be repeated the following year, and perhaps for a few more years. Sharing the expense across many universities could make this financially feasible.

This should be seen as an opportunity, not for PR or fundraising, but for sharing a national academic vision of "The Idea of a University," and why academic ideas are important to every American. This is a moment when universities can rise to an important occasion and stand tall—at least to the height of the Goodyear blimp.

If this video is engaging and done with a light touch, viewers may well both hold off getting their next beer from the fridge, and/or hold their urine until the video is finished. But even if 90 percent of viewers can't wait with these urges, the un-urged 10 percent would still constitute the largest audience any university has ever had. Every week for the whole football season! Aw heck, let's add the basketball season as well.

So I'm suggesting that universities play hardball with football broadcasters. Millions of TV sports fans this coming season could hear the "real score" from academia.

Incidentally, I'm not the least bit embarrassed to offer this suggestion, despite the advice I received from the savvy broadcasting experts.

Here are a few related suggestions. Perhaps all university games played across the nation on a given Saturday could feature a particular academic subject—English this week, History next week, Law the week after that. Each week's subject would focus on one core idea from that subject. Create a national "Academic Idea of the Week." Sell T-shirts, sweatshirts, hats on all the campuses the week before, as well as during each game, all inscribed with the featured great idea. Thus, hundreds of thousands of students across the nation become billboards for the same great university idea. Make sure the camera scans people wearing these shirts, and scans the idea written on them, during the games. Solicit on-camera comments, serious or silly, about the week's great idea from happy students enjoying the game. Print the same idea on the game tickets. If the idea happens to be about, say, Shakespeare, get the cheerleaders to create a special cheer for old Will ("We've got the Will to win" or some such), and get that on camera. In short, turn university football into an event about both universities and football. Announce at the game and on the air, and print on the tickets, that the websites of all participating universities have more information about the week's idea. Hand out fliers explaining the idea of the week at public events on campus such as public lectures, concerts, theater, and museum programs. Put up a big sign in the student union announcing the idea of the week.

Best to be prepared for some professor's claim that the proposed "Academic Idea of the Week" trivializes and disrespects higher learning. Perhaps we could reply that introducing millions of Americans each week to an important academic idea, even if superficially, with even just a small percentage of these people following up on the Web or elsewhere, would represent a positive contribution of academia to society. Do you agree?

"And Radio"

Radio in America began in earnest in the 1920s, long before the invention of television. Most of the first radio stations were located at mid-western land grant universities. Thus, from its very outset, American broadcasting was an academic enterprise.[30]

The land grants viewed the new form of communication as a way to help fulfill their mission of outreach to the citizens of their state, including news, agricultural information, and educational programs. But at some land grant universities, the mission went further. For instance, the University of Wisconsin intended "to carry 'the university atmosphere'—programming representing the values and standards of the university—to all corners of the state."[31] By 1930, over 200 non-commercial stations had been FCC-licensed, many of them at academic campuses.

But the newborn non-commercial enterprise was to suffer one near-death experience during its infancy, and another during its adolescence, before making a modest recovery toward the end of the 20th century. And now in the 21st, the death knell tolls again, though this time with strong hints of re-incarnation into a very different life form.

The first near death experience was a product, in part, of universities not placing a high priority on broadcasting, and thus not investing very much in the new medium. Most station managers were university professors who regarded broadcasting as a hobby at best, and had little professional aspiration for either radio or their role in it. But other factors contributed to ringing the knell—the 1930s' Great Depression, the growth of commercial radio during the same period, and intensive Washington lobbying by commercial broadcasters who, according to one analyst, "massively outspent the educators, outmaneuvered them in Washington, and out-produced them on the air."[32]

A devastating event for non-commercial radio was the passing of the Communications Act of 1934. It directed commercial stations, by teaming up with professors, to become the nation's providers of educational programming. With this proposal effectively sidelining non-commercial stations, by mid-decade, more than three quarters of them had closed down.

Several high profile academics actually did join hands with the commercial stations for educational broadcasting, as the Communication Act had urged. Many of these cooperative ventures were supported by the Carnegie Corporation. Notably, NBC broadcast academic lectures, interviews and discussions. Perhaps not surprisingly, most of these programs were flops, partly because most professors were not microphone-savvy. Soon the networks started backing down on their prior promises to hold some primetime slots for the profs. The commercial/academic relationship went on the rocks. There was some temporary relief for the educators; in contrast to Carnegie's support of commercially based educational radio, the Cleveland-based Payne Fund supported independent, non-commercial educational stations during the 1930s. But these funds were insufficient to revive the moribund non-commercials.

After World War II, the Ford Foundation held out a life line to non-commercial radio stations, mostly those at mid-western land grant universities. A new spirit of learning filled the land, and educational radio was seen as a suitable adjunct to formal schooling. Thus, the non-commercials survived, though barely. Ford funds also supported 100 new FM non-commercial stations that opened in the 1960s. The good news was that FM stations could provide higher fidelity than AM, thus improved transmission of both classical music and conversations. The bad news was that these advantages were largely irrelevant, as most people didn't have an FM receiver! Thus, for about two decades, these hi-fi signals wafted right past most potential listeners.

Non-commercial radio's second near death experience came in 1967. The exciting story of how it survived this crisis is one of intrigue, involving a few heroes with deep commitment and a good share of hubris, who acted boldly to preserve non-commercial radio for future generations.[33]

As mentioned above, the 1967 Public Broadcasting Act signed into law by President Johnson had originally been recommended by the Carnegie I Report of the same year. That report actually had called for a Corporation for Public *Television*, not public *Broadcasting*. And in the congressional bill's original wording, radio was not mentioned once.

Had the bill gone through congress as originally proposed, public radio probably would have received no federal funding and almost certainly would have died. The Ford Foundation, which had been keeping non-commercial radio marginally alive, had recently decided that the future was in TV, not radio.

But a few people at the University of Michigan's non-commercial, educational radio station got wind of the Carnegie I Report, and fought back. They organized what has been called "a guerrilla operation to slip the words 'and radio' into the public television bill recommended by Carnegie I. They would adopt a stealth strategy that involved misrepresentation, temper tantrums, and an inside connection in the Johnson administration."[34] Nearly everywhere in the proposed bill that the word "television" appeared, they inserted the words "and radio." With just two days left before the bill was to go to Congress, public radio had been resuscitated. Or so these guerrilla fighters thought.

What happened? Through the work of some mysterious, unidentified counter-revolutionary group, every insertion of the words "and radio" was erased from the text. But alas, the guerrillas discovered these erasures, and with one day to go, just as mysteriously, they re-inserted these two, now famous words, "and radio" every place where they had been erased. And that's how Congress received the bill for consideration. Radio was in, and ultimately the bill, which was named the Public *Broadcasting* (not *Television*) Act, created the Corporation for Public *Broadcasting* (not *Television*), which to this day supports public TV and public radio. CPB created National Public Radio (NPR) in 1970, one year after it had created PBS for television. From the beginning, though, PBS has received the lion's share of the financial support from CPB—currently three times what NPR receives.

Public radio's third, and current, near-death experience, and its likely reincarnation, is explained by Vivian Schiller, past President/CEO of National Public Radio:

> We don't call ourselves National Public Radio anymore. We're NPR....That used to mean radio, but we don't think we should be limited to that anymore....We [want] to reach more people, on more platforms. We want to make it as widely available as possible....This is a huge change and we should embrace it. Mobile [hand-held devices] will play a big part.[35]

Don't throw away your radio receiver yet, but make sure you are *au courant* with computer and mobile technology if you want to keep up with National Public Radio (oops, I mean NPR).

One significant difference between public radio and public TV is relevant to our discussion. NPR has no common carriage policy with the public radio stations, as PBS does with its TV stations. Thus, each NPR-affiliated station is free to broadcast what it wants, when it wants. As an extreme example, NPR station KUSC in Los Angeles airs almost exclusively classical music, with virtually none of the available NPR programming.

How many people actually listen to public radio, compared with those who tune in to commercial stations?[36] Approximately 1.5 percent of the American population listens to NPR for at least five consecutive minutes at some time on an average day. The figures available for commercial radio are collected from week-long samplings, rather than day-long samplings, complicating comparisons. But given that 190 million Americans, including 74 percent of those over 18, listen to commercial radio at least once a week, NPR garners only a tiny percentage of the overall radio audience.

What does this small listening audience hear on public radio? The most listened to NPR program is its weekday news broadcast, *Morning Edition*, which is also the most listened to news program on American radio, public or commercial.[37] To support its news programming, NPR employs the largest world-wide news gathering staff in all of American radio. The second most listened to NPR program is *All Things Considered*, a news and public affairs magazine-style program. NPR's past President Schiller defines both *Morning Edition* and *All Things Considered* as news programs. Former NPR president Kevin Klose and present senior host of *All Things Considered* Robert Siegel both added that NPR in general is about news and public affairs.[38]

Who listens to NPR? Is it largely an elite audience, like that of PBS? Note that both *Morning Edition* and *All Things Considered* are specifically timed to coincide with people's commute to and from work. A common expression among NPR broadcasters is the "driveway moment," a pause outside one's house to catch an interesting item on *All Things Considered*, at the end of the homeward commute. But who drives to and from work, rather than taking a bus or subway, riding a bike or walking? And who lives in a house with a driveway, rather than in an apartment? People who can afford a home, usually in the suburbs, who are usually not poor.

Nearly three times as many NPR listeners hold professional jobs, more than twice as many have at least a bachelor's degree, and about 4 times as many have a graduate degree, than among the general population.[39] A remarkable two thirds of NPR listeners are baby boomers, born between the end of WWII and 1964. In that era, attaining an undergraduate, and certainly a graduate, degree was more rare than it is today, so baby boomers with these degrees—common among NPR listeners—are a smaller population segment than younger people with these same degrees. One expert comment sums up what most analysts say, "...public radio [has] always been the province of America's most educated and discerning people...."[40]

For a further take on NPR's target audience, I asked Robert Siegel with whom he visualizes himself speaking when he broadcasts on *All Things Considered*.

"My parents," he replied.

"Really? Tell me about them."

"They were school teachers, and my father became a school principal in the New York City system. First generation Jewish Americans, their own parents came from Latvia. For them, speaking perfect English, with neither a Latvian nor a Brooklyn accent, was a strong drive, and to achieve this they took speech courses."[41]

Strongly driven, articulate, urban educators—not exactly your average folks. I received a similar answer from public radio host Ira Flatow of *Science Friday* in New York, who envisions himself speaking to "a highly educated listener."[42]

But just as I had inquired regarding public television, I asked NPR's Vivian Schiller, "Would a listener to an NPR station broadcasting from a university have the sense of the university behind the voice."

"Not at all," she replied. "Usually the university is not engaged with the station. The General Manager is responsible for the station. He or she may be paid by the university, but is not there to serve its mission. He or she is usually a radio professional, not an academic, and is trained or experienced in media management."

Suspecting some residual negative feelings at NPR about the early, old fashioned, formal, university broadcasts, I asked Schiller, "Is the memory of educational radio still with us?"

"Yes it is, and it's boring," she replied.[43]

As with public television, few academics are involved in leadership roles of public radio on the national level, despite the long history of academic leadership—and despite the fact that the whole public radio system was saved by people from the University of Michigan! Today, most of the system's leaders are journalists or other broadcast professionals. For instance, the two most recent NPR Presidents, Vivian Schiller and Kevin Klose were previously journalists. Eight out of fifteen NPR board members are station managers, while only two are associated with academia—Board President Howard Stevenson, who is a Harvard business professor, and Kent State University President Carol Cartwright. A leading author on NPR states that it has long been "the station managers and journalists who truly owned the enterprise."[44]

Wouldn't it be positive to restore academia's involvement in public radio? The expertise is there in departments of communications and journalism staffed by the very people who train those ending up as NPR leaders. These university people have the skills and the breadth of vision to join the leadership of this important channel of communication.

Here's one bright spot in this rather bleak picture. Alan Chartock, president of Albany's NPR station WAMC, has created *The Academic Minute*, broadcast twice daily by professors from around the country and the world, who present ideas emerging from their research and other academic work. The program is introduced by Mount Holyoke College President and Philosophy Professor Lynn Pasquerella, and the college helps support the project. It is available worldwide by podcast.[45] May the WAMC example be widely emulated.

In summary, although you can catch an occasional prof on NPR or PBS, more on some shows than on others, these national public broadcasting systems are not particularly effective in sharing academic ideas with a wide public. They reach remarkably few people—a few percent of Americans on a given day, and probably mostly the same people on the next day. As I have indicated, public broadcasting does not strongly connect this small audience to academia and its ideas. I have suggested several ways to improve this situation.

Part of the good news about public broadcasting is its availability on the Internet. You can select from a wide variety of *Frontline, American Experience, NOVA,* and other TV shows, as well as radio programs such as *Science Friday*. As broadcasting will increasingly involve the Internet, we turn next to the expanding role of this extraordinary medium in sharing university ideas with the public.

Notes

1. Jonathan Nichols-Pethick, "The Dynamics of Local Television," in *Beyond Prime Time: Television Programming in the Post-Network Era,* ed. Amanda D. Lotz (New York: Routledge, 2009), 156-179, http://www.fcc.gov/cgb/consumerfacts/digitalradio. html.

2. Shelly Palmer, *Television Disrupted: The Transition from Network to Networked TV,* 2nd ed. (Ryebrook, New York: York House Press, 2009), xvi.

3. http://money.cnn.com/2006/09/06/commentary/sportsbiz/index.htm; Victoria E. Johnson, "Everything New is Old Again: Sport Television, Innovation, and Tradition for a Multi-platform Era," in Lotz (ed.), *Beyond Prime Time,* 121.

4. Nichols-Pethick, "The Dynamics of Local Television."

5. Nielson Media Research, Television Audience 2009, and data from Neilson ratings, summarized at http://www.csun.edu/science/health/docs/tv&health. html.

6. A few other broadcasting varieties are found at some colleges and universities, but will not be discussed here. These include closed circuit systems for on-campus use only, as well as weak broadcasting stations with hardly any range outside of campus, often student-operated and sometimes serving a teaching role in a communications or journalism department. Also, some campuses have a fully outfitted, modern television production studio, but without any broadcast facilities. These permit high quality taping of programs that can be made available to broadcast stations elsewhere, such as a different campus of a multi-campus university.

7. These 357 stations operate under 166 licenses, some of which cover more than one station. Of these, 54 licenses, just under one third, are held by university stations.

8. The history of American TV, especially public TV, presented here is drawn primarily from the following sources: James Day, *The Vanishing Vision: The Inside Story of Public Television* (Berkeley: University of California Press, 1995); Lotz, (ed.) *Beyond Prime Time*; Laurie Ouellette, *Viewers Like You: How Public TV Failed the People* (New York: Columbia University Press, 2002); Palmer, *Television Disrupted.*

9. Putnam, *Bowling Alone,* 217.

10. Lyndon B. Johnson, "Remarks Upon Signing the Public Broadcasting Act of 1967," *The American Presidency Project*, November 7, 1967, 474. http://www.presidency.ucsd.edu/ws/index.php?pid=28532&st=public+broadcasting&stl=.

11. Beth Walsh, Director of Research, PBS, Washington, DC., personal communication. The PBS statistics are based on the number of people listening for at least six minutes at some point during prime time. The Nielson Media statistics are based on the number of people who tuned in during an average minute. This difference probably accounts for the disparity in the percentages obtained. As many as 40 million people (about 13 percent of Americans) occasionally tune in to a single program. Well over 100 million (over 30 percent of Americans) are generally found to be viewing some program at that same moment, and presumably many more than this tune in to commercial TV at some moment during primetime on a typical evening.

12. Day, *Vanishing Vision*, 332.

13. Ibid., 357.

14. Laurie Ouellette, "Reinventing PBS: Public Television in the Post-network, Post-welfare Era," in: Lotz, *Beyond Prime Time*, 190.

15. Beth Walsh, personal communication.

16. Ouellette, "Reinventing PBS," 190.

17. Interviewed by the author at PBS, Arlington, VA, April 14, 2010.

18. Interview by the author at the University of California, Berkeley, April 7, 2010.

19. E-mail from WGBH, July 1, 2010.

20. One program especially deserving mention, even though it almost always plays outside of primetime, is *Charlie Rose*. Charlie is a highly talented interviewer of leaders in politics, business, the arts, and (approximately 20 percent of his guests) academia. As a neurobiologist, I was particularly pleased by the remarkable 12-part series that he and Columbia University Nobel Laureate Eric Kandel co-produced, that brought to the screen 12 small groups of academic research neurobiologists for informal round-table discussions about different topics related to the brain.

21. Day, *Vanishing Vision*, 340, 344-5.

22. Beth Walsh, e-mail message to the author, September 23, 2010.

23. Interviewed by the author at UNC-TV, April 16, 2010.

24. Interviewed by the author at University of North Carolina, April 15, 2010.

25. Interviewed by the author at PBS, Arlington, VA, April 14, 2010.

26. Interviewed by the author at UCSD TV, April 6, 2010.

27. Interviewed by the author at CUNY, August 8, 2007.

28. http://www.nytimes.com/2009/02/28/business/media/28network.html.

29. Nick DeSantis "U. of California TV Station Will Develop Original Content for YouTube," *The Chronicle of Higher Education*, March 19, 2012.

30. The history of radio presented here is drawn primarily from the following sources: Eugene E. Leach, "History of Public Broadcasting in the United States: Tuning Out Education," *Current* (Feb-March 1983); also available at http:///www.current.org/coop/coopl.shtml); Michael P. McCauley, *NPR: The Trials and Triumphs of National Public Radio* (New York: Columbia University Press, 2005); Jack W. Mitchell, *Listener Supported: The Culture and History of Public Radio* (Westport, CT: Praeger, 2005); Lisa A. Phillips, *Public Radio: Behind the Voices* (New York: CDS Books, 2006).

31. Mitchell, *Listener Supported*, 15.

32. Leach, *History of Public Broadcasting*.

33. This amazing story is dramatically reported in Mitchell, *Listener Supported*, 33-38.

34. Ibid., 34.

35. http://www/current.org.

36. The data presented here are from a telephone interview with Vivian Schiller, former President and CEO of NPR, and from Arbitron, Inc., the leading evaluator of radio audiences, http://arbitron.mediaroom.com/index.php?s=43&item=711.

37. This would appear to contradict the statement that NPR attracts only a tiny fraction of the listeners. However, the people listening to news on stations other than NPR are divided among a great many different national networks and local stations; thus, each of these has fewer listeners than *Morning Edition*.

38. Each of these three was interviewed by the author during April, 2010—Schiller by telephone, Klose at the University of Maryland, Siegel at NPR, Washington, DC.

39. McCauley, *Trials and Triumphs*, 115.

40. Ibid., 113.

41. Interviewed by the author at NPR, Washington, DC, April 14, 2010.

42. Interviewed by the author, New York, NY April 21, 2010.

43. Telephone interview by the author, April 22, 2010.

44. McCauley, Trials and Triumphs, 91.

45. http://www.insidehighered.com/academic-minute; http://www.wamc.org/academic-minute.html.

CHAPTER 9. THE WEB AND FLOW OF UNIVERSITY IDEAS

Once upon a time, before personal computers, you surfed at the beach, and browsed in a store, windows were made of glass, programming was on radio and TV, a website was the location of a spider's home, and you wouldn't dream of placing your hand on a mouse. If someone mentioned "algorithms," you'd try to think which song they'd recorded.

Today, like 2 billion Internet users, I sit at my computer—the one on which I am typing these words—communicate worldwide, and hook into vast informational resources—things unimaginable a few years ago. The Internet has transformed academic work, as it has so many other endeavors. This chapter focuses on how the Internet is beginning to transform the way academia shares its ideas with the public. "Beginning," because academia has been slow to develop this use of the Web. In examining this development, once again I look at things anthropologically, this time as a Margaret Mead of the Web.

Here's one indication I have discerned of academia' slow start in sharing its ideas over the Internet. Remember the questionnaire I sent to American Red Cross employees? The respondents stated they use the Internet far more than any other means to learn about subjects that interest them; and the subject that interested them by far the most was current affairs. So I did a quick web-check of universities in terms of two current affairs topics that were then hot—in November, 2009. I Googled "Iraq War" and "Afghanistan." For each subject, I searched the first 100 sites that appeared on the screen. The results might surprise you.

For "Iraq War," only three among the first 100 sites were from universities, and they did not appear on the first screen that included the first 10 websites, pretty much all that most casual browsers glance at. These three appeared in positions 29 (University of Michigan Library), 51 (East Carolina University Library) and 96 (Dartmouth Library). For "Afghanistan" there was only one site, located in position 88 (University of California, Berkeley Library). All four of these sites were listings of academic library resources and links. None was an article, a blog, or an audio- or video-taped lecture, discussion, or interview of a university professor about either subject. That is, no university experts in political science, government, military history, sociology, or any other relevant subject were there to share ideas about two of the world's hottest topics. Not via a Google browse, at least. Most of the websites were from media or government organizations, politically oriented organizations, and non-academic bloggers. When I Goggled "Afghanistan blogs," I picked up some academics, but diluted by a great number of other bloggers, many of whose "credentials" were an undergraduate degree in political science, a recent return from military service, or some rough equivalent. Google Scholar, by contrast, offered many articles by academics, but nearly all were scholarly, directed to professional experts.

In August, 2012, I did a quick re-check. Of the first 50 sites for Iraq War there were none from universities, and for Afghanistan there was one. I also examined the first 25 sites for four more specific subjects—"Causes of the Iraq War", "Reasons for the Iraq War", "Afghanistan War" and "Afghanistan Culture"—a total of 100 sites. Three were from universities.

So everybody except universities is talking to the general public about these two hot topics via the Internet. True, universities and colleges reach the public via the Internet in other ways. The six ways listed below, each followed by a question in parenthesis, are the subjects discussed in this chapter.

- University and college websites. (Where are the ideas?)

- Videos on the Web. (Are they a breakthrough?)

- Reader-friendly university articles on the Web (Are they a panacea?)

- Online course enrollment. (Why are so few people getting the ideas?)

- OpenCourseWare. (Why are so few courses putting out ideas?)

- Social networking. (Who's an expert?)

Before returning to this list, here's an important, though probably obvious, comment. Computers, other digital devices, the Internet, and related software are developing so rapidly that by the time this book reaches your hands, some of my observations may have become irrelevant, some of my suggestions may already have been implemented, or replaced by better ones. That's progress.

University and College Websites (Where Are the ideas?)

Every accredited university and college probably has a website. Do these effectively share their ideas with the public? To answer this, we first need to define the intended audience. Websites are intended primarily for the institution's major stakeholders—current students and faculty (for whom the website provides much useful information), prospective students and their parents (who are invited to visit the campus as part of the application process), alumni (some of whom donate money and/or assistance), and other potential donors (on whom it is wise to make a good impression).

The information for a university's website is usually organized by the public relations, or public communications, department, a non-academic unit staffed by people with PR, writing, and administrative skills, but untrained in academic research or teaching. Comments by PR heads at two universities summed up their website's goals. Lori Doyle, Vice President for University Communications at the University of Pennsylvania, told me, "My job is to enhance the reputation of the University of Pennsylvania."[1] Nancy Connell, Director of News and Information Services at the University of Michigan, said, "The news [that we send out on the Internet and elsewhere] is as much entertainment as it is news."[2]

To me, some of the articles are interesting and well written, but most have a glitzy, sound-bite quality and avoid anything deep or controversial. Others are written in hyper-academe-speak that makes little sense to me, and probably to most others. Here's one illustration. On January 13, 2010, the University of Illinois posted the following announcement on their homepage: "Two University of Illinois professors are among 100 young researchers named...as recipients of [the United States] Presidential Early Career Awards for Scientists and Engineers, the highest honor bestowed by the U.S. government on young professionals at the outset of their independent research careers." Sounded impressive, so I read on. Next was a quote from President Obama: "These extraordinarily gifted young scientists and engineers represent the best in our country....With their talent, creativity, and dedication, I am confident that they will lead their fields in new breakthroughs and discoveries and help us use science and technology to lift up our nation and our world."

Great, but what did they actually do? One of them, I read, works in "Experimental mechanics at the nanoscale; mechanical reliability, fracture, and fatigue of micro-electromechanical systems; deformation and damage mechanics of polymer nanocomposites and soft nanophase materials." Sounds like this means "How little things break," but I haven't understood the explanation. Likewise for the description of the other young professor's work. Though admittedly an extreme example, looking for academic ideas on university websites has its frustrations.

This is particularly so when one looks for academic ideas on a given subject. Suppose you take an interest in global warming, and want to sample a range of academic ideas from various universities on the subject. How would you find such material, written for a general, non-technical reader, on university websites? You'd have to sample many sites and hope to find a few relevant articles. How inefficient!

The next two sections describe efforts to overcome this inefficiency, first regarding video material, and then written material.

Videos on the Web (Are they a breakthrough?)

Some university websites present videos of entire courses, or lectures by visiting scholars, or brief statements by faculty about their work. (Stanford is a leader in this field.) However, there remains the problem of how to find ideas about specific subjects, like global warming, not just at one university but at several. Solving this problem was to require a website with video material gathered from not one, but many universities, with a keyword-searchable function. But nobody had come up with this concept. Nobody, that is, except a Yale undergraduate named Richard Ludlow.

Ludlow was having trouble understanding a courses in linear algebra at Yale. On the Internet, he happened upon MIT's "OpenCourseWare," (described below) and found the videotaped lectures of MIT's linear algebra course, taught by Professor Gilbert Strang, the author of the textbook used in the Yale course through which Ludlow was suffering.[3]

Twenty-year-old Ludlow had a gutsy idea: Why not collect and display, on a single website, videotaped courses from many great universities? But how would he get his hands on all those videos for his own website? Turned out this was no problem. Many universities create their videos under Creative Commons licenses. Rather than an "all rights reserved" status, these licenses permit one to obtain and post on the Web the videos for free, though only for educational, and not commercial, purposes. Thus emerged the organization, and the website, called Academic Earth.

Academicearth.org presents, free of charge, videos of entire courses as well as guest lectures from many universities, including several of the nation's best ones. The site is keyword searchable in the sense that it directs you to courses within which your keyword appears. A list of 79 courses popped up when I typed in "global warming." Though it's hard to know where during an entire course a particular subject is discussed, a list of each lecture's main subject provides a useful guideline.

Launched in early 2009, Academicearth.com claimed over a million website visits within its first three months. The average time visitors remained on the site (calculated after removing all those visits that lasted less than 10 seconds—that is, those who were just wafting through) was an impressive 27 minutes, which means that many people were sticking with the lectures for a decent duration, and no doubt some until the prof's final "See you next time."

This created a breakthrough in bringing university ideas to the public. However in 2011, Academic Earth was acquired by the firm Ampush Media, whose founders were former investment bankers. Suddenly, along with the free video courses from Yale, Stanford and other outstanding schools were online certification courses or degree programs, mostly in job-related subjects, and decidedly not for free, from the likes of Marian, North Central, and Roseman Universities (raise your hand if you've ever heard of these schools.) How the fee is split between Ampush and these institutions, for which Ampush's Academic Earth is now serving as a marketing platform, is not clear.

One problem with this arrangement is that only the latter group of courses provide Ampush with income. Thus, the free courses from the distinguished universities, while still present on the site, are at risk of descending to second class citizenship, lacking upkeep and further development. A second problem is that this website could lose free access to further Creative Commons licensed videos of outstanding university courses, now that it is more decidedly a money-making venture. Even if this doesn't happen, Academic Earth is beginning to look like a for-profit online conglomerate, with a menu including offerings from many undistinguished schools, damaging the reputation for excellence that Ludlow and his associates had built. Time will tell whether this breakthrough in sharing academic ideas continues to serve its initial function. I can't help thinking, though, that these problems might have been avoided if Academic Earth had been conceived and developed from the outset as a university initiated and guided venture, either a company or a non-profit organization. Both types have come into being, one in 2011, the other in 2012.

Coursera, launched in 2011, was conceived by two Stanford professors of computer science, established as a Silicon Valley company in cooperation with a consortium of top universities, and financed by venture capitalists. It began by offering free courses on the Web to anyone, initially in math, computer science and engineering. Unlike with Academic Earth, students are expected to read the course material, do the assignments, and take quizzes and exams, all of which are graded online. A student is expected to spend about 12 hours per week studying a given course. There is no one-on-one interaction with the professor, and no course credit is offered.

In its first year, with just Stanford and three other leading research universities, Coursera offered 43 courses to 690,000 students in 190 countries. By the autumn of 2012 its roster of 16 top research universities offered over 100 courses in a wider range of subjects, including history, poetry and philosophy. Coursera may pursue financial sustainability by selling certificates (not degrees) to students who successfully complete one or more courses. Also, companies may be offered, for a fee, access to Coursera's most successful students. [4]

Unlike Coursera, edX, developed in 2012, is a not-for-profit enterprise, initially of MIT and Harvard, and later including Berkeley. Like Coursera it is beginning with interactive courses on technical subjects, and it may offer students certificates but not course credit. [5]

Today, there are other websites offering a variety of academic videos. For instance, there's YouTube EDU, but most of its videos are under 10 minutes long, some under a minute, and many are pure PR. Then there's iTunes U, whose unimpressive selection of videos, tasteless design, and low ease navigation make it, in my view, well worth missing

As academic video websites begin to proliferate, distinguished universities are beginning to place their courses on more than one site. Courses on the Web for free from the top universities will surely compete effectively with courses for a fee from mediocre, for-profit or not-for-profit, Web-based universities.

Free academic courses on the Web are clearly a breakthrough. Yet with no demographic studies available so far to determine the age distribution of Coursera's or edX's online students, it remains questionable whether, for continuing education adults, the time demands of these courses will exceed the interest level of the general public.

Reader-friendly University Articles on the Web (Are they a panacea?)

What Academic Earth created for video material, Futurity.org—launched the same year, 2009—is doing for written articles about research-based ideas from many universities. But with a big difference.

Futurity is a non-profit, inter-university project that sells nothing on its website. It shares, for free, breaking news from academic research. An initiative of Stanford and Duke Universities and the University of Rochester, Futurity now includes 64 highly ranked universities, all but 13 in the USA. Each pays annual dues (currently $3,000) to participate and share its breaking news, mostly about research in the natural and social sciences. The project's spokespersons mention the ongoing decline in newspaper coverage of university science and technology research as a main motivation for the project. Duke's spokesperson comments, "It's not often you see high-powered universities working together in such a collaborative way. That fact alone is one indication of the project's significance."[6]

Here's one way to measure Futurity's usefulness. Recall that when I searched Google for material from universities about the Iraq War and Afghanistan, I found almost nothing. By contrast, in 2012, nine months after US troops had withdrawn from Iraq, I searched the Futurity website via the key phrase "Iraq War," and 46 articles popped up, each about an aspect of university research on the war. For "Afghanistan," the count was 155 articles!

But how many people actually use, or even know about Futurity? What is its impact level? I used browser visit data presented for the different articles from 2012, presented on the website, to obtain a crude measure. I then calculated the average number of visits a Futurity article receives. In the first week after appearing on the website, an average article received 540 visits. During its first ten months, this increased to 1,470 visits. These numbers seem low, either compared to Academic Earth, or if one imagines how many people might have read these same articles, had they been printed in major national newspapers—in spite of newspapers' declining readership.

Most Futurity authors are journalists from the public relations offices of the participating universities. Acceptance of articles and some modifications of those accepted are tasks of Futurity's small editorial staff. Although the researchers are not writing the pieces, they are heavily quoted in most articles. In my view, most articles are well-written. Links are presented to the researchers' own articles, published in professional journals, about the same subject. The site is interactive, with the option for visitor comments.

I have high praise for Futurity, though with three reservations. First, I hope it will manage to increase its readership, with its website will becoming a staple of Internet browsing. Second, I wish the site included articles on the humanities as well as the sciences; new university ideas emerge from a wide range of research areas, and all should be brought to public attention. And third, I wonder whether the site's founders considered having the researchers write their own articles, rather than placing journalists between the researchers and the public. True, researchers' articles would need a good editing by professional journalists, and this would increase costs. However, this arrangement would provide a more authentic research voice, and might include explanations of the evidence adduced in the research, such as: "To address question A, we carried out experiment B; here's how we did it. Control C was necessary for such-and-such reasons. The experiment's result was D. We interpret this to mean E because of F. G shows the limitations of this conclusion, and H is a possibility for overcoming these limitations in the future." Discussions about evidence, as I suggested earlier, are important for the general public, and it is primarily researchers, not journalists, who would likely include such information and get it right.

In 2011, a similar project, called The Conversation, was launched at the University of Melbourne, Australia. Like Futurity, it presents articles about research-based ideas from universities, though mostly those in Australia. Claiming to present "academic rigor, journalistic flair," most of the articles are written by the researchers themselves, whose photo portraits appear beside the article. Articles are edited by a staff of journalist-editors working for The Conversation. The site presents entries from other nations, though these are different—mostly reprints from university websites, scientific journals or other sources. The Conversation's regular articles are well-written, though no doubt high in editorial costs.

Other Internet sources for printed science news exist. Google News, for instance. Its articles tend to be more superficial than those on the two academic websites discussed above. Many of the Google News articles are about science policy, not the actual research findings. Eurekalert!, a website of the non-profit American Association for the Advancement of Science (AAAS) strays in the opposite direction; its articles are a bit more technical than those of Futurity or The Conversation. Their target audience is reporters, science writers, and the scientific community; the average non-scientist would find some of the material hard going. For sharing ideas based on university research with the general public, Futurity comes closest to the mark.

You may wonder why I am focusing on these multi-university websites, given the enormous availability of blogs, some by academic researchers. Blogs often state the blogger's opinions, are not necessarily evidence-based, and are widely scattered among the Internet's more than 50 million blogs, many written by people with little expertise in the subjects discussed.

Is the availability of reader-friendly articles such as those in Futurity a panacea for the general lack of university idea sharing with the public? No. Not yet, at least. That would partially depend on a significant increase in the site's readership. Moreover, some people may not want to read articles on the Web, when they can watch videos on Academic Earth, Coursera, edX or other programs. I'm keeping my fingers crossed for all these developments.

Online Course Enrollment (Why are so few people getting the ideas?)

Some people claim that the college or university campus is a dinosaur on its way to extinction, to be replaced by academia on the Web. They point out that online courses—sometimes called e-learning—are reaching into the most isolated communities throughout the nation and around the world, offering a wide range of attractively presented, interactive learning opportunities suited to different learning paces, styles, and study schedules—all at relatively low cost. I am not referring to free video courses such as those on some campus websites or on Academic Earth, but to courses taken for a fee, usually for credit, in which the student interacts in some fashion with the professor and perhaps the course's other Internet students. Some courses are part of a program that terminates with earning a badge, or a certificate of competence in a job-related subject, if not an actual degree. There are courses for undergraduates, graduate students, and continuing education students.

These Internet courses are catching on fast. Investments in education software companies and projects rose from less than $100 million in 2007 to more than 400 million in 2011, in spite of the continuing economic recession.[7] Why, some people are asking, would undergrads continue to relocate to a distant campus for four years and pay exorbitant tuition costs?

Some students won't continue to do so. In an insightful analysis of e-learning's rapid development, Harvard Business School's Clayton Christensen and coauthor Henry Eyring explain that e-learning is upending traditional college education in a manner familiar to the business world.[8] In that world, small firms with new technologies can upend more traditional industrial giants. Christensen calls this process "disruptive innovation." While traditional firms often focus on continuing to do what they do best, the upstart firms capture more and more of the market by undercutting prices and by recognizing and fulfilling new customer needs. Ultimately, upstart becomes giant, as the former giant shrinks.

In academia, Christensen and Eyring see the traditional universities and colleges as counterparts of the industrial giants, and institutions with newer learning technologies—especially the ever improving e-learning—as the upstarts. These authors recognize that the top research universities and liberal arts colleges—the ones *A Dam in the River* is about—will not be upended, because they offer something of value that students who can either afford them or win a scholarship will continue to want.

Thus, although e-learning offers a very important addition to the menu of diverse learning options for America's diverse society, the campus experience at a great university or college remains the gold standard of higher education. Nothing beats being there. Nothing ever will. That's why, when quality communication is essential, academics, business people, and heads of state will travel half way around the world to talk with one another in person. World leaders don't negotiate peace treaties on Skype.

Even co-authors Tapscott and Williams, whose popular Internet book *Wikinomics* promotes online courses and Web-based social networking, recognize the importance of being there for a college or university experience: "Proximity creates personal familiarity and fosters trust. Body language, intonation, and general demeanor play an important role in human interaction. Moreover, it's easy to underestimate the degree to which tacit learning and knowledge creation are enhanced by face-to-face contact. These are all valid considerations, and will remain true for as long as we remain human."[9]

Yet online courses are here and growing in popularity, including among continuing education students—the adult learners this book is first and foremost about. At most universities, the majority of online courses, whether for regular or continuing students, are primarily career-oriented or technical in subject matter. Sloan-C, an organization highly regarded for studying and promoting online education, claims that only 30 percent of fully online degree programs are idea-based (in the liberal arts, general studies, humanities, social sciences); 70 percent are technical, skills-based and career-oriented (in business, computers, engineering, the health professions).[10] Although technical, skill-based and career-oriented courses transmit *some* ideas—it is hard to imagine totally idea-free teaching—the essence of a course in marketing, or nursing, or lab technology is to teach the students how to *do* marketing, nursing, or lab technology, not to explore these subjects from a historical, anthropological, literary, or other broadly interpretive perspective.

I wanted to look further into the Sloan-C claim of the low percentage of online idea-based courses, but specifically in continuing education programs. I selected as a case study the impressive listing of continuing education courses on the University of Illinois website. Based on each course's title and descriptive blurb, I counted those courses that appeared to be: a) primarily idea-based; b) primarily practical or technical, or c) difficult to classify.[11] Although there are clearly inaccuracies in my classification, the results are instructive. Out of 164 courses, 60 were idea-based (that's 37 percent) not far from the Sloan-C count of 30 percent). There were 74 practical or technical courses (47 percent), and 30 difficult to classify.

To check out my classification, I emailed Faye Lesht, head of the University of Illinois Continuing Education Program that runs the courses I had categorized. I requested the same classification of her program's offerings. I was surprised by her estimate, namely, that only 10 percent of the online courses taught are in "general/liberal studies, not focusing mainly on practical or technical skills or tasks." And only 10 percent of the students in their program are enrolled in these courses. The remaining 90 percent of both the online courses taught, and the student enrollments, are "mainly practically or technically oriented, relevant to job skills, personal skills, or other skills or tasks."[12]

How many adult Americans are taking idea-based continuing education courses online? In Chapter 4, I calculated that roughly 1 in 60 adults are taking *in-class*, idea-based, continuing education courses at American universities and colleges, and 1 in 1,200 are doing so at the 100 top research universities. Data from the National Center for Education Statistics lead to the estimate that only about half as many are taking such courses online. That's 1 in 120 at all schools or one in 2,400 at the 100 top research schools![13] Thus, anyone who claims that online, idea-based, continuing education courses are having a pervasive effect on American society needs to recognize that the numbers refute this claim.

All this seems to be no news to experts in the online course business. One such expert, Drexel University's Francis Harvey, asked rhetorically, "Which adults study on line?" and answered pointedly, "Adults who want to advance in the work they're already doing. It's all about getting certified."[14] This was further shown in a recent study of the preferences of three age groups of continuing education students at UCLA—older (aged 49 to 66), middle (aged 28 to 48) and young (aged up to age 27). For all three groups, the most commonly indicated reason for engaging in continuing education was "to advance my career". This was a bit surprising for the older group, many of whom are nearing traditional retirement age. Moreover, none of the three age groups selected strictly online courses as their preferred learning format; all had high regard for in-class learning.

OpenCourseWare (Why are so few courses putting out ideas?)

In 2001, MIT became the first major university to give away its knowledge on the Web, big time, for free. It launched an Internet program called OpenCourseWare, abbreviated OCW. MIT engineering professor Richard Larson related to me the origin of this revolutionary idea: "I sat on the Provost's committee to decide what we at MIT were going to do about an online presence. There was a lot of chatter in the room. Then someone—I don't remember who—said, 'What would it be like if we just gave away all our course materials on the Web for free?' The chatter suddenly stopped. After a while, someone said, 'That would be interesting.' And that was it" (interviewed by the author at MIT, March 24, 2008).

You don't take courses through OCW, or earn college credit or a degree. There are no tutors, interactions with professors or students, and no assigned homework. Rather, OCW posts on the Internet information about almost every MIT course—more than 1900 of them—that you can access and use as you like. Postings vary course to course. For some it is the course description, syllabus, and reading list, whereas others include homework assignments, exams and their answers, the professor's lecture notes, or a photo gallery. For a limited number of courses, the lectures are fully videoed.

The OCW website receives nearly a million visits per month, 40 percent from the USA, and 20 percent from China. About half of the USA visits are from students or faculty at other universities and colleges. Much of the material is useful for lecturers trying to improve their own courses and thinking, "Let's see how it's done at MIT," and for students struggling through these same courses at other schools, for whom it has provided both useful insights and inspiration, as in the case of Richard Ludlow. Not only are course materials free, but the OCW software is "open," meaning that teachers in other institutions can modify it for use in their own courses. Moreover, although MIT was the first to develop open courseware, they have encouraged over 200 institutions, many overseas, to join an OCW Consortium, a nonprofit organization that supports OCW goals. Its member universities and colleges are also placing their own course materials online for free.

Steve Carson, OCW's External Relations Director, showed me around their facilities. I was impressed by (among other things) the many very smart technical people I met, and I realized this had to be an expensive operation. Carson explained that OCW began with $26 million in grants from the Hewlett and Mellon Foundations and a further $6 million from MIT. Now that most of the software design, legal matters, and other technical issues have been resolved, OCW's annual operating budget is $4 million, of which half is covered by MIT, and the rest by donations that MIT actively solicits.

MIT is appropriately proud of OpenCourseWare. Charles Vest, President at the time of OCW's founding, writes, "As our faculty had hoped, today there is an emerging open-courseware movement....Consistent with our open philosophy, MIT OCW has actively worked to encourage and assist this movement...."[15] MIT receives well-deserved kudos from around the world, thereby elevating its already through-the-roof global prestige. To quote former MIT mathematician and satirical songster Tom Lehrer, the school is "doing well by doing good."

How effective is OCW in doing what *A Dam in the River* urges—opening the campus sluice gates to let the ideas flow, not just to profs and their students, but deeply into society? One way to check this is to dig deeply into OCW's website.

For a broad sharing of ideas with the public, I believe that the videos of course lectures are by far OCW's most valuable resource. Others think similarly; although less than 1 in 20 of the courses on the website include lecture videos, 16 of the 20 courses most frequently visited include such videos.[16] Recall, you don't take a course on OCW, so you can sample one lecture or as many as you wish. The majority of the video-taped courses are on technical subjects—courses like *Multivariate Calculus,* or *Thermodynamics and Kinetics*—stuff MIT students eat for breakfast. In fact, of the 20 most visited courses, eight are in computer science, five in math and four in physics. None of these 20 are in the humanities. Although MIT offers 379 humanities courses—in Anthropology, History, Literature, Political Science, Women's and Gender Studies, Writing, and Humanistic Studies—videotaped lectures are presented on OCW for just five of these courses. That's 5 out of 379! And for these 379 humanities courses, there's a real dearth of other types of material on OCW. These are MIT's most broadly idea-based courses, the ones most accessible to a general audience, yet they barely have a presence on the OCW website.

Thus, although OCW is a remarkable resource for instructors and students and anyone else interested in technical subjects, to date—and this could change—it is not serving as a significant opener of the sluice gates for university ideas of widespread interest to the general public. According to Susan Hockfield, MIT President until 2012, "We do not yet know the full potential of OCW and its ultimate impact on global education. But it is clear to us that by thinking of knowledge as a public good for the benefit of all...we can make a difference."[17] The infrastructure is in place to steer OCW toward making an even broader difference by more focus on the MIT courses that can speak directly to society at large.

This chapter concludes by examining the most popular aspect of Internet culture, social networking, and raises broader questions about expertise.

Social Networking (Who's an expert?)

When I was a kid, my parents regarded our family physician, Dr. Zucker, sitting behind his large desk in his Park Avenue, Manhattan office, as the guardian of our family's wellbeing and the embodiment of professional wisdom. They would never presume to know something about health, disease, or a variety of family matters that Dr. Zucker didn't know far better.

Today, there's been a measure of equalization between doctor and patient. It's not that doctors know less than before—actually, they know much more. But now even people with no medical training can readily learn about health issues, at least on a non-technical level, on the Internet. Moreover, many doctors obtain much of their updating from the Internet, further equalizing the doctor/patient relationship.[18]

The altered patient perception of doctors is but one example of a much wider shift in how the public relates to experts, including academic experts. In Chapter 2, I suggested that an academic expert is someone who knows, based on extensive training and research experience, how to obtain and evaluate evidence for ideas within a given field of specialization, and to some extent in related fields. As such, academic experts have an important educational and leadership role to fulfill.

In this section we'll see how the Internet is helping to convince people that this extensive training and experience are irrelevant because now everyone is said to be an expert. Please place the phrase—*everyone's an expert*—in your short-term, not your long-term, memory. I will refer to this phrase several more times, but at the end of this chapter, I will invite you to expunge it permanently from your mind.

The Internet is clearly making available a vast range of information, some of which was previously sequestered in inaccessible professional archives, obscured by academic or other traditions, sometimes debated behind closed doors. With the ascendancy of wikis, blogs, and social network programs, almost everyone is not only a recipient, but potentially a provider of information—a homegrown "expert," some would say. They might also say the Internet has turned expertise on its head.

Underlying these changes is hi tech computer research, much of it at universities, designed to expand the range of Internet technologies by which people can share their knowledge. To help bring myself up to speed in this field, I attended the Ed-Media 2009 Conference, which focused on the use of, and research about, the Internet in academia. Given the common practice of surfing the Web, the conference was held, fittingly, at one of the world's greatest surfing sites, Honolulu's Waikiki Beach. ("No really, I need to go," I explained to my dean.) I was a bit distressed to find that, with so many new ideas bantered about at the conference, I had trouble integrating everything. Imagine my relief as I kept hearing the hi-tech people say, "I just can't keep up with all this new tech stuff." *They* can't keep up?

An idea frequently discussed at the conference, a synthesis of the various knowledge-democratizing trends, was "collective [or] distributed intelligence." With people sharing information on the Web in groups, the knowledge, or the intelligence, is said to be located in the group, more or less equally parceled out among its members. A central, defining principle about such groups is that no one person stands out—this would be regarded as undemocratic. This may be interpreted in one of two ways: Either there's no such thing as an expert (since an expert would stand out); or, you guessed it, *everyone's an expert* (in which case, again, no one would stand out). This mantra permeated the conference, hushed along hallways, confided over coffee, and whispered wisely to newcomers, often preceded by, "Ya know, don't ya, that...." But it struck me most directly during the Q&A period after Stephen Downes' lecture.

Downes is a social network analyst with the National Research Council of Canada. It was clear within the first few moments of his talk that he is smart, well informed, and inventive. And, as I have the hubris to suggest, misguided.

Downes' research focuses on developing a theory of, and a program to create, a "personal learning environment," which he abbreviated PLE. This program would facilitate a learner's access to and integration of knowledge about any subject, derived from a wide range of sources, mostly on the Internet, in a highly interactive manner. Downes intends PLE to be used in both college and continuing education courses, where it would basically replace the professor, and by anyone who wants to learn just about anything.

In a course using PLE, rather than having a curriculum and class meetings, each learner determines his/her own content within the course's broadly defined subject. Doing so means utilizing an ever fluctuating network of Internet information options to take a learning journey, each student journeying in his/her own direction. The experience is entirely learner-centered. There is no body of knowledge decided upon by the teacher to be learned by the whole class.

The learner reaches out via the Web to blogs, social networks, and especially to "meshworks." A meshwork differs from a social network by its more dynamic, less stable, grouping of people. The learner joins a meshwork if it posts, or has recently posted, information the learner finds useful at that moment. Once received, the learner transforms that item into a form suited to his or her purpose (remember, it's the learner, not predetermined content, that matters); that is, the learner (to use an au courant term that makes me reach for my Dramamine) *re-purposes* the item, and sends it back to those one-mouse-click-old mesh "friends," who further re-repurpose the item and bounce it back again to the learner. Moments later, the learner may well flit off in search of another meshwork. Knowledge acquisition Downes-style is chaotic, not something you could neatly outline, because you'd barely have started your outline when some new thought from some meshwork "friend" would repurpose *you*.

I was pleased that the conference organizers had left a whole hour for audience questions following Downes' talk, something done only for star speakers. My hand shot up first. I mentioned that, as a biologist and not a social network analyst, I felt like an outsider. However, I said, I believe there are lots of fascinating ideas in biology, among other fields, that interest learners in college or in the general public, but some of these ideas are complex and would need an expert to explain them properly. Where, I asked, do experts fit into the PLE concept?

Silly me. He looked me straight in the eye and burst forth with—you guessed it— "Everyone's an expert." He clarified, "A mother is an expert about her own kids. And I myself am an expert about how to make a hot dog, because I used to work in a hot dog factory." Then he stopped and looked at me.

So I'm thinking, kids, hotdogs, *and?*

But there was no and.

This "expert" thing had me stumped. These smart people surely knew that a professor of, say, astrophysics who has just discovered a new planet in the universe, or a professor of biology who has just developed a new anti-cancer drug would have expert knowledge of broad interest to many learners. How could they deny the significance of such expertise?

Some insight into this question derives from another media guru, Harvard Law School's David Weinberger, who one-ups Downes regarding experts in his book, *Everything in Miscellaneous*. Weinberger seems angry. See if you agree, based on several short quotes from his book:

- "We call them experts and we give them clipboards."

- "...their institutions are no longer in charge of our ideas."
- "Control has changed hands. The new rules...are in effect, transforming the landscape in which we work, buy, learn, vote, and play."
- "Authorities have long filtered and organized information for us...."
- "...citizens are not waiting for permission to take control of finding and organizing information."
- "The result is a startling change in our culture's belief that truth means accuracy, effectiveness requires adherence to clear lines of command and control and knowledge is power."[19]

Could it be that Downes, Weinberger and others of like mind are so enamored by the democratization of learning through social networking, so pleased with its anti-authoritarian, anti-institutional, anti-establishment nature that they remains loyal to it at all costs? Just a hypothesis, but I can't come up with a better one.

Andrew Keen, an insightful commentator on the digital world, sees things differently. To him, all this social networking is "creating an endless digital forest of mediocrity." And "...democratization, despite its lofty idealization, is undermining truth, souring civic discourse, and belittling expertise, experience and talent."[20]

It seems likely that most of the "everyone's an expert" claimants would seek out a true expert if needed. If one were, unfortunately, to become a cancer patient, he or she would be knocking on the door of the biology professor with that new anti-cancer drug. Blog browsing, networking, and meshing around might be useful, but the expert may have an answer no one in meshland knows. And one's life may depend on it.

However, to bring this discussion full circle, the cancer biologists and the other experts in academia are unlikely to be fully appreciated until they show a serious presence on the Internet, in a language and style suitable to a general audience.

OK, this is where I invite you to expunge from your short term memory the phrase I mentioned above—I dare not state it again, for this could cause it to slip permanently into your long term memory. But you know the one I mean—it begins "Everyone's...." Done? Phrase gone? What phrase, you ask? Good.

Notes

1. Interviewed by the author at the University of Pennsylvania, May 5, 2008.

2. Interviewed by the author at the University of Michigan, March 19, 2007.

3. Reuters, "Academic Earth Launches Website Offering Free Video Lectures From Leading Universities," http://www.reuters.com/article/idUS157269+24-Mar-2009+PRN20090324.

4. Tamar Lewin, "Universities Reshaping Education on the Web," *New York Times*, July 17, 2012, http://www.nytimes.com/2012/07/17/education/consortium-of-colleges-takes-online-education-to-new-level.html; Jordan Weissman, "The Single Most Important Experiment in Higher Education," *The Atlantic*, 156: July 18, 2012, http:www.theatlantic.com/business/archive/2012/07/the-single-most-important-experiment-in-higher-education/259953.

5. https:www.edX.org/

6. http://news.stanford.edu/news/2009/september14/futurity-website-launch-091709.html; Evan Lerner, "The Science Journalism Community Weighs In as a New Website Blurs the Line Between Reporting and Public Relations," *Seed Magazine*, http://seedmagazine.com/content/article/futurity_imperfect/; E-mail correspondence with Jenny Leonard and Bill Murphy of the University of Rochester, June, 2012.

7. Nick DeSantis, "A Boom Time for Education start-Ups," *The Chronicle of Higher Education*, March 18, 2012.

8. Clayton M. Christensen and Henry J. Eyring, *The Innovative University: Changing the DNA of Higher Education from the Inside Out* (San Francisco: Jossey-Bass: 2011).

9. Don Tapscott and Anthony D. Williams, *Wikinomics: How Mass Collaboration Changes Everything* (New York: Portfolio, 2006), 264.

10. I. Elaine Allen and Jeff Seaman, *Staying the course: Online Education in the United States, 2008* (Newburyport, MA: The Sloan Consortium, 2008) http://www.sloan-c.org/publications/survey/staying_course.

11. Examples of two courses I categorized as idea-based are Race and Ethnicity, and Understanding Visual Culture. Examples of courses I categorized as practical or technical are Personal Financial Planning, and Reproductive Management of Livestock. And a course I found difficult to classify is Natural Resources for Teachers.

12. Faye Lesht, e-mail message to author, January 5, 2010. I thank her and her associate Ken Gustin for also providing the following information. The total number of students in the University of Illinois' continuing education online courses during 2010 was 1020, of whom 771 were taking degree programs and 249 were taking courses not for a degree. The program does not offer courses to credential students with certificates in professional skills or tasks.

13. National Center for Educational Statistics, *National Household Educational Surveys Program of 2005: Adult Education Participation in 2004-2005*, http://nces.ed.gov/pubsearch/pubsinfo.asp?pubid=2006077.

14. Interviewed by the author at Drexel University, May 5, 2008.

15. Vest, *American Research University* (see chapt. 4, n. 68), 100.

16. http://ocw.mit.edu.

17. http://ocw.mit.edu/OcwWeb/web/about/president/index.htm.

18. One widely used Internet source used for updating physicians is MedPageToday, of the University of Pennsylvania Medical School. It posts about 12 stories per day, which are certified for their accuracy by Prof. Zalman Agus. As he explained to me, doctors use this service to maintain their accreditation—they take a simple test to prove that they have read a given article. This process is free and easier to carry out than taking courses, which are rarely free. About 400,000 single stories, each about 75 words in length, are read per year on this program. (Dr. Agus was interviewed by the author at the University of Pennsylvania, May 5, 2008.)

19. David Weinberger, *Everything is Miscellaneous: The Power of the New Digital Disorder* (New York: Henry Holt, 2007). The six quotes are, respectively, from pages 101, 102, 106, 132, 133, and 229.

20. Keen, *Cult of the Amateur*, 3, 15.

Chapter 10. Creating a Plan of Action

I began *A Dam in the River* with two claims. First, that America's outstanding universities and colleges are home to a "huge and expanding reservoir of ideas... arguably the world's deepest source of knowledge about the widest range of subjects." Second, that ideas are critically important—they can "change a mind, change a life, change the world." Yet, throughout this book, I have presented evidence that only a very small percentage of adults encounter ideas from academia. Less than one percent take online continuing education courses in idea-rich subjects. Similarly low percentages take idea-rich in-class courses, tune in to public radio or public TV, read online articles from universities about their research ideas, or buy university press books. Probably even fewer engage in idea-rich visits to university campuses. One can safely presume that many of the people who participate in any of the above activities also participate in others; thus, the overall number of people engaged with academic ideas is not a sum of all these low percentages, rather a quite low overall percentage.

America's leading colleges and universities, by and large, do not take the sharing of their ideas with the public as a significant part of their mission. The academic culture does not hold this sharing as a priority. I have encountered this cultural roadblock on many occasions during my research for this book. Here is the most recent occasion.

In 2012, I attended annual conference of the University Professional and Continuing Education Association in Portland, Oregon. Almost all the sessions—lectures, panel discussions, and workshops—were about job-related or technical courses. (These related to the word "Professional" in the association's name.) Only one session, a panel discussion, was about promoting liberal arts and idea-oriented education. Yet all four academics on this panel stressed that liberal education is important because it makes the students more employable, as industry increasingly wants and needs well-rounded employees.

Frustrated and a bit depressed, I asked the panelists, "To what extent do you feel that the effect ideas can have on an individual's mind and life should be a major basis for promoting liberal education?" To my amazement, the audience wildly applauded my question, as though it had released some pent-up disaffection with the seemingly ever-present notion at the conference—and increasingly in academia—that ideas are good because they satisfy the boss.

While substantially ignoring the American adult public, many US universities have been running after foreign students, not only with online courses and residential studies on US campuses, but also by building entire new campuses in foreign countries. As of now, 60 American universities have built 78 overseas campuses in 39 nations, with 13 more in the planning stage.[1] These foreign campuses offer important educational opportunities abroad and can be financially rewarding for their stateside institutions. University presidents speak proudly of their institution's "global presence," while smiling all the way to the bank. I would suggest that, while plowing new fields abroad, more attention should be paid to sowing seeds at home.

Throughout *A Dam in the River*, I have described various initiatives, many incipient, for sharing academic ideas with the public, and have suggested additional initiatives. A key to their success is cooperation, on various levels—cooperation within a campus to improve, for instance, the writing of academics; cooperation among universities in projects such as Coursera, Futurity, and the Academic Idea of the Week; and cooperation between academia and the public as in the 4PM and its ramifications. Aspects of academic culture—such as the notion that academics know best and that I, as an academic, know better than most other academics—tend to work against cooperation. Overcoming these constraints is important for producing the advances advocated in *A Dam in the River*.

35 Suggested Actions

The suggestions for new initiatives are scattered throughout the previous chapters. They are of several types, in terms of the particular subject matter addressed, who would implement them, and the magnitude of their cost and their intended benefit. Given this scattering and diversity, I have codified these suggestions, 35 in all, in a user-friendly format which can help individuals, groups, whole campuses, or groups of campuses, select items for discussion and possible implementation. No one size fits all; a given suggestion will be best suited to a given campus depending on its unique characteristics. However, some suggestions would involve several campuses working together.

In the following table, the left-most column, "Suggested Action," lists the 35 suggestions. The second column, "Pages in Text," cites the page location where the suggested action is described. In some cases the text description continues for several pages. In other cases the description is brief, though the context of its discussion in the text can be instructive. The third column, "Who Decides?," indicates who, among the campus hierarchy or those off campus, are the people most likely to consider implementing the particular suggestion. In this column, the term "Central Admin." implies that the university Chancellor, President, and/or Provost would decide. When "Central Admin." is followed by another person or group in parentheses, the central administration would probably encourage or appoint this person or group to implement the suggestion. If the parentheses contain the term "Inter-university," the central administrations of several universities and/or colleges should consider implementing the suggested action together.

Finally, the fourth through sixth columns offer an approximate cost/benefit evaluation of implementing each suggestion. The fourth column lists the cost on a 1 to 5 scale, where 1 means little or no cost at all, and 5 means moderate to substantial cost. The fifth column, "Benefit," presents an assessment of the expected outcome on a similar 1 to 5 scale. When the benefit would be felt primarily by the local community, the maximal benefit score entered is 3. When a national benefit is a possible outcome, the maximal score entered is 5. Within these constraints, the greater the expected benefit—that is, affecting more people and/or affecting them more deeply—the higher the score entered. The sixth and final column, "Benefit to cost Ratio," summarizes how great an effect relative to cost (bang per buck) can be expected from implementing each suggestion. Clearly, a higher number in this column hints at a financially attractive suggestion. The benefit and cost analysis is subjective, and should be used only as a rough guideline.

Given the telegraphic nature of the information presented in the table, it can neither fully explain, nor place in a broader context, the various suggestions, as they are described in the text. Thus, the table is intended as a kind of Yellow Pages guide to the book's earlier chapters. The entries are grouped according to the types of goals they are meant to achieve. A brief explanation of the goals appears, within the table, before each group of entries.

Here's item 36. Copy this list and post it on your bathroom mirror.

I offer two cautions regarding the items in this table. First, it would be easy to subvert their objective from public education to public relations. That is, ideas could be shared merely to impress, not to enlighten, the public. Second, it would also be easy to subvert some of the items into purely academic exercises. For instance, faculty discussions, inter-disciplinary centers, national organizations and professional journals about university ideas might fascinate many academics but fail to impact on society. I suggest that, in implementing any of the above suggestions, the public be kept firmly in mind as the target audience.

Suggested Action	Pages in Text	Who Decides?	Cost (1 to 5 scale)	Benefit (1 to 5 scale)	Benefit/Cost Ratio
Suggestions 1 through 8 are designed to gain campus support for the sharing of academic ideas with the public, to discover what kinds of academic ideas would be best shared, and how these are likely to be received by, and to affect, the public.					
1) Interested university or college students gather and start a student organization to promote the sharing of academic ideas with the public. Propose to your campus faculty and administrators that your institution become a national leader in this regard. Follow up on your proposal.	105	University or college students	1	4	4
2) Interested faculty members gather to discuss sharing academic ideas with the public. Write a proposal for your deans and central administrators. Follow up.	105	Faculty members	1	5	5
3) Develop an inter-disciplinary center on campus for the study of university ideas, best methods of sharing them with, and their expected effects upon, the general public.	105	Faculty members	2	5	2.5
4) Develop a national academic society and academic journal for research on university ideas, best methods of sharing them with the public, expected effects on the public, and evaluation.	105	Faculty members	3	5	1.75

5) Gather a group of alumni to discuss your alma mater's sharing academic ideas with the public. Send a proposal to the chief administrators. Propose that your alma mater become a national leader in this regard. Hold your donations until you get a satisfactory response.	105	Alumni	1	4	4
6) Local residents gather to discuss how to gain greater access to academic ideas from a nearby campus. Write a proposal and send it to one or more deans. Follow up.	105–106	Residents living near a major academic campus	1	3	3
7) Develop a support organization of on- and off-campus partners to motivate and guide the sharing of university ideas with the public.	106	On and off campus partners	1	4	4
8) Carry out market research to test public interest in university ideas, and ways of delivering them.	153	Central Admin. (Business School)	2	4	2

Suggestions 9 and 10 seek specific changes in administrative procedure regarding the sharing of academic ideas with the public.

9) Administrators accept *true excellence* in writing, lecturing, broadcasting or other activities for the public as valid academic work, considered in evaluations for faculty hiring, tenure, and promotion. Develop criteria for judging excellence in these areas, which is different from judging academic work.	157–158	Central Admin.	1	5	5

10) Request that applicants for faculty jobs offer a public presentation (lecture, broadcast, essay, or other) in addition to a research seminar, during job interviews.	158	Central Admin.	1	3	3

Suggestions 11-20, the largest group in this table, are intended to enhance the experience of visitors to universities and colleges. Although several items would serve primarily a local audience (hence, their entries in the benefit column are no higher than 3), items 11-13 would likely draw a larger—at least a state-wide—audience, and items 14-15, being inter-university projects, would likely have a national impact (thus, for entries 11-15, the value shown in the Benefit column can be as high as 5).

11) Develop an "open-campus museum."	123–125	Central Admin.	2	5	2.5
12) Develop or enhance a Campus Visitor Center.	127	Central Admin.	5	4	0.8
13) Develop a program for public visits to individual course lectures ("Visitor Invitation Program," VIP).		Central Admin. (Inter-university)	2	5	2.5
14) Develop an inter-university "Academic Idea of the Week" program, for presentation at all public campus venues—sports events and their broadcasts, lectures, concerts, plays, museums, websites, etc., across the nation.	118–120	Central Admin. (Inter-university)	2	5	2.5
15) Develop an annual weekend—"Open Campus Idea Festival."	118	Central Admin.	2	3	1.5
16) Develop an academic course on tour guiding, prerequisite for all campus guides.	112	Central Admin. (Relevant deans)	1	3	3
17) Develop one or more idea-rich guided general campus tours, and/or audio-visual presentation for the general public, distinct from those for student applicants and their families.	112	Campus Tours Admin.	2	3	1.5
18) Incorporate academic ideas in existing campus tours.	112	Campus Tours Admin.	1	3	3

Suggestion	Pages	Responsible			
19) Discover how tour visitors relate to tour subject, and use this to connect visitors to the presentation (i.e. use the "4PM").	131–134	Campus Tour Admin.	1	3	3
20) Develop an idea-rich, printed brochure for self-guided walking tours.	111	Central Admin. (Public Relations Office)	1	3	3
Suggestions 21-24 concern academic writing for the public, and publication of this writing by university presses.					
21) Develop a course ("Not Unlike Good Writing") to improve writing for the public by faculty, postdocs, and graduate students. Where possible, university press editors help teach the course.	154–156	Central Admin. (Deans)	1	5	5
22) University press develop closer campus ties, and court more home campus authors.	157	University Press	1	4	4
23) Relocate offices of university press to central site on main campus, to increase contact with potential home-campus authors.	157	Central Admin.	4	4	1
24) Commit to audience expansion for the Futurity website.	190–191	Central Admin.	2	5	2.5
Suggestions 25-28 concern TV and radio broadcasting of academic ideas by faculty.					
25) Develop popular inter-university video of academic ideas for halftime of nationally broadcast university football and basketball games.	173–175	Central Admin. (Inter-university)	5	5	1
26) Use local public or commercial radio and TV stations to broadcast university ideas in a creative format.	173	Central Admin. (Deans of Communication, Journalism)	1	3	3
27) Train faculty in speaking on radio and TV.	173	Deans of Communication, Journalism; Public Relations Director	1	4	4

28) Universities become nationally active once again in administering public broadcasting—NPR, PBS.	170, 180	Central Admin. (Deans of Communications, Journalism)	1	4	4

Suggestions 29-32 concern academia's use of the Internet and continuing education courses.

29) OpenCourseWare: add more materials from idea-rich courses in humanities, arts, etc. to the OCW website.	195–196	OpenCourseWare directors (at MIT and elsewhere)	2	4	2
30) Create more idea-based (as opposed to technical or skill-based) continuing education courses, in-class and online.	87–88	Continuing Education Deans	2	4	2
31) Incorporate broad ideas from the humanities into technical and career oriented continuing education courses, in-class or online.	88	Continuing Education Deans	1	4	4

Suggestions 32-35 involve modifying several different types of existing campus programs to share academic ideas more effectively with the public. These programs are Cooperative Extension networks operated by land grant universities, oral and public history programs, science technology and society programs, existing campus museums, and civic engagement programs.

32) Use the Cooperative Extension network to share great university ideas at land grant universities with the state-wide public.	87	Coop. Extension Deans at Land Grant Universities	1	4	4
33) Develop richer academic programs in oral and public history, to permit more idea sharing.	91–92	History Department Chair	3	3	1
34) Develop more outreach activities in science technology and society (STS) programs to engage the public more fully.	93–94	STS Chair	3	3	1
35) Civic engagement teams inform local communities of the ideas behind team projects, and progress.	84	Civic Engagement Directors	1	3	3

Will It Work?

Even if a good number of these 35 suggestions were implemented at many universities and colleges, how can we know in advance if they will produce the desired effects—broadening people's horizons, improving analytical thinking, expanding a sense of wonder, creating a more enlightened citizenry, elevating public discourse, and improving decision making on issues of national importance? Can these suggestions really "change a mind, change a life, change the world?"

The short answer is we can't know. Even after implementation, it will be difficult to judge, because many of the anticipated effects are subjective and difficult to measure. How do you measure the extent to which an idea broadens one's horizons or changes one's life? Yet, serious discussion among interested parties, and research on how to maximize the likelihood of success, are called for. Suggestions 1 through 8 in the table are all about such discussion, with items 3, 4, and 8 stressing research on this subject.

Some critics might argue that in the absence of certainty, it would foolish to implement this, or any other, plan of action that takes a university into largely uncharted terrain. I find it hard to imagine that placing the enormous array of great ideas from academia in the public's hands can be anything but good. That's my educated guess. Many of the great developments in history originated as educated guesses. Did the Founding Fathers *know* that the nation would survive its great test of independence and democracy? Did President Lincoln *know* that the nation could be healed, and slavery terminated? Did Daniel Coit Gilman *know* that the German research university could be transplanted successfully to the American shore, as described in Chapter 7? And did Vannevar Bush *know* that basic research, carried out primarily in universities under federal support, would become a key to America's academic success, as detailed in Chapter 2? But imagine how America would look today if each of these educated guesses had been abandoned, for fear of uncertainty.

I hope that *A Dam in the River* has inspired you to contribute to the important changes discussed, and has helped point ways to do so. At stake is the nation's greatest resource—the American mind. This resource's future can be secured only through the involvement of many people, both on and off campus. Are you one of these people?

Notes

1. Justin Pope, "New Caution for US Universities Overseas," October 20, 2011; Karin Fisher, "Report says number of overseas branch campuses continues to climb," *The Chronicle of Higher Education*, January 11, 2012.

Appendix. Institutions Visited and People Interviewed for This Book

Many of those interviewed hold several official titles, or responsibilities, at their home institution, and these titles often shift with time. The one or two titles listed for each person below are the ones most relevant to the interview. For each institution, administrators are listed before faculty. All interviews were carried out by the author. Most were carried out in person. Those labeled "T" were telephone interviews. At institutions labeled "CT," I took part in the student-guided campus tour.

Colleges and Universities

Amherst College (CT)

Anthony Marx, College President
Greg Call, Dean of the Faculty
Peter Crowley, Director, Natural History Museum and Professor of Geology
Betsy Siersma, Interim Director, Mead Art Museum
Scott Laidlaw, Director, Campus Outreach Program
Jan Dizard, Professor of Sociology
Stephen George, Professor of Biology
George Greenstein, Professor of Astronomy
John Servos, Professor of History
Arielle Philips, Research Associate in Astronomy

Bennington College

Elizabeth Coleman, College President

Ron Cohen, Professor of Psychology
Elizabeth Sherman, Professor of Biology

City University of New York (CUNY)

Matthew Goldstein, University Chancellor
Robert Isaacson, Executive Director, CUNY TV
Brian Camp, Program Manager, CUNY TV

Columbia University (CT)

Nicholas Lemann, Dean, Columbia School of Journalism
David Stone, Executive Vice President for Communications
James Jordan, Director, Columbia University Press
Robert McCaughey, Professor of Intellectual and Academic History (T)
Kate Wittenberg, Director, Electronic Publishing Initiative at
    Columbia
Jane Knitzer, Director, National Center for Children in Poverty

Cornell University (CT)

Prof. Frank Rhodes, University President Emeritus
G. Peter LePage, Dean, School of Arts and Sciences
Susan Henry, Dean, School of Agriculture and Life Sciences
Glenn Altschuler, Dean of Continuing Education and Summer Sessions (T)
Stephen Hamilton, Assoc. Provost for Outreach
Ronald Seeber, Vice Provost for Land Grant Affairs
Kraig Adler, former Vice Provost and Professor of Biology
John Ackerman, Director, Cornell University Press
Catherine Penner and Ralph Janis, current and past Directors, respectively,

Cornell Alumni University (T)

Medha Devar, Assoc. Director, Vivo Project (T)
Amanda Kittelberger, Associate Director, Cornell Outreach Page
Terry Ehling, Director, Center for Innovative Publishing, Cornell
    Libraries
Carl Hopkins, Professor of Biology
Howard Howland, Professor of Biology
Scott Peters, Professor of Agricultural Education

Drexel University

Daniel Dougherty, Director, Center for Civic Engagement
Francis Harvey, Professor of Education, distance learning
Rebecca Clothey, Director, Higher Education Program, distance learning

Duke University (CT)

Harvard University (CT)

Thomas Lentz, Director, Harvard Art Museums
James Hansen, Director, Museum of Comparative Zoology
Michael Fisher, Editor-in-Chief, Harvard University Press
Jon Rosenberg, Editor, Harvard Magazine
Thomas Sander, Assoc. Director, Saguaro Seminars, John F. Kennedy School
    of Government
Andrew Zelleke, Assoc. Director, Center for Public Leadership, John F.
    Kennedy School of Government
Neil Gross, Professor of Sociology (T)

Massachusetts Institute of Technology (MIT)

Richard Larson, Professor of Civil and Environmental Engineering and co-
    founder, MIT OpenCourseware
Steve Carson, Director, MIT OpenCourseware
John Durant, Director, MIT Museum
MacKenzie Smith, Associate Director For Technology, MIT Library
Frank Levy, Professor of Urban Economics

New York University (NYU)

Carol Mandel, Dean, Division of Libraries
Daniel Walkowitz, Professor of History
Jack Tchen, Professor of History

North Carolina State University

Johnny Wynne, Dean, School of Agriculture
Joe Zublena, Director, North Carolina Cooperative Extension Service

Pomona College (CT)

David Oxtoby, College President
Gary Kates, Dean of the College
Cynthia Peters, Director, Media Relations
Rachel Levin, Professor of Biology

Princeton University (CT)

Kristin Appelget, Director, Community and Regional Affairs
Karen Woodbridge, Director, Community Relations
Trisha Thorme, Director, Community Based Learning Initiative

Smith College

Richard Olivo, Professor of Biology

Swarthmore College

Constance Hungerford, Provost
Rachel Merz, Professor of Biology
Julie Hagelin, Professor of Biology

University of Arizona (CT)

Eugene Sander, Dean, College of Agriculture and Life Sciences, and VP for Outreach
Michael Proctor, Associate Dean for External Relations
Alexis Faust, Executive Director, Flandrau University Science Center
Jennifer Fields, Director of Education, Flandrau University Science Center
Giovanni Battistini, VP for Technology, Flandrau University Science Center
John Hildebrand, Chairperson, Department of Neurobiology

University of California Berkeley (CT)

Lowell Bergman, Professor of Journalism, Documentary Film Producer—PBS, *Frontline*
Robert Full, Professor of Biology

University of California Riverside (CT)

Thomas Baldwin, Dean, Natural and Agricultural Sciences
Kris Lovekin, Director, Media Relations
Vicki Gomer, Marketing Coordinator
Ryan Kuchler, Web Coordinator
Kathy Barton, Medical School Development Officer

University of California San Diego

Marye Anne Fox, University Chancellor
Mary Walshok, Associate Vice Chancellor, Dean and Director, University Extension
Lynn Burnstan, Director, UCSD-TV
Arthur Ellis, Vice Chancellor for Research
Gabriele Wienhausen, Associate Dean for Education
Barry Brown, Professor of Communications
Eduardo Macagno, Professor of Biology
Allen Selverston, Professor of Biology

University of Chicago

Robert Zimmer, University President
Robert Rosenberg, Director, Public Communications
Cary Nathenson, Associate Dean, Graham School of General Studies
Jose Quintans, Professor of Biology
Randy Landsberg, Department of Astronomy Outreach Director

University of Maryland

Kevin Klose, Dean, College of Journalism, President Emeritus of National Public Radio

University of Michigan (CT)

Paul Courant, former University Provost; Director, University Library
Rebecca McGowan, University Regent
Cynthia Wilbanks, Vice President for Governmental Relations
Marvin Krislov, University Counsel
Rebecca Blank, Dean, Gerald R. Ford School of Public Policy
Douglas Kelbaugh, Dean, School of Architecture and Urban Planning
Bryan Rogers, Dean, School Art and Design
James Woolliscroft, Dean, Medical School
John Burkhardt, Director, National Forum on Higher Education for the Public Good
James Steward, Director, University of Michigan Museum of Art
Amy Harris, Director, Exhibit Museum of Natural History
Robert Grese, Director, Mathaei Botanical Gardens and Nichols Arboretum
Brenda Johnson, Director of Public Services, Hatcher Graduate Library
James Kosteva, Associate Vice President for Research
Nancy Connell, Director, Public Relations

University of North Carolina

Steve Volstad, Director of Communications, UNC TV
Shannon Vickery, Head of Production, UNC TV
Diane Lucas, Head of Programming and Outreach, UNC TV
Tom Linden, Professor of Journalism, Producer and Host of Science and Health, UNC TV
John Sweeney, Professor of Journalism

University of Pennsylvania

Michael Delli Caprini, Dean, Annenberg School for Communication
Zalman Agus, Associate Dean, Continuing Medical Education
Lori Doyle, Vice President for University Communications
Ira Harkavy, Associate Vice President, Center for Community Partnerships

John Prendertgast, Editor, The Pennsylvania Gazette Alumni Magazine
Peter Agree, Editor-in-Chief, University of Pennsylvania Press
Jessica Lowenthal, Executive Director, Kelly Writers House
Matthew Hartley, Professor of Education

Williams College (CT)

Yale University (CT)

Sheila Pastor, Director, Meade Visitors Center
Michael Donoghue, Director, Peabody Museum of Natural History
Jessica Sachs, Education Director, Yale University Art Gallery

Additional Academic Institutions

American Association for the Advancement of Science, Washington, DC

Tiffany Lohwater, Director, Public Engagement

American Association of Universities, Washington, DC

Robert Berdahl, President; former Chancellor, University of California, Berkeley; former President, University of Texas, Austin

American Association of University Professors, Washington, DC

Jonathan Knight, Director, Dept. of Academic Freedom, Tenure and Governance

Campus Compact, Providence, RI

Maureen Curley, President

Ithaka, New York, NY

Kate Wittenberg, Project Director, Client and Partnership Development

JSTOR, New York, NY

Michael Spinella, Executive Director
Roger Schonfeld, Research Manager

National Academies, Washington, DC

Maureen O'Leary, Director of Public Information
Jay Labov, Senior Advisor for Education and Communications

National Public Radio, Washington, DC

Vivian Schiller, past President and CEO (T)

Robert Siegel, Senior Host, *All Things Considered*

Public Broadcasting System, Arlington, VA
Paula Kerger, President and CEO

Shifting Baselines Ocean Media Project, Los Angeles, CA
Randy Olson, Science documentary film producer (T)

Society for Neuroscience—Washington, DC
Todd Bentson, Director of Public Information
Nick Spitzer, Academic Chairman, Public Education and Communication
Committee (T)

Talking Science, New York, NY
Ira Flatow, Producer and Host, NPR's *Science Friday* and other science
productions

WETA Public Television, Washington, DC
Jeff Bieber, VP for News and Public Affairs

People Interviewed in Person, Away from their Home Institutions

Laura Brown, Ithaka, and former Editor, Oxford University Press, USA
Sean Carroll, Professor of Biology, University of Wisconsin
Leslie Hannah, Professor of Arts, Sciences and Business, Kansas State
University
Adriana Kazar, Professor of Higher Education, University of Southern
California
Yaakov Nahmias, Research Associate in bioengineering, Harvard Medical
School
Baldomeo Olivera, Professor of Biology, University of Utah
Sheldon Rothblatt, Professor of History, U. Cal. Berkeley
Arthur Sacks, Professor of Liberal Arts and International Studies, Colorado
School of Mines
Jean Sideris, Outreach Coordinator, Union of Concerned Scientists
Suzanne Thurston, Education Officer, American Association for the
Advancement of Science
Susan Volman, Health Sciences Administrator, National Institutes of Health
Joshua Wallman, Professor of Biology, CUNY

Acknowledgments

The Hebrew University has given me the opportunity to establish and direct the unique "open-campus museum" called the Nature Park & Galleries on its Edmund J. Safra Science Campus. Through this experience, together with the related university course I have developed and taught on museum guiding, and the further training of the museum's guides, I acquired a deepened awareness of the public in relationship to both museums and universities. This awareness has strongly informed my research and analysis for *A Dam in the River*. Thanks go to the many people who approved, and those who helped create, this museum: three university presidents, three provosts, four deans, three general university managers, and other administrators, as well as my faculty colleagues who have offered moral and intellectual support, the curators and other workers of the university's National Collections of Natural History, and the university's non-academic staff, including horticultural experts, gardeners and buildings-and-grounds personnel. I further thank the many excellent staff of the Nature Park & Galleries, from whom I have learned a great deal. And a very special thanks to the many donors to the Nature Park & Galleries, without whom this project—and thus, this book—could never have come about.

Much of my museum learning has been informed by the advice and moral support I've received from two professionals, Zahava Doering of the Smithsonian Institution, Washington DC, and Glenn Sujo of London. I thank the 155 American academic leaders (listed in the Appendix) who took the time to sit with me for in-depth interviews. I also thank the librarians at the Bentley Library at the University of Michigan, the Frost Library at Amherst College, and the New York Public Library for assisting me in finding essential materials. Helpful conversations and correspondence with Amy Avgar, Chris Comer, Robert Cooper, Seth Dubin, Seth Nelson-Levy, Judith Margolis, Avraham Mossari, and Bob

Slater are also much appreciated. Carol Bell was extremely gracious in lending me her New York apartment during two full summer research trips.

My sincere thanks go to the many people who have read parts or all of the manuscript and provided extremely useful feedback. Brief sections were read by Laura Brown, Jeremy Camhi, Marshall Devor, Jeff Dodick, Mike Frisch, Charles Knapp, John Servos, and Elizabeth Sherman. Longer sections or the entire manuscript were read by Russell Berman, Zahava Doering, John Falk, Marye Anne Fox, Charles Greenbaum, Dudley Herschbach, Alice Huang, Donald Kennedy, Laurin Lewis, Frank Rhodes, Susan Volman, and Mary Walshok. Felice Kahn Zisken did an excellent job editing the final draft. It has been a complete pleasure working with the staff of Algora Publications.

My greatest fan and supporter, my wife Jane Camhi, read and wisely edited the first few drafts of the entire book. Jane also has my deepest thanks for putting up with me for the five years of this project, including the many times I was away on research trips for the book, and the many times when, although I was physically at home, my mind was away on a research trip. Thanks also to my kids and grandkids for their patience with me.

Suggested Readings

Introduction

Arum, R. and J. Roksa. 2011. *Academically Adrift.* Chicago: University of Chicago Press.

Hofstadter, R. 1962. *Anti-intellectualism in American Life.* New York: Vintage.

Posner, R. D. 2001. *Public Intellectuals: A Study of Decline.* Cambridge, MA: Harvard University Press.

Walshok, M. L. 1995. *Knowledge Without Boundaries: What America's Research Universities Can Do for the Economy, the Workplace, and the Community.* San Francisco: Jossey-Bass.

Chapter 1. The Idea of a University

Bérubé, M. 2006. *What's Liberal About the Liberal Arts? Classroom Politics and "Bias" in Higher Education.* New York: Norton.

Cole, J. R. 2009. *The Great American University: Its Rise to Preeminence, Its Indispensable National Role, Why it Must be Protected.* New York: Public Affairs.

Keeling, R. P. and R. H. Hersh. 2012. *We're Losing our Minds: Rethinking American Higher Education.* New York: Palgrave Macmillan.

Moody, C. 2005. *The Republican War on Science.* New York: Basic Books.

Chapter 2. Ideas From the Disciplines

Bush, V. 1945. *Science the Endless Frontier.* Washington, DC: United States Government Printing Office. http://www.nsf.gov/about/history/vbush1945.htm.

Falk. J. H. and L. D. Dierking. 2002. *Lessons Without Limits: How Free-Choice Learning is Transforming Education.* Walnut Creek, CA: AltaMira.

Gardner, H. 1983. *Frames of Mind: The Theory of Multiple Intelligences*. New York: Basic Books.

Kandel, E. R. 2006. *In Search of Memory: The Emergence of a New Science of Mind.* New York: W. W. Norton.

Chapter 3. Value-Based Ideas

Bloom, A. 1987. *The Closing of the American Mind.* New York: Simon and Schuster.

Lawrence-Lightfoot, S. 2000. *Respect: An Exploration.* Cambridge, MA: Perseus.

Thelin, J. R. 2004. *A History of American Higher Education.* Baltimore: Johns Hopkins Press.

Young, R. B. 1997. *No Neutral Ground: Standing by the Values We Prize in Higher Education.* San Francisco: Jossey-Bass.

Chapter 4. The Low Flow of Ideas

Bok, D. 1982. *Beyond the Ivory Tower.* Cambridge, MA: Harvard University Press.

Fish, S. 2008. *Save the World on Your Own Time.* Oxford: Oxford University Press.

Kerr, C. 2001 (rev. ed.). *The Uses of the University.* Cambridge, MA: Harvard University Press.

Kezar, A. J., T. C. Chambers, and J. C. Burkhardt. 2005. *Higher Education for the Public Good: Emerging Voices From a National Movement.* San Francisco: Jossey-Bass.

Chapter 5. Visiting Universities, I: A "Margaret Mead" on Campus

Allitt, P. 2005. *I'm the Teacher, You're the Student: A Semester in the University Classroom.* Philadelphia: University of Pennsylvania Press.

Hein, G. E. 1998. *Learning in the Museum.* New York: Routledge.

Knudsen, D. M., T. T. Cable, and L. Beck. 2003. *Interpretation of Cultural and Natural Resources.* State College, PA: Venture.

Levy, B. A., S. M. Lloyd, and S. P. Schreiber. 2001. *Great Tours! Thematic Tours and Guide Training for Historic Sites.* Walnut Creek, CA: AltaMira.

Chapter 6. Visiting Universities, II: Blessed be the Guests

Doering, Z. D. 1999. Strangers, Guests or Clients? Visitor Experiences in Museums. *Curator, The Museum Journal* 42 (2):74-87.

Pekarik, A. J. 2010. From Knowing to Not Knowing: Moving Beyond "Outcomes." *Curator, The Museum Journal* 53 (1):105-115.

Schwarzer, M. 2006. *Riches, Rivals and Radicals: 100 Years of Museums in America.* Washington, DC: American Association of Museums.

Tsybulskaya, D. and J. Camhi. 2009. Accessing and Incorporating Visitors' Entrance Narratives in Guided Museum Tours. *Curator, The Museum Journal* 52 (1): 81-100.

Chapter 7. Books, "The Greatest Things We Have"

Germano, W. 2008 (2nd ed.). *Getting it Published*. Chicago: University of Chicago Press.

Sagan, C. 1980. *Cosmos*. New York: Random House.

Schiffrin, A. 2000. *The Business of Books*. London: Verso.

Thompson, J. B. 2005. *Books in the Digital Age*. Cambridge, UK: Polity Press.

Chapter 8. Public Radio and TV: A "Broad Casting" of University Ideas?

Day, J. 1995. *The Vanishing Vision: The Inside Story of Public Television*. Berkeley, CA: University of California Press.

McCauley, M. P. 2005. *NPR: The Trials and Triumphs of National Public Radio*. New York: Columbia University Press.

Mitchell, J. W. 2005. *Listener Supported: The Culture and History of Public Radio*. Westport, CT: Praeger.

Ouellette, L. 2002. *Viewers Like You: How Public TV Failed the People*. New York: Columbia University Press.

Chapter 9. The Web and Flow of University Ideas

http://academicearth.org

http://theconversation.edu.au

http://www.futurity.org

Keen, A. 2007. *The Cult of the Amateur: How Today's Internet is Killing Our Culture*. New York: Doubleday.

Walsh, T. 2011. *Unlocking the Gates: How and Why Leading Universities are Opening Up Access to Their Courses*. Princeton, NJ: Princeton University Press.

INDEX

Y

Z